Ideas, Institutions, and Trade

Ideas, Institutions, and Trade

The WTO and the Curious Role of EU Farm Policy in Trade Liberalization

Carsten Daugbjerg and Alan Swinbank

OXFORD
UNIVERSITY PRESS

OXFORD
UNIVERSITY PRESS

Great Clarendon Street, Oxford OX2 6DP

Oxford University Press is a department of the University of Oxford.
It furthers the University's objective of excellence in research, scholarship,
and education by publishing worldwide in

Oxford New York

Auckland Cape Town Dar es Salaam Hong Kong Karachi
Kuala Lumpur Madrid Melbourne Mexico City Nairobi
New Delhi Shanghai Taipei Toronto

With offices in

Argentina Austria Brazil Chile Czech Republic France Greece
Guatemala Hungary Italy Japan Poland Portugal Singapore
South Korea Switzerland Thailand Turkey Ukraine Vietnam

Oxford is a registered trade mark of Oxford University Press
in the UK and in certain other countries

Published in the United States
by Oxford University Press Inc., New York

© Carsten Daugbjerg and Alan Swinbank 2009

The moral rights of the authors have been asserted
Database right Oxford University Press (maker)

First published 2009

British Library Cataloguing in Publication Data
Data available

Library of Congress Cataloging in Publication Data
Library of Congress Control Number: 2009928971

Typeset by SPI Publisher Services, Pondicherry, India
Printed in Great Britain
on acid-free paper by the
MPG Books Group, Bodmin and King's Lynn

ISBN 978-0-19-955775-2

To Line, Esben, Asta Marie, Sidsel, Melissa, and Timothy

Contents

Preface

Although agriculture has a small, and declining, importance in employment and income generation within the EU, it has a political importance well beyond its economic impact. In particular, the EU's common agricultural policy (CAP) has often been the source of conflict between the EU and its trade partners, within first the GATT (the General Agreement on Tariffs and Trade), and then the WTO (World Trade Organization).

Most recently, in the Doha Round of multilateral trade negotiations in the WTO—the *Doha Development Agenda*—agriculture proved to be a sticking point resulting in setbacks and delays in the Round. It was one of the key issues that could not be resolved in the last-minute intensive negotiations in Geneva that failed to close the Round in December 2008. As this book goes to press it remains uncertain whether (and when) the Doha Round can be resuscitated from its deep freeze. Whilst the abortive discussions in 2008 had focused on Indian and US farm trade concerns, the EU's stance on farm policy had undoubtedly contributed to the long-drawn-out negotiations and periodic setbacks. Whatever the final outcome of the Doha Round, disagreements over agricultural policy are likely to figure in future trade disputes and trade rounds, with the CAP the focus of much controversy. Thus the politics of European agriculture remains a crucial component both of international trade negotiation and diplomacy, and of the European construct where farm policy, and the budgetary transfers arising from the CAP, has long been the source of many tortured negotiations between the member states. This is the theme of our book.

It is a collaborative endeavour between a political scientist (Daugbjerg) and an agricultural economist (Swinbank) who share long-standing research interests in the causes, consequences, and interrelationships of CAP reform and GATT/WTO trade negotiations and disputes. In retrospect it is clear that the project began in late summer 2003 when we tried in the limited space of a journal article to explain the genesis and consequences of the CAP reforms agreed earlier that summer. It was clear that the WTO had played an important role, but it was difficult to understand the WTO process without an appreciation of how that interacts with EU decision making. Most of the accounts in the literature are essentially descriptive, and unable to produce analytical frameworks that provide insights into the causal mechanisms driving the design of farm trade agreements. This shortcoming motivated our research, and set our objective of writing a book that provided useful insights into international trade relations. We suggest that the position of the EU in agricultural trade negotiations is pivotal. Due to the comparatively limited competitiveness of the EU's agricultural sector, and the EU's institutionally constrained ability to undertake CAP reform, the CAP sets limits for agricultural trade liberalization within the WTO. This blocks progress across the full compass of the WTO agenda. Therefore, the farm trade negotiation, with the CAP at its core, is the key to understanding the dynamics of trade rounds in the WTO.

Structure

In Chapters 1 and 2 we set out the research questions and the theoretical framework of the book. Chapter 1 defines the key concepts of agricultural exceptionalism and agricultural normalism, which are competing assumptions on the nature of agricultural production and markets. Agricultural exceptionalism—a term current in the political science literature—holds that the farming industry is different from most economic sectors in modern societies, contributing to broader national interests and goals, and warranting extensive state intervention. This view was the ideational underpinning of national agricultural policies in the post-war period, and it remained embedded in GATT farm trade rules from 1947 to 1994.

In Chapter 2, we develop a dynamic analytical framework in which the interrelationship between ideational and institutional change is given prominence in explaining, on the one hand, the evolution of WTO farm trade rules and, on the other, CAP reform. We suggest that CAP reform is in part driven by GATT/WTO imperatives; the reforms then define the EU's farm trade negotiating position; but this in turn sets limits for subsequent changes to WTO farm trade rules that can be negotiated.

We begin Chapter 3 by accounting for the roots of agricultural exceptionalism in the GATT, and show how it was spelt out in GATT trade rules. The remainder of this chapter examines the specific provisions of the Uruguay Round Agreement on Agriculture (URAA), in which we demonstrate the erosion of agricultural exceptionalism in comparison to the 'old' GATT provisions, and we also show how the URAA allowed WTO members considerable leeway to maintain high levels of agricultural support and protection.

In Chapter 4, we explain *how* agricultural exceptionalism was eroded in the Uruguay Round (UR). From the early 1960s, the United States had attempted to align trade rules for farm products with those for other industries, but unsuccessfully; and it was not until the UR, negotiated and implemented as a *Single Undertaking*, that trading partners were able to agree a new trade regime for agriculture. The chapter concentrates on identifying and examining the factors bringing about change.

In Chapter 5, we analyse the implementation of WTO farm rules within the WTO dispute settlement system in order to determine the extent to which the Dispute Settlement Body's rulings have brought about further farm trade liberalization. We highlight the important change from a consensual to a quasi-judicial system, and assess cases in which the CAP has been directly or indirectly challenged.

Chapter 6 moves from the global to the EU level in order to analyse the way in which the ideational shift of the global farm trade regime has influenced the development of EU agricultural policy institutions and the CAP. We demonstrate that the changed global context, emerging in the early 1990s, increasingly influenced CAP decision-making institutions, which, in turn, affected the design of agricultural support measures.

In Chapter 7, we show how CAP reform, whilst driven by WTO concerns, also feeds back into the WTO negotiations, setting limits to what can be agreed, but also providing enhanced opportunities for agreement. From being defensive within the 'old' GATT, attempting to limit the damage that an agricultural agreement could cause to the CAP, the EU became more offensive in its relationship with the WTO.

In Chapter 8, we summarize our theoretical contribution and our most important findings, and assess the post-Doha trade agenda in light of the difficulties experienced in concluding the Doha Round as a Single Undertaking, and of the possible *renaissance* of agricultural exceptionalism triggered by the 2008 world food 'crisis'.

Acknowledgements

Over many years we have absorbed the thoughts and theories of fellow academics, policy makers, and analysts, and hope that in this text we have made due acknowledgement of our intellectual debt. We apologize for any inadvertent lapse or misrepresentation. Students, conference participants, and others have sometimes unwittingly contributed to the development of our ideas. These were elaborated when we met not only in Reading and Aarhus, but also in various locations throughout Europe and North America (Leeds [the United Kingdom], Copenhagen [Denmark], Princeton [the United States], Stavanger [Norway], Victoria [Canada], Ghent [Belgium], and Viterbo [Italy]) at conferences and meetings presenting papers that underpin the book.

It has been an iterative, symbiotic process: conference papers have emerged from, and then been absorbed back into, the text; and they have spun off journal articles that in turn have been shaped by word limits and editors' and referees' preferences, before again feeding back into the book. Thus some of the paragraphs in this text have appeared before. In particular, a paper we gave to the International Political Economy Society in Princeton in 2006, and to the Agricultural Economics Society in Reading in 2007, was the basis for our paper in *The World Economy* (Daugbjerg and Swinbank 2008a): the latter is spread through Chapters 1, 4 (the Single Undertaking), 5 (on dispute settlement), and 7. Similarly, a paper for the international conference *Agricultural Policy Changes: Canada, EU and World Trade Organisation*, in Victoria in 2007, was the basis for material in both the book (Chapters 2 and 6) and a paper in the *Journal of European Integration* (Daugbjerg and Swinbank 2009). Paragraphs from *Comparative European Politics* (Swinbank and Daugbjerg 2006) can be found in Chapter 6, and ideas previously expressed in *Comparative Political Studies* (Daugbjerg 2008) can be found in Chapter 7. As necessary, text has been updated and edited, and expanded. We are grateful to our referees, editors, and publishers for helping us publish our work; and we trust we have kept within the terms of the various publishing agreements we have signed over the years.

We are particularly indebted to a number of people who motivated our work and assisted in turning our ideas into a book. Arlindo Cunha helped us understand the complexities of the EU decision-making process, and appreciate Portuguese cuisine and wine. Dominic Byatt, our commissioning editor at Oxford University Press, was particularly supportive. Annette B. Andersen quickly and efficiently turned a somewhat scrappy manuscript into OUP house style. Finally, we thank our families for, yet again, their patience, understanding, and support.

List of Figures

List of Tables

List of Boxes

List of Abbreviations

ABARE	Australian Bureau of Agricultural and Resource Economics
ACP	African, Caribbean, and Pacific States
AIE	Analysis and Information Exchange
AMS	Aggregate Measurement of Support
CAP	Common Agricultural Policy
CCC	Commodity Credit Corporation
CRS	Cumulative Recovery System
DDA	Doha Development Agenda
DSB	Dispute Settlement Body
DSU	Dispute Settlement Understanding
EBA	Everything but Arms
EC	European Communities
ECSC	European Coal and Steel Community
ECU	European Currency Unit
EEC	European Economic Community
EPAs	Economic Partnership Agreements
FAO	Food and Agriculture Organization of the United Nations
GATS	General Agreement on Trade in Services
GMOs	Genetically Modified Organisms
GSP	Generalized System of Preferences
IAC	Industries Assistance Commission
IACS	Integrated Administration and Control System
IMF	International Monetary Fund
ITO	International Trade Organization
LDCs	Least Developed Countries
MEP	Member of the European Parliament
MFN	Most Favoured Nation

List of Abbreviations

MTO	Multilateral Trade Organization
NAMA	Non-Agricultural Market Access
OECD	Organisation for Economic Co-operation and Development
OEEC	Organisation for European Economic Co-operation
OTDS	Overall Trade-Distorting Domestic Support
PFC	Production Flexibility Contract
PSE	Producer Support Estimate
QMV	Qualified Majority Voting
RTAs	Regional Trade Agreements
SCM	Subsidies and Countervailing Measures
SPS	Sanitary and Phytosanitary Measures
TBT	Technical Barriers to Trade
TRIPS	Trade-Related Aspects of Intellectual Property Rights
TRQs	Tariff Rate Quotas
UNCTAD	United Nations Conference on Trade and Development
UNICE	Union of Industrial and Employers' Confederations of Europe
UR	Uruguay Round
URAA	Uruguay Round Agreement on Agriculture
USDA	United States Department of Agriculture
USTR	United States Trade Representative

Chapter 1

An Introduction to Agricultural Exceptionalism in EU Farm Policy and the GATT

There is no escaping the fact that the intensive efforts the whole membership has been putting in over the last days with the aim of establishing modalities in Agriculture and NAMA [non-*agricultural market access*] have failed. Members have been unable to bridge their differences despite more than a week of hard work.

Much has been achieved this week. We were very close to finalizing modalities in Agriculture and NAMA. A very few issues...led us not to establish modalities, but a huge amount of problems which had remained intractable for years have found solutions. Negotiators have been prepared to reach out beyond their entrenched positions and seek compromise, which they did. However...we were not able to find convergence in the area of the Special Safeguard Mechanism [*on agricultural imports into developing countries*]. And we did not even get around to discussing Cotton. As a result we have not been able to establish the Agriculture and NAMA modalities this week. (WTO Director-General Pascal Lamy's statement to the Trade Negotiations Committee after the suspension of the Doha Round negotiations on 30 July 2008).

The Uruguay Round (UR in this text), the eighth round of multilateral trade negotiations under the auspices of the GATT, was launched in Punta del Este, Uruguay in September 1986, and concluded in Marrakesh, Morocco in April 1994. It was the last and also the most difficult trade round under the GATT. The UR became a turning point in international trade negotiations, and in the implementation of trade agreements. First, the UR expanded the agenda to include new issues. Previous rounds had successfully reduced tariffs on trade in most manufactured goods, but attempts to set rules for trade in agricultural goods, steel, footwear, and

1

textiles had been less successful, 'largely as a result of the extensive inter-vention by governments in these sectors' (Barton et al. 2006: 91). The UR expanded the agenda to include these difficult issues, and also non-tariff trade barriers including technical barriers to trade (e.g. relating to food safety). In addition, new issues such as trade in services, trade in products which embody intellectual property, and trade-related investment meas-ures were put onto the agenda (Barton et al. 2006: Chapter 4). Second, while previous trade agreements were concerned with trade barriers at the border, mainly tariffs, the UR negotiations extended the agenda to trade barriers behind the border such as domestic rules on investment, intellec-tual property, food safety, animal and plant protection, service provision, and domestic farm support (Barton et al. 2006: Chapter 5). One of the outcomes was the Uruguay Round *Agreement on Agriculture* (URAA).

Third, the UR resulted in a revised Dispute Settlement Understanding (DSU), ousting the old system that had tried to resolve disputes by con-sensus, and installing instead a new quasi-judicial procedure that WTO members could not easily block. Finally, it should be noted that the entire endeavour was treated as a *Single Undertaking*, in that a single package deal was negotiated (*nothing was agreed until everything was agreed*) that had to be accepted by all participants if they wished to become members of the new WTO, and that all the WTO agreements would then be implemented as a single entity.

Thus, the UR was an unusually broad and ambitious round. The Doha Development Agenda (DDA), more commonly known as the Doha Round, commenced in November 2001 and was also negotiated as a Single Under-taking. Originally it had a fairly broad agenda, including trade in services, non-agricultural goods and agricultural products as well as contested issues like investment protection, competition policy, and transparency in government procurement (the Singapore Issues[1]). Developing countries were reluctant to discuss the three last-mentioned issues and, after the failure at the WTO Ministerial in Cancún in 2003, the European Union (EU) reluctantly agreed to exclude them from the agenda. It was in par-ticular on the insistence of the EU that these issues had been included in the first place, to improve the EU's opportunity to achieve balance in the forthcoming negotiations which otherwise would have focused on agri-culture, as mandated by the URAA. The United States would have been satisfied with a narrow round based on agricultural trade, but this would have been impossible for the EU because of the difficulty of legitimizing unilateral concessions on agriculture to its domestic farm constituencies. By contrast, in a more broadly based round, concessions on agriculture could be portrayed as the price that had to be paid for improved access to foreign markets for other sectors of the EU's economy.

Despite the relative unimportance of agriculture in modern Western economies, disputes over farm trade liberalization can thwart the whole WTO process. Lack of progress in the farm trade negotiations brought both the UR and the Doha Round to a halt on several occasions, and it was not until the farm trade negotiations moved forward that the rounds could continue. From a pure welfare economics perspective it seems odd that farm trade could become such a pivotal issue in trade negotiations. Throughout the 1980s agricultural economists working in universities, government research centres, and in the Organisation for Economic Co-operation and Development (OECD) successfully and repeatedly demonstrated that trade liberalization in agriculture would provide considerable economic welfare gains.[2] These gains would not only be distributed to competitive agricultural exporters such as Australia, New Zealand, Brazil, and Argentina, but also to countries with high degrees of agricultural protection that undertook trade liberalization. By importing cheaper food from the world market, economic resources tied up in agriculture could be redirected to more profitable employment in other economic sectors, thereby increasing national income. In particular, the EU would be likely to reap such benefits because of its high level of agricultural protection. Of course, European farmers would bear the brunt of the adjustment costs.

However, economic argument did not carry as much weight as the political argument. Throughout GATT's history, farm trade has been a difficult issue.[3] This was certainly the case in the UR, following its inclusion on the agenda in Punta del Este in September 1986, and subsequently within the WTO. During the UR, lack of progress in the agricultural trade negotiations caused trouble in all phases of the round, but it was particularly the case when the Round was approaching its planned conclusion in late 1990 that the farm trade issue's pivotal role became evident. Up until then, there had been little progress on agriculture. EU farm policy was at the core of this bottleneck. The inability of the EU to table an offer that could salvage the talks scheduled for the ministerial conference in Brussels in December 1990 was the direct cause of the breakdown of the Round (Paemen and Bensch 1995: Chapter IX). It was not until the EU had embarked upon a meaningful reform of its agricultural policy, culminating in agreement on the MacSharry reform in May 1992 that the Round progressed again.

During the Doha Round, agriculture again became a key issue and caused similar difficulties. The pivotal role of agriculture was clearly demonstrated by a German research team that interviewed 124 delegates at the Cancún (2003) and Hong Kong (2005) WTO ministerial meetings. It reported that 38 per cent of respondents considered farm trade as the most important issue of the Doha Round (Feindt and Müller 2007). An early setback to the agriculture negotiations was the failure to agree on a draft outline for a new agriculture agreement by 31 March 2003, the original deadline that had been set. Attempting to appease in part its international critics, and avoid being blamed for failure at the Cancún ministerial conference in September 2003, EU farm ministers adopted a Common Agricultural Policy (CAP) reform in June 2003 which, in the view of the EU Commission, would shift direct payments into the so-called *green box*—a WTO domestic farm support category not subject to expenditure limits, which we explain in Chapter 3. Though farm trade played its role in the failure in Cancún, it was not the only issue causing the conference to be unsuccessful. Disagreements on the Singapore Issues, and negotiation procedures, also played their role.

Realizing that the future of the round was at stake, agricultural negotiators were able to reach a framework agreement on agriculture in Geneva in late July 2004, which was sufficient to allow the Round to continue (Anania and Bureau 2005). Further progress was achieved in the Hong Kong Ministerial in December 2005, but an overall agreement on the modalities (the architecture) of an agricultural agreement was not yet in sight because this would necessarily involve agreement on market access (problematic for the EU and others) and domestic support (a US concern). In particular, the EU was reluctant to give concessions that would really open up trade. Nevertheless the negotiations continued, but unsuccessfully, and in July 2006 the trade round was suspended without a date set for its resumption. In announcing the suspension, the WTO's Director-General squarely placed the blame on agriculture, saying that it was 'clear that the main blockage is on the Agriculture legs of the triangle of issues' (these being market access and domestic support, and non-agricultural market access (NAMA)) that a small group of countries (referred to as the G6: the United States, EU, Brazil, India, Australia, and Japan) had been trying to address (Lamy 2006). In past negotiations the EU had been castigated as the scapegoat when apportioning blame for the lack of progress in agricultural trade negotiations, but on this occasion the EU skilfully passed the ball to the United States.

Despite the expectations of many pundits, the negotiations were re-sumed in February 2007, and the most optimistic EU negotiators opined that there was a chance of closing the round in early 2008. However, despite this optimism, a meeting of a grouping known as the G4 (Brazil, India, the EU, and the United States) in Potsdam, Germany, in June 2007, failed to advance the negotiations. Nonetheless the chair of the agricul-ture negations, Crawford Falconer, published his *Draft Possible Modalities on Agriculture*, which was further refined over the following months (see e.g. WTO [2008a]). Despite considerable progress, when ministers met in Geneva in July 2008 in a further attempt to conclude the Round they failed to do so, with the proximate cause for failure said to be a rift between India and the United States over market access arrangements for agricul-tural products into developing country markets (see again Pascal Lamy's comment at the beginning of this chapter).

As the above account shows, and despite much drama and the prolonga-tion of negotiations, the agricultural issue did not totally deadlock the UR, resulting in ultimate failure; and the DDA might yet be completed suc-cessfully. In the UR, after tough negotiations, agricultural negotiators were able to resolve the most urgent problems and avoid collapse of the Round. This progress was conditional on reform of the EU's CAP. The 2003 reform of the CAP, although far from paving the way for a new agricultural agreement, did help prevent an early collapse of the Doha Round.

Thus, to understand why and how agricultural trade negotiations since the mid 1980s have become a key source of conflict in GATT and WTO trade rounds, capable of bringing them to the brink of failure, we must understand the nature of agricultural trade conflict and the way the issue is dealt with within the GATT/WTO. In particular, we need to understand how the EU's CAP—a policy system set up to protect one of the least competitive agricultural sectors of the major agricultural trading powers—evolves and sets limits for the agricultural negotiations in the GATT and the WTO. Equally importantly, we need to understand how the CAP's evolution has been influenced by developments within GATT and the WTO.

Agricultural exceptionalism

When analysing the agricultural negotiations, the academic literature concentrates on the difficulties of agreeing on the specific commitments to reduce agricultural support and protection (e.g. Moyer 1993; Paarlberg

1993, 1997; Josling et al. 1996; Swinbank and Tanner 1996; Patterson 1997; Meyerson 2003; Meunier 2005). We argue that the problem of agriculture goes deeper than disputes over tariffs and subsidies. It is about fundamentally different views on the nature of agriculture. Basically, the conflict over agriculture can be put down to the question of whether agriculture is a unique economic sector with special market and production conditions which deserves special treatment because it contributes to national goals, or whether it is an industry with market and production conditions which are not fundamentally different from those of other economic sectors. From the economic depression of the 1930s up until the 1980s, the ideational underpinning of agricultural policy in liberal democracies was characterized by the former view, which in the political science literature is known as *agricultural exceptionalism* (Skogstad 1998: 467–70).

The concept of agricultural exceptionalism is often used to describe the special treatment of agriculture in the nation state and in the EU (Grant 1995; Skogstad 1998; Halpin 2005), but it can also be applied at the global level. It is an *elite assumption*, or idea, on the nature of agricultural production and markets. To some extent, this assumption, or idea, is supported by logical reasoning and evidence, such as theories on the farm income problem and the treadmill providing the intellectual underpinnings of agricultural exceptionalism. At an *ideational* (or abstract) level, agricultural exceptionalism holds that the farming industry is different from most economic sectors in modern societies. First, farming is subject to unstable weather and market conditions, which are beyond the control of the individual farmer. Climatic factors, and plant and animal diseases and pests, can have a marked impact on farm production, resulting in sharp fluctuations in market prices (because of the low price elasticity of demand for farm products) and potentially unstable farm incomes. Furthermore, farmers may collectively overreact to market price movements, with high prices following a harvest failure inducing farmers to increase their plantings for the next season, when prices collapse because of oversupply, etc. Second, it has often been argued that farm incomes could be chronically low ('the farm income problem') in a growing economy. Because of the low income elasticity of demand, there will be little increase in the demand for farm products as the economy grows. Consequently, farms have to get larger, and farmers and farm workers have to quit the land if income levels in the farm sector are to match those in the rest of the economy. However, if farm labour and other farming assets are 'locked in' to the sector, unable to exit and earn higher returns elsewhere in the economy, their income earning capacity may be depressed. Moreover, given that farming is characterized by many small farmers, each of whom is a price-taker, there is a 'treadmill' of competition as each farmer seeks to reduce costs by adopting new technologies, thereby fuelling oversupply which drives down market prices.[4] Thus 'the first rationale for treating agriculture as an exceptional sector is tied to the *specific interests and needs* of farmers' (Skogstad 1998: 468).

The second defining feature of agricultural exceptionalism is that the farming sector 'contributes to broader national interests and goals' (Skogstad 1998: 468). A secure and safe food supply, and stable and reasonable food prices, are highly valued. In the agricultural exceptionalist view, unregulated markets will fail to deliver these valued objectives in food supply. The importance of food security to the world's high-income developed economies decreased during the second half of the twentieth century as a result of changes in the technology of war, the globalization of food supply chains, the international acceptability of global currencies together with the purchasing power of high-income economies, and major productivity gains in agriculture and the food supply chain (Swinbank 1992). Food production increased and relative food prices decreased, so that food shortages, and high food prices, were no longer seen as an immediate risk for high-income consumers (and economies).[5] Accordingly, newer versions of agricultural exceptionalism emerged that emphasized the public goods provided by the agricultural sector. These include care of farmed landscapes, maintenance of biodiversity, flood control, and the viability of rural communities that preserve the country's cultural heritage. By the late 1990s, policy makers and analysts were referring to the *multifunctionality* of agriculture (a term we will return to at various stages in the text).

As an elite assumption on the nature of agricultural production and markets, agricultural exceptionalism underwrites a distinct agricultural policy paradigm and thus legitimizes exceptional treatment of agriculture in terms of public policy (Skogstad 1998: 465–6). A policy paradigm 'specifies not only the goals of policy and the kind of instruments that can be used to attain them, but also the very nature of the problems they are meant to be addressing' (Hall 1993: 279). This distinct agricultural policy paradigm has been variously phrased, for example, the *state-assisted paradigm* (Coleman et al. 1997: 275), the *dependent agriculture paradigm* (Moyer and Josling 2002: 33), and the *interventionist policy paradigm* (Daugbjerg 1999: 418). Despite the lack of an agreed term, the definitions are strikingly similar, all emphasizing a distinct policy paradigm in which the price mechanism is seen as 'a suboptimal means of achieving an efficient and productive agricultural sector' (Coleman et al. 1997: 275). We shall use the term 'state-assisted paradigm' throughout the book.

When the state-assisted paradigm underpins agricultural policy, governments intervene in agricultural markets to ensure farm incomes (Moyer and Josling 2002: 33). This dictates a crucial role for the state. Farm incomes (the policy makers hope) can be maintained or increased by a myriad of measures, used singularly or in various permutations. They include revenue-increasing and cost-reducing measures, such as:

- establishing border protection (by the use of tariffs, variable import levies,[6] import quotas, or quality regulations);
- restricting domestic supply, using quotas and planting restrictions for example, or giving farmers collective monopoly powers in the domestic market in the form of marketing boards;
- intervening to maintain domestic market prices, through intervention purchases, subsidies for the use of food products as animal feed, etc.;
- direct payments to producers: linked to production (e.g. deficiency payments), input use (e.g. area payments), location (e.g. in mountainous regions), or supposedly decoupled from production (e.g. the Single Payment Scheme introduced by the EU in 2003);
- export subsidies, either in explicit form, or for example, via the operation of state-trading enterprises;
- cost-reducing measures, such as subsidies on fertilizers, fuel, seeds, and irrigation water; and
- investment grants, sometimes in the form of subsidized credit, including payments for replanting vines, converting from conventional to organic production, etc.

However, these measures to increase and stabilize incomes are all a bit of a policy chimera, because the increase in farm *revenues* engineered by these schemes, and similarly the full benefit of the input subsidies, will not be matched by a similar increase in farm *incomes*, as land (and other input) prices will rise, and more inputs such as fertilizers and fuel will be purchased as output expands. Moreover, unless targeted at small farmers, and/or farms in disadvantaged regions, the benefits of such schemes are likely to be highly skewed, with a minority of farm businesses reaping the bulk of the benefits (not that small farm businesses are necessarily associated with 'poor' farmers: rich city-types running a hobby farm on the land surrounding their country home, for example). Understandably, the beneficiaries are eager to see support continued.

The state-assisted policy paradigm does not dictate a particular policy design, but leaves room for a variety of agricultural policies. For instance, the way the state-assisted policy paradigm was manifested in the original EU policy model was to support farm incomes indirectly through artificially high market prices, while the dominant model in the United States was direct payment schemes.

The idea of agricultural exceptionalism also led to formation of exceptional political and administrative institutions in the agricultural policy sector. In most industrialized countries, until fairly recently, special ministries have been dedicated to serve agriculture, and ministers of agriculture have been appointed (Halpin 2005: 10). In many countries, s/he often became the minister *for* agriculture rather than the minister *of* agriculture. Special administrative bodies were also set up to administer agricultural policies and these often integrated farm associations in the policy administration, forming close networks consisting of agricultural civil servants and group officials. The policy process was characterized by a corporatist policy style. In some cases, the responsibility for implementing agricultural policy was delegated to farm associations, in particular in the dairy sector.

While agricultural support and protection measures benefited farmers, landowners, and other businesses associated with farm production, they also brought about economic welfare losses for society as a whole. The measures prevent food from being grown where it could be produced most efficiently, which means that the economy is not as productive as it could be, and impose costs on consumers (who pay excessively high prices for food) and taxpayers. Agricultural policies also distorted trade, to the disadvantage of competitive suppliers elsewhere, including many developing countries which cannot afford to provide the same level of support to their farmers. High tariffs prevent them from exporting commodities, in which many have a comparative advantage, to the highly protected markets in developed countries. For instance, cane sugar, which can be produced in many developing countries with a tropical climate, can easily compete with sugar produced from beets grown in the temperate climate of the EU. But an EU tariff on sugar in excess of 200 per cent prevented overseas producers of cane sugar from competing with sugar produced within the EU, apart from a select group of developing countries from the ACP (African, Caribbean, and Pacific States) that had privileged access to the EU's market.

When countries resort to export subsidies to sell their farm surpluses on world markets, it is not comparative advantage but rather the generosity of the finance ministry's funding that determines market share. But at the same time that farmers in competitive countries have suffered from the loss of export markets, producers can even be priced out of their own domestic markets by the subsidized exports of surplus production. For example, Oxfam International (2005: 12) claims that, in the Dominican Republic 'around 10,000 farmers are thought to have been forced out of business during the past two decades due to the dumping of European milk products'. Little wonder that Johnson (1973) talked about *World Agriculture in Disarray*.

Agricultural exceptionalism has been institutionally embedded in GATT since 1947. The fundamental idea underpinning GATT 1947 is that of market liberalism and free (or, at least, freer) trade. The overarching ideational foundation of the GATT was based on comparative advantage. GATT's Preface had declared that the objectives of its Contracting Parties were those of 'raising standards of living, ensuring full employment and a large and steadily growing volume of real income and effective demand, developing the full use of the resources of the world and expanding the production and exchange of goods'. To this end they agreed to enter 'into reciprocal and mutually advantageous arrangements directed to the substantial reduction of tariffs and other barriers to trade and to the elimination of discriminatory treatment in international commerce'. The overall aim was to allow producers with a comparative advantage to expand their market share, giving consumers access to a wider range of more competitively priced products. Though appealing from an economic perspective, the smooth transformation to such a situation can prove difficult, because it puts severe pressure on industries that had previously benefited from protection. In particular, agriculture proved to be one of the main sectors of many economies that strongly resisted free trade. Thus, agriculture was given exceptional treatment in GATT. Articles XI and XVI meant that agriculture was shielded from the full force of rules regarding the use of quantitative import restrictions, and export subsidies. Thus, the farming industry has had exceptional treatment in the international trade rules in force since 1947, mirroring the domestic agricultural policies in many of GATT's Contracting Parties, including the United States and the European countries which a decade later formed the European Economic Community (now the EU). Agricultural exceptionalism in the GATT implied that international trade rules played only a minor role in shaping the CAP. Though this may lead one to think that global agricultural trade operated in a lawless state, it is not quite true: GATT regulated trade in all goods, *including* agriculture, but the rules on agriculture were less tightly drawn, and applied, than they were on other goods, as we outline in Chapter 3.

The origins of agricultural exceptionalism

Throughout the twentieth century agriculture was one of the most protected sectors in developed countries. A 'wave of protectionism' had swept across Europe in the 1880s as governments tried to protect European farmers from overseas competition (McCalla 1969: 332; Tracy 1982: Part I). The railways had opened up the American prairies, and had brought cheap Russian grain to the Baltic ports. From 1877 North America had 'four consecutive seasons in which harvests were excellent' (Tracy 1982: 20). Sharp reductions in freight rates, as a result of new technologies, facilitated the shipment of grain to west European ports, triggering a 'dramatic collapse in grain prices in 1879' (Thirsk 1997: 149), in a year in which western Europe faced a disastrous harvest, with more poor years into the 1880s. Meat imports followed, with Burnett (1979: 134–5) suggesting 1880 as a pivotal date when the 'first really successful cargo of frozen beef and mutton' arrived in London from Melbourne. For British agriculture these developments led to near collapse, particularly on arable farms, but the cheaper food prices led to dramatic changes in the diet of the working class (Burnett 1979: 135). Denmark embarked upon a 'fundamental transformation' of its farm sector (Tracy 1982: 116), focusing on livestock production based on cheap imported grains. But many European countries tried to protect their farmers from this competition by reinforcing or introducing trade restrictions: 'In Germany large-scale agriculture sought and obtained protection for itself. In France, ... agriculture as a whole successfully defended its position with tariffs. In Italy the response was to emigrate' (Kindleberger 1951: 37).

A second wave of agricultural protectionism was triggered by the collapse of commodity prices after the First World War, and then during the world slump following the Wall Street Crash in 1929 (Tracy 1982: Part II). New tariffs and other trade restrictions, and various sorts of income support were introduced, not just in Europe but in many parts of the world. For example, in the United States, commodity support programmes were introduced by Roosevelt's New Deal policies of 1933 (McCalla 1969: 335–6; Orden et al. 1999: 12). Many of these schemes still exist today and form the core of current agricultural policies in many developed countries. During the Second World War and its immediate aftermath, food was again scarce, particularly for importing countries with non-convertible currencies, and this persisted into the commodity price boom of the Korean War (1950–3). Having extolled their farmers to produce more, and having experienced food shortages, governments were reluctant to break their promises and expose their farm sectors to the vagaries of world market price fluctuations when those prices fell. In the United Kingdom, for example, the *Agriculture Act, 1947*, 'constituted a clear commitment...to intervene on behalf of agriculture even in peacetime and was an assurance that there would be no repetition of the events of 1921' (Tracy 1982: 235) when the guarantees stemming from the First World War had been abandoned. It was in this febrile atmosphere that GATT was conceived.

From agricultural exceptionalism to agricultural normalism?

In the 1980s, agricultural exceptionalism came under pressure. A new basic understanding of the nature of agricultural markets and production was emerging, which we refer to as *agricultural normalism*. In agricultural normalism, agricultural markets are perceived to be basically stable and capable of providing society's desired outcomes. Imbalances and instability in agricultural markets are the consequence of government intervention, not the result of imperfections in agricultural markets. Both agricultural markets and production operate in a similar fashion to those of other economic sectors. The world market is stable, and not necessarily characterized by depressed prices, and indeed there is a growing market for processed and differentiated foods offering good returns. Price instability on world markets could be decreased by encouraging increased linkage of national markets: by reducing or removing the tariffs, non-tariff barriers, and export subsidies which in effect isolate domestic markets from price movements on a small and residual world market. On a larger and more representative world market, prices would be less sensitive to fluctuations in demand and supply. Government support creates surplus production, resulting in both depressed and unstable world markets (Johnson 1975).

These alternative basic assumptions underwrote a new agricultural policy paradigm, the *market-liberal policy paradigm*, which prescribes a very different role for the state in the agricultural sector. In this paradigm:

> market allocation takes precedence over state intervention, and efficiency over equity. The central tenets are as follows: first, agriculture should be understood as an economic sector like all others and

agricultural policy should not be premised on serving other policy goals; second, competitive markets, in which only supply and demand determine prices, should be the source of producers' incomes; third, only those producers who can earn an income from the sale of commodities in these free markets should remain active in agriculture; and finally, individual producers should be responsible, mainly through private insurance markets, for protecting themselves against income losses due to natural conditions (Coleman et al. 1997: 275–6).[7]

The role of the state under the market-liberal paradigm differs significantly from that of the state-assisted policy paradigm. Agriculture is not seen as being in need of permanent income support and therefore the role of the state is simply to correct for market failures or imperfect markets. Policy instruments would be very different from those stemming from the state-assisted agriculture paradigm. For instance, 'farmers may still need state support in correcting for imperfect insurance markets if incomes (or revenue streams) are chronically unstable' (Coleman et al. 2004: 103). Consequently, while the market-liberal paradigm to a large extent underpins Australian agricultural policy, the state plays an important role in drought relief (Botterill 2003). Since the state-assisted policy paradigm prevailed for a long period in most industrialized countries its support instruments could not be abolished overnight, but have to be phased out over a certain period. Therefore the market-liberal policy paradigm allows for the use of decoupled compensation payments in the transition period (Coleman et al. 2004: Chapter 4).

Agricultural normalism became the ideational underpinning of the URAA. Coleman et al. (2004: 106) convincingly argue that agricultural normalism 'became globally institutionalized in the set of rules in the WTO's Agreement on Agriculture negotiated in the UR. Behind these rules stands the belief that world markets in agriculture will be essentially stable if domestic policies are reformed to conform to the competitive [*market-liberal*] paradigm'.[8] Change in the farm trade regime was fundamental, not so much because of the constraints in terms of specific commitments to reduce farm support and protection which it put on WTO member states, but rather in terms of the underlying perception of agriculture. It significantly altered the debate about the future of agricultural policies and international farm trade rules. As Tangermann (2004: 40) argues: 'The Uruguay Round has not only resulted in new legal rules and quantitative reduction commitments in the areas of market access, domestic support and export competition. It has also affected the nature of the policy debate in agriculture. The WTO has become a relevant factor in agricultural policy making'. National policy makers had to consider how URAA commitments impacted on existing farm policies, and envisage how future rounds of trade negotiations (e.g. that foreshadowed in the URAA) might reshape the URAA and therefore set a framework for various farm policy reform options that WTO members might consider. Quoting Tangermann (2004: 37) again: 'while in the past the four letters "GATT" were unknown to many participants in the agricultural policy debate, the term "WTO" can now be heard even when farmers chat to each other in the local pub!'

However, the URAA was characterized by ambivalence. In the short term the URAA had a very limited impact on trade because it allowed countries to maintain high levels of subsidies and import protection. As Tangermann (2004: 39–40) remarks:

> the point has often been made that most of the quantitative commitments established in the Uruguay Round were so generous that they did not yield much in the way of trade liberalization. As a matter of fact, levels of support provided to agricultural producers in OECD countries, as measured within the OECD's framework of PSE[9] analysis, have not, on average, declined significantly after the Uruguay Round, though they decreased somewhat while the Uruguay Round negotiations were still going on.

Thus the Agreement was both a remarkable shift in the perception of agriculture, *and* a major disappointment for those hoping for a rapid elimination of agricultural support and protection. Therefore, when analysing the URAA it is useful to distinguish between its *ideational and operational levels, or layers*. The former refers to the ideas that underpin the Agreement while the latter refers to the specific commitments to reduce farm support and protection (Daugbjerg 2008: 1268). Even though ideational change was significant, few have analysed it. By contrast, in this book we turn our attention to this neglected side of the URAA—its ideational underpinning and it impacts.

The pivotal role of EU farm policy in the WTO

As argued earlier, the CAP plays an important role in the WTO, with a pivotal position in agricultural trade negotiations. Not only has the EU emerged as the major agricultural trading power, but among the major players it has (or has had) one of the least competitive agricultural sectors.

This is illustrated in Table 1.1 that shows the six largest exporters and importers of agricultural products in 2003, the year the Fischler reforms were agreed, with—for selected OECD countries—the respective Producer Support Estimates (PSEs) for 1986–8 (the base period for the URAA reduction commitments) and 2003–5. Although Japan has a much higher percentage PSE than the EU, it is not a significant exporter of agricultural products, and its import role is less. A caveat is in order, however: Although the PSE measures the level of support received by the farm sector, it does not differentiate between the types of support that may have rather different effects on production and hence trade. The EU's 'old' CAP in the 1980s, ☆ for example, relied heavily on market price support that heavily impacted on trade. The MacSharry reforms of 1992 introduced a much more benign system of support that had less impact on production and hence trade; and the Fischler reforms of 2003–4 further decoupled EU support. These changes are not reflected in the PSE figures reported in Table 1.1.

Nonetheless, the high level of support, and its reliance on subsidized exports, indicates that the EU is the major trading power most affected by the negotiation of new trade agreements limiting the ability of WTO members to protect their farm sectors. Therefore 'Agriculture is the issue on which the EU is most on the defensive; it is the EU policy for which the Doha Round has the most serious implications' (Young 2007: 804).

Another important factor making the evolution of the CAP a key issue in WTO negotiations is the EU's institutional framework for determining

Table 1.1 Top six agricultural importers and exporters, 2003, and PSEs for selected OECD countries

	Per cent of world imports 2003	Per cent of world exports 2003	PSE per cent 1986–8	PSE per cent 2003–5
EU	13.6*	10.9*	41	34
US	10.7	11.3	22	16
Japan	8.1	nl	64	58
China	4.2	3.3		
Canada	2.5	5.0	36	22
Korea	2.2	nl	70	62
Brazil	nl	3.6		
Australia	nl	2.4	8	5

*Excludes intra-EU trade, but all the figures are expressed as percentage of total world (including intra-EU) trade.
nl: Not listed in top 15 importers/exporters.
Source: Per cent of world agricultural trade: WTO (2004a).
PSE per cent: OECD data as published in Agra Europe, 23 June 2006: EP/7.

15

trade policy. The EU is a member of the WTO in its own right, and negotiates on trade policy as a single entity: the member states have delegated to the EU the responsibility for trade policy. But there is a double delegation of responsibility, because it is the Commission that undertakes the negotiations on behalf of the EU, on the basis of a *mandate* established by the member states through the Council of Ministers, and it is then the Council of Ministers that must conclude any agreement. Moreover, GATT/ WTO negotiations on agriculture extend beyond the traditional concerns of trade negotiators: the URAA negotiations, in which the Commissioner for Agriculture (Ray MacSharry) took the lead for the EU, also resulted in agreements to limit domestic support to farmers, and export subsidies; and the agreement to reduce import protection itself had implications for the 'old' CAP's variable import levy mechanisms which were seen as an integral part of a managed market. Thus agreement on the URAA inevitably involved farm ministers, in their grouping as a Council of Ministers. Where the EU has conservative trade interests, as with farm trade, and where the norm of consensual decision making in the Council of Ministers is very strong, which it is in agricultural politics, the EU's negotiating position will set limits for a WTO agreement. Consequently, WTO agreements on agriculture cannot readily be accepted by the EU unless there is also agreement on CAP reform, whilst CAP reform is, to a large extent, driven by pressure from the GATT/WTO negotiations.

Research questions and the argument of the book

Agricultural exceptionalism survived for almost half a century in the GATT. Although agricultural trade liberalization was on the agenda of the Dillon (1960–2), Kennedy (1963–7), and Tokyo (1973–9) Rounds, it was not until the UR that agricultural exceptionalism was seriously questioned, and eroded. As a hegemonic actor in the post-war period, the United States had ensured that agricultural exceptionalism was institutionally embedded in GATT 1947. However, as Goldstein (1993: 223) notes: 'By the 1960s, American opinion had changed. But GATT rules had not. Thus, the problem for the United States thereafter was to attempt, through diplomacy, to establish new operating procedures by which to liberalize trade'.[10] During the UR, the United States was more committed than earlier to liberalizing farm trade. President Reagan's Zero-2000 proposal was a clear expression of agricultural normalism because, if it had been adopted, world market shares would henceforth have been determined by comparative advantage rather than agricultural subsidies.

Since the consensus rule applied in deciding new rules in GATT rounds, as it still does in the WTO, one may wonder why the EU allowed the idea of agricultural exceptionalism, as a defence of the CAP, to be eroded as the ideational underpinning of the international farm trade regime. The EU believed that agricultural markets were not particularly effective in generating desired social outcomes, and consequently that government intervention was required. Whilst the EU's proposal for the UR negotiations acknowledged the need to reduce market distortions, its tenor nonetheless emphasized a managed market approach. For example, it said that 'it cannot be conceivable to set up a general "decoupled" support arrangement, which without an adequate price stabilization mechanism would have the same perverse effect on production as the current régimes' (GATT 1989c: 3). The consensus rule of GATT implied that all members had veto power, including the EU, which also has additional bargaining power as a result of its large market (Steinberg 2002). Despite these bargaining advantages, the EU accepted an erosion of agricultural exceptionalism in world trade rules. So, in Chapter 4, we address the question: *Why and how was agricultural exceptionalism eventually eroded in the UR?*

Although, as argued earlier, the specific reduction commitments of the URAA were only expected to have limited immediate impact upon domestic farm policies, disputes over the legal interpretation of the UR texts inevitably arose, and the new DSU was called into play. This institutional change brought into the WTO system by the UR enables actors dissatisfied with progress in trade negotiations to bring about further agricultural trade liberalization by successfully challenging policies in dispute settlement. Under the old GATT system, disputes were settled by consensus (tempered by power diplomacy), giving the contracting parties veto power. This implied that it was very difficult to enforce GATT rules unless all the countries involved in the dispute accepted the panel's decision. The UR resulted in a break with the past in the dispute settlement system. The new system is based on a quasi-judicial procedure implying that individual disputants cannot block rulings as they could under the GATT. Countries are expected to bring their policies into conformity with WTO rules (or face retaliatory trade sanctions). In other words, 'soft' law has been replaced by 'hard', or harder, law. So, the second question to be answered is *Have proceedings in the Dispute Settlement Body resulted in further farm trade liberalization?* This is the theme of Chapter 5.

As argued earlier, the EU's farm policy occupies a pivotal, even blocking, position in WTO negotiations. But the evolution of the CAP does not take place in isolation from the broader international context within which it is embedded. The URAA, with its agricultural normalist ideational underpinning, influences domestic agricultural policy debates and sets the direction for domestic reform. The URAA legitimized the demands of advocates of reform who, for whatever reason, wanted to reduce agricultural support. From being primarily an EU domestic exercise, EU agricultural policy evolution is now increasingly taking WTO rules and processes into consideration. From 1995 on, policy makers designing CAP reform would strive to ensure conformity with WTO agreements, and perhaps even attempt to anticipate future developments in the WTO. Thus the *context* of EU agricultural policy making has evolved and continues to do so. Therefore, in Chapter 6, we ask as our third question: *In what way has the ideational underpinning of the URAA influenced EU agricultural policy institutions and CAP reform?*

The causal relationship between CAP reform and WTO agreements on agriculture is not unidirectional. The evolution of the CAP influenced in turn developments in the WTO, enabling further liberalization in agricultural trade. Due to the comparatively limited competitiveness of the EU agricultural sector and the EU's institutionally constrained ability to undertake CAP reform, the CAP sets limits for agricultural trade liberalization within the WTO. Thus our fourth question, which we address in Chapter 7, asks: *How do CAP reforms feed back into the WTO negotiations, setting limits for what can be achieved?* The way the CAP reforms and trade disputes and negotiations interact has important implications for the outcome of negotiations on farm trade liberalization.

In Chapter 8, we summarize the theoretical challenges and the most important findings and analyse the post-Doha trade agenda in the light of the difficulties of the Single Undertaking in bringing about a conclusion of the Doha Round, and the 2008 food crisis.

The EU, its institutions, and decision-making procedures

To many Europeans, let alone citizens of other regions of the world, the EU in its various manifestations, its institutions, and its decision-making procedures, remains mysterious. Thus, for readers less familiar with the EU, we include a brief overview.

The European Economic Community (EEC) came into being on 1 January 1958 under the Treaty of Rome, providing the foundation for the trade policies, and the CAP, referred to in this book. From 1967 the EEC, the European Coal and Steel Community (ECSC, which has now lapsed), and the European Atomic Energy Community (EURATOM) were run as a single entity: the European Communities (EC). Over the years its membership has expanded from the original 6 member states in 1958 to 27 on 1 January 2007, with others hoping to join, and through a series of treaty changes its competences have expanded and its decision-making rules have changed, giving in particular progressively more powers to the European Parliament. Following ratification of the Maastricht Treaty two further 'pillars' were added to the European edifice—a common foreign and security policy, and cooperation in the fields of justice and home affairs—and the name European Union (EU) was assumed. In Lisbon on 13 December 2007 a new treaty was signed by the EU's leaders (the *Treaty of Lisbon amending the Treaty on European Union and the Treaty establishing the European Community*),[11] which, had it been ratified by all 27 member states, would have made further changes to the EU's competences and decision-making procedures, but the rejection of the Treaty by Ireland in a referendum has placed its future in doubt. Legally it is the EC (rather than the EU) that is a WTO member, and so WTO documents refer to the EC. So, *EEC, EC, or EU*? In this book our usual practice has been to use the acronym *EU*, even when talking about events prior to adoption of the Maastricht Treaty, and to its activities in the WTO, but we have used *EEC* when this seemed more appropriate particularly in Chapter 4, and we have preserved other authors' usage in quotations.

From the outset, the Treaty of Rome conferred on the EU the exclusive competence to determine a CAP. It was a customs union, with a common external tariff, 'with a common commercial policy towards third countries' (Article 3 EEC). There were four main institutions: a Commission (which now styles itself as the European Commission), a Council, a Parliament, and a Court of Justice.

The Commission, headed by a College of Commissioners, is the EU's civil service. It is arranged into a number of *Directorates-General*, and other services: the Directorate-General for Agriculture and Rural Development (once known as DG VI), and the Directorate-General for Trade, are the directorates most closely associated with the narrative in this text. The College of Commissioners is appointed for a fixed term of office: in the current College (2005–9) there are 27 Commissioners, one from each member state; but, supposedly, they are *not* there to represent the interests

Table 1.2 EU commissioners (president, agriculture and trade) 1985–the present

Period	President	Agriculture	Trade
1985–8	Jacques Delors	Frans Andriessen	Willy De Clercq
1989–92	Jacques Delors	Ray MacSharry	Frans Andriessen
1993–4	Jacques Delors	René Steichen	Leon Brittan
1995–9	Jacques Santer*	Franz Fischler	Leon Brittan
2000–2004	Romano Prodi	Franz Fischler	Pascal Lamy**
2005–9	José Manuel Barroso	Mariann Fischer Boel	Peter Mandelson*** Catherine Ashton

*The Santer Commission resigned on 15 March 1999, following allegations of corruption within the Commission. Mario Monti served as president in an interim capacity, and Franz Fischler and Sir Leon Brittan retained their responsibilities, until the Prodi Commission took over in September 1999.
**Subsequently Director-General of the WTO. He had served as *Chef de Cabinet* for Jacques Delors through the three Delors Commissions.
***Resigned 3 October 2008 to join the British government. He was replaced by Baroness Ashton (Catherine Ashton).

of the member state. Each has responsibility for a particular policy field: Table 1.2 lists those responsible for Agriculture, and GATT/WTO Trade negotiations, from the UR to the present.

The Treaties empower the Commission with a number of responsibilities, in particular the power of initiative. Accordingly it is commonly said that *the Commission proposes, and the Council disposes*. Thus the Commission, broadly speaking, has the sole prerogative to propose new legislation: the proposal then passes to the Council and the European Parliament for decision. In the original formulation, the powers of the European Parliament were rather limited; and—without the provisions of the Lisbon Treaty—this remains the case for the CAP, although in related areas of policy (e.g. food law) the European Parliament and the Council are the joint decision makers, and this has long been the case with regard to the budget.

The Council, served by a small permanent secretariat, is made up of a representative from each of the member states, and tends to meet in different configurations to reflect the items on the agenda.[12] Thus matters relating to the CAP are dealt with by farm ministers meeting as the Agriculture and Fisheries Council. The presidency of the Council rotates on a six-month basis (though the Lisbon Treaty would have changed this). Council meetings are attended by the appropriate Commissioner, who presents and defends the Commission's proposal; and, when changes are required before a proposal proves acceptable to the Council, it is the Commissioner and the Council President who will broker the changes.

Table 1.3 Member states' voting weights, EU12, 1992

Member states	Weight	Member states	Weight
Belgium	5	Ireland	3
Denmark	3	Italy	10
Germany	10	Luxembourg	2
Greece	5	The Netherlands	5
Spain	8	Portugal	5
France	10	United Kingdom	10

In some areas of EU policy, unanimity is required. Increasingly, however, qualified majority voting (QMV) was provided for by the original Treaties and subsequent treaty amendments, and this has been the case for the CAP since its earliest days. Under QMV the votes of the member states are weighted in (very) rough proportion to their populations: details have varied through treaty changes and successive enlargements, but by way of example the weightings in 1992, when the MacSharry reforms were adopted, are listed in Table 1.3. A qualified majority was 54: so if member states with a total vote of 54 or more were in favour of a Commission proposal, it could be adopted by qualified majority vote. This meant that a blocking minority was 23: together France, the United Kingdom, and Denmark, for example, by voting against, abstaining, or refusing to take part in a vote, could block a decision.

From the outset, QMV was contentious and led to one of the major crises in the history of the EU (and the CAP). It occurred in 1965, in the so-called *empty-chair crisis*, when France left the Council chamber, and it was only resolved some months later with the so-called *Luxembourg compromise*. Much has been written about this early history of the EU: see for example, the not uncontested account by Moravcsik (2000*a*, 2000*b*) and subsequent papers in the *Journal of Cold War Studies*. Suffice to say the other five member states basically agreed not to outvote France, even though the Treaties might permit QMV, should France declare the matter to be of vital national importance. Paradoxically, this power of *veto* was reinforced by the accession of the euro-sceptical Denmark and the United Kingdom in 1973, because if the three acted in concert, and refused to take part in a vote, collectively they did command a blocking minority (Swinbank 1997: 66).

It is doubtful whether a member state could successfully invoke the Luxembourg compromise today, but there have been suggestions that they might try.[13] For example, it is reported that, in 2003, the French president said of the proposed Fischler reform package: 'The current proposal from the Commissioner is not acceptable....It is not accepted by France. This means everyone has to move, including the Commissioner' (*Financial Times* 21 June 2003: 8). If accurate, it suggests that France (or at least Mr. Chirac) believed that France should not be outvoted on matters of supreme importance.

In practice, however, the Council and Commission strive hard to reach consensus, thereby avoiding the need to go to a vote. For example, Heisenberg (2005: 71–3) suggests that 81 per cent of all Council decisions are made by consensus; and, as pointed out by Cunha (2007: 78), the unanimity norm in EU agricultural policy has 'proved to be an important help for ministers *explaining* at home why they had supported certain decisions which were negative to their farmers'.

The Council of Ministers is not the only forum in which member states deliberate on proposals from the Commission. In addition there are regular meetings of the Heads of State and Government, in a grouping now known as the European Council. Its *modus operandi* is to take strategic decisions, on the future of the EU and its policies, which then need to be enacted into EU law by the appropriate Council of Ministers (with or without the European Parliament, depending on whether a co-decision rule applies). In effect the European Council proceeds on the basis of consensus, trading off the interests of one member state on a particular issue against those of other member states on issues of importance to them; and elsewhere we have suggested that when CAP reform is pushed onto the European Council's agenda the outcome is likely to be a dilution of the reform package (Daugbjerg and Swinbank 2007).

The Treaty of Rome introduced a double delegation of powers with respect to trade policy. Not only did the creation of the customs union involve the member states granting exclusive competence to the EU to negotiate and conclude trade agreements, but it also gave the Commission particular powers. Thus the Commission was to submit proposals to the Council 'for tariff negotiations with third countries'; the Council would 'authorise the Commission to open such negotiations'; and the Commission would then undertake the negotiations 'in consultation with a special committee...and within the framework of such directives as the Council may issue to it' (EEC Articles 111 and 113). Originally known as the *113 Committee*, this is now known as the *133 Committee* following the renumbering of the Treaty Articles by the Nice Treaty. Finally, trade agreements would be 'concluded by the Council on behalf of the Community' (EEC Article 114). Throughout, the Council was authorized by the Treaty to decide by QMV (after an initial period in the early days of the EEC when the unanimity rule applied).

Thus the Commission, usually led by the Commissioner with responsibility for trade, and a professional cadre of trade negotiators, negotiates on behalf of the EU on the basis of a mandate given by the member states. As the UR was a Single Undertaking, involving policy arenas beyond trade in goods, there was a complicated debate about the ratification process, the applicability of QMV in these non-traditional areas, and the role of the European Parliament, which we do not discuss here. For details on the role of the Council, Commission, and the European Parliament in the negotiation and ratification of trade agreements see Woolcock 2005.

The EU was not itself a member of GATT 1947, but the Commission was accepted as the EU's negotiator, representing the member state GATT signatories. Following the creation of the WTO on 1 January 1995, the EU became a member of the WTO in its own right, whilst the member states retained their membership. Ministerial meetings (such as Seattle in 1989 and Cancún in 2003) are a bit of a jamboree, with a large EU team clustering around the Commission negotiators: ministers and others representing the member states, members of the European Parliament (MEPs), NGOs, and other representative groups. When sessions move into the real negotiations, either professional trade negotiators meeting in Geneva or elsewhere, or ministers meeting in closed or restricted sessions at ministerial meetings, it is the Commission negotiators who take their place in the room, leaving the representatives of the member states outside, to be briefed or consulted later.[14] This means that the Article 133 Committee, and/or the Council of Ministers, might be meeting frequently in some foreign location, as the member states jostle to exercise control over the Commission negotiators, who in turn try to maintain their room for manoeuvre.

23

Chapter 2

Ideas, Institutions, and Policy:
A Theoretical Framework

In the previous chapter, we set out to explain: (*a*) why and how ideational change occurred; (*b*) how this impacted on the implementation of the Uruguay Round Agreement on Agriculture (URAA); (*c*) how the ideational change influenced the European Union's (EU's) agricultural policy evolution; and (*d*) how such domestic policy change feeds back into the WTO farm trade negotiations. To guide our empirical study we outline in this chapter an analytical framework consisting of four components to answer these four research questions. Though ideational theory is still in its infant phases, it has potential to direct us towards the key factors bringing about ideational change in world farm trade rules.

The first two components of the analytical framework are developed to analyse ideational and institutional change in the WTO while the last two address the interrelationship between such changes at the global and the domestic level. The *first component* identifies the theoretically relevant factors explaining ideational change in the WTO. The *second component* focuses on the relationship between ideational change and change of WTO institutions given responsibility for overseeing trade agreements. Since there is little evidence that the URAA led to rapid and full-scale liberalization of domestic agricultural policies, the *third component* of the framework develops an analytical model which can be applied to analyse gradual and cumulative institutional and policy change at the domestic level as a consequence of ideational change at the global level. Recognizing that agricultural trade liberalization is a gradual process, likely to stretch over a long time period in a sequence of trade rounds, the *fourth component* of our framework suggests how evolution of EU agricultural policy sets limits for WTO farm trade agreements.

Before outlining this theoretical framework, we give a general and brief overview of the academic literature on agricultural trade liberalization, dominated as it is by a 'free-trade' perspective based on neoclassic trade theory. After this, we review the literature analysing the relationship between EU decision-making processes on trade policy and the constraints this places on the EU's negotiating capacity in the WTO; and we then explore the role of ideas in public policy.

The free-trade perspective on agricultural trade liberalization

After agricultural trade became an integral part of the Uruguay Round (UR) in the mid-1980s, social scientists began paying much more attention to the issue and as a result a number of books and articles on the agricultural trade negotiations and the agreement itself were published. These works are characterized by a descriptive approach, accounting for the way the negotiations unfolded (e.g. Josling et al. 1996; Swinbank and Tanner 1996) and legal expositions of the agreement (e.g. Desta 2002). Many agricultural economists concentrated on estimating the Agreement's likely impacts on trade volumes, world prices, and economic welfare, using a variety of partial and general equilibrium modelling techniques: for a review of this literature covering the period from the early 1980s through to 1999, see Sumner and Tangermann (2002: Section 4). Somewhat alarmingly Sumner and Tangermann conclude that the 'models economists use are, on the one hand, complex enough to defy comprehension of what drives the results, and on the other hand, so simple that they cannot incorporate crucial features of a complex policy reform' (p. 2039). This strong quantitative approach was continued in the run-up to, and during, the Doha Round, with various attempts made to capture more of the complexities of preferential tariff structures and other subtleties of farm and trade policies: Anderson and Martin (2006) provide a recent overview. Much of this modelling is based on neoclassical trade theory. Consequently, the general thrust of the results is that trade liberalization would improve the general well-being of humankind; and economists 'have continued to preach the efficiency benefits derived from the full use of comparative advantage, free consumer choice, and uninhibited international trade flows' (Sumner and Tangermann 2002: 2001).

This 'free-trade' perspective can also be seen in the writings of some political scientists. For example Davis (2003: 4–5) introduces her book by claiming 'agriculture stands out as a sector where countries stubbornly defend domestic programs... Collective action incentives guarantee that farmers wield political strength beyond their numbers', but the 'costs of the resulting agricultural protection include expenditures for higher prices and taxes'. There is also a moralistic, even mercantilist, tone when she writes: 'Protection also closes off valuable markets for agriculture exporters, which include the United States and many developing countries... Although many developing countries have a comparative advantage in agriculture and agricultural exports could play a major role in poverty reduction, the subsidies and trade barriers of rich countries have prevented these gains from trade' (pp. 5–6).[1]

But governments have been reluctant to liberalize, and so—from this free-trade perspective—the political economy literature has attempted to explain why governments continue to intervene, why policy is biased against trade, and why inefficient policy instruments persist (de Gorter and Swinnen 2002). Kindleberger (1951: 30) had suggested that 'a useful tool of analysis might be found in group behavior'. One of the basic assumptions underpinning the concept of perfect competition is that all actors are perfectly informed, but Downs (1957: 236) suggested that consumers and taxpayers might well be *rationally ignorant* when policies have only a marginal impact upon them: 'Any concept of democracy based on an electorate of equally well-informed citizens is irrational.' These, and other contributions, helped develop the notion of a political marketplace in which interest groups, voters, politicians, and bureaucrats interact in pursuit of their own interests. This results in *government failure*, in that policies are not designed to address the economist's traditional concerns of market failure or equity, but instead respond to the rent-seeking activities of various interest groups (Brooks 1996). However, such a relatively narrow theoretical perspective neglects the importance of institutions and ideas in policy making. Further, the political economy literature has mostly focused on domestic (and EU) policy-making processes and is not designed specifically to analyse decision-making processes simultaneously taking place at the domestic and international level. In political science much attention has been directed towards understanding such two-level games.

Two-level games and trade negotiations

A political science approach much applied to international trade negotiations is the two-level game model developed by Putnam (1988). Several studies have applied this framework in analysing the UR negotiations on agriculture. For instance, Paarlberg (1993, 1997), Moyer (1993), Meyerson (2003), and Meunier (2005) apply the framework.[2] Putnam argues that international negotiations can best be conceived of as two-level games. Negotiators are simultaneously subject to domestic and international pressures. At the domestic level, various types of groups or individuals seek to put pressure on the negotiator to reach agreements which are favourable to them, or at least do not burden them. At the international level, 'national governments seek to maximize their own ability to satisfy domestic pressures, while minimizing the adverse consequences of foreign developments' (Putnam 1988: 434).

International negotiators on both sides of the negotiating table are constrained by the fact that the agreements made must be ratified domestically. Therefore, international negotiators must consult domestic groups, such as interest groups, politicians, and public authorities, in order to establish what could be ratified in the domestic political arena. Applying the terminology of Putnam, they must define their win-set, which is 'the set of all possible . . . [international] agreements that would "win"—that is, gain the necessary majority among the constituents' (p. 437). States in which few agreements are supported by a majority have small win-sets, while large win-sets occur where several possible agreements can attract the support of a majority. To reach agreement in international negotiations, the win-sets of the states must overlap, and 'the larger each win-set, the more likely they are to overlap' (p. 438). In other words, the more possible outcomes that are acceptable to domestic constituencies, the easier it is to find solutions at the international level which can be ratified domestically (p. 438).

The relative size of win-sets influences the bargaining power of the negotiator at the international level. As Schelling (1960: 19) had argued: 'the power of a negotiator often rests on a manifest inability to make concessions and to meet demands'. This counter-intuitive statement is often referred to as the Schelling conjecture (Meunier 2005: 50). A negotiator representing a state with a small win-set can forcefully claim that certain proposals stand a limited chance of being ratified domestically and this gives him/her a bargaining advantage. In contrast, the negotiating positions of states with large win-sets can more easily be moved because their negotiators cannot put forward a similarly forceful argument. Therefore, international agreements tend to accommodate the interests of states with small win-sets. The Schelling conjecture has been criticized by Meunier (2005: 50–3), who argues that it is not a proposition that can be universally applied, but is valid only in certain circumstances. She also claims there is limited evidence to suggest that the strategy of converting small win-sets to bargaining power is widely used in practice (see Meunier 2005: 53 for references).

The two-level game model pays insufficient attention attention to the way in which membership of international trade regimes impact on *domestic* policy reform processes which in turn may enable states to change their negotiating positions and thus alter the game in future negotiations within the regime. For instance, it is of little help in explaining how or why the EU's negotiating position has changed over time. Comparing the Uruguay and Doha Rounds, for example, we note a number of contrasts. First, whereas the EU's position in the UR was essentially reactive (Ingersent et al. 1994: 61), the EU adopted a proactive negotiating stance in the Doha Round. Second, in the Fischler reforms of 2003, by decoupling its direct payments, the EU adopted a position in the Doha Round that would have been unthinkable during the UR.[3] Third, in Hong Kong in December 2005, the EU agreed to phase out export subsidies by 2013 if an overall agreement could be secured. The institutionalization of export subsidies into GATT 1947 had been one of the emblematic features of agricultural exceptionalism: indeed, Sumner and Tangermann (2002: 2023) suggest that the UR negotiations were to a significant extent 'driven by the grain trade war between the United States and the European Union' that had erupted in the 1980s. During the UR any suggestion that the EU's negotiators were contemplating an elimination of export subsidies would undoubtedly have provoked a French veto.

When focusing on the EU's engagement with its trading partners over a single agreement on agricultural trade liberalization, such as the URAA, the two-level game model with its Schelling conjecture makes analytical sense. However, if one wants to explain why the EU's negotiating position has evolved substantially over time and to show how this has influenced the discussion on agricultural trade within the GATT/WTO, we need a more dynamic perspective on two-level games. Another weakness of the two-level game is that it assumes that international negotiations are one-dimensional, focusing on the specific commitments of an agreement to reduce tariffs and support. As Young (1997: 298) correctly points out: 'No matter how complex regimes become, in the final analysis they generally rest on a dominant vision or discourse.' Thus in Chapter 1 we argued that the UR negotiations on agricultural trade involved both an operational and an ideational layer, the latter referring to the ideas that underpinned the URAA, whilst the former referred to the specific commitments to reduce farm support and protection.

Ideas and institutions in public policy

Recent theoretical developments within political science have drawn attention to the role of ideas in explaining institutional and policy change. To explain how trade rules in agriculture develop we need to have a dynamic model in which ideas and institutional evolution are the main driving forces explaining the development of agricultural trade rules over time. Thus, we need an analytical model that takes account of the fact that the domestic and international contexts within which negotiations are conducted evolve, and that this then changes the setting for each event in the sequence of trade policy making.

> Keynes (1936: 383–4) closed his *General Theory* reflecting on the role of ideas as determinants of policy change:
>   ...the ideas of economists and political philosophers, both when they are right and when they are wrong, are more powerful than is commonly understood. Indeed the world is ruled by little else. Practical men, who believe themselves to be quite exempt from any intellectual influences, are usually the slaves of some defunct economist. Madmen in authority, who hear voices in the air, are distilling their frenzy from some academic scribbler of a few years back. I am sure the power of vested interests is vastly exaggerated compared with the gradual encroachment of ideas...soon or late, it is ideas, not vested interests, which are dangerous for good or evil.

Though Keynes highlighted the power of ideas, policy analysts have tended to give priority to interest-based theories rather than to ideational theories when explaining public policies. Indeed Brooks (1996: 367) suggests that 'the political economy perspective is a theoretical rebuke to Keynes'. Usually, the interests of the key actors have been derived from their structural position in the economy. Public choice theory is perhaps the most prominent example of such an approach to public policy analysis. During the last two decades or so, policy analysts have shown a renewed interest in institutions and the way they influence key actors' opportunities to shape public policies. Most scholars using these theories would agree with Schattschneider (1975 [1960]: 69), who states: 'organization is the mobilization of bias: Some issues are organized into politics while others are organized out'. For instance, following this line of argument, Hall (1986: 266) argues: 'organisational structures [tend] to lead policy-makers into some courses of action and away from others; and each course of action tends to favor the interests of some social groups over others'.

Classic institutional theory concentrated on analysing the influence of formal institutions such as constitutional rules. New institutionalism has put much more emphasis on informal institutions such as procedures, codes, and norms. For instance, the Council of Agricultural Ministers is a *formal* body, while the agricultural policy network in the EU is an *informal* institution (see Daugbjerg 1999). Formal and informal rules of decision-making bodies specify how decisions are to be made, narrow down the agenda being discussed, prescribe certain types of solutions, and specify actors' obligations and even roles to play. By performing these functions, institutions provide a certain degree of certainty by structuring expectations on other actors' behaviour and the issues being addressed, how they are processed and, not least, how decisions are made and implemented. In the institutionalist literature, institutions have an independent effect on policy decisions since they constrain certain actions and facilitate others. However, there is disagreement on the extent to which institutions influence human behaviour. Are they to be seen as devices that constrain and facilitate certain actions of rational and instrumental actors attempting to maximize their self-interest? Or are institutions devices that not only constrain and facilitate certain actions, but also define the interests and rationality of political actors? Basically, this disagreement is a reflection of the classic structure–agency problem in the social sciences. In the extreme, the key question in this debate is: 'Are ... actors unwitting products of their context, helpless individuals with minimal control over their destiny, floundering around in a maelstrom of turbulent currents; or are they knowledgeable and intentional subjects with complete control over the settings which frame their actions?' (Hay 1995: 189).

Nonetheless, institutionalists agree that institutions matter in public policy making; they preclude some actions and facilitate others. Political institutions affect the range of options available to policy makers by setting 'limits on what some agents can do, and enable other agents to do things they otherwise would not have been able to do ...' (Rothstein 1992: 35; see also March and Olsen 1989, North 1990: 23, 33). Thus, institutions constrain political actors, such as the EU Farm Commissioner or the US Trade Representative in offering certain concessions in the WTO. In the EU an important informal decision-making rule is that WTO offers should be based on a consensus within the Council of Agriculture Ministers, or at least it should have the acceptance of France even if some (smaller) EU member states have to be voted down. Similarly, it makes a major difference for the autonomy of the US Trade Representative whether or not Congress has granted the president trade promotion authority (also known as fast track). Under this authority Congress votes on the whole trade package by a simple majority vote. If this authority has not been granted, Congress would be entitled to vote on each issue embodied in a trade agreement. Under these circumstances the US Trade Representative would be unable to trade off concessions on one issue for gains on another, because it would be much easier for those opposed to the concessions to mobilize a majority in Congress than it is to muster sufficient votes to reject the whole trade package.

The theoretical approaches focusing on interests and institutions proved able to explain political stability, but as they were applied to explain the neo-liberal policy reforms of the 1980s and 1990s it became clear to many that they only partially explained policy change. Therefore, some policy analysts turned to ideas as the key to understanding policy change that could not be explained by existing theories. Thus, there was a return to the ideas on ideas that Keynes had voiced in the 1930s, and research on ideas is now a growing theme within political science. However, an agreement on how to address the role of ideas in relation to interests and institutions, and policy change, has not emerged. Some policy analysts ascribe only a limited role to ideas, while others view them as key.

In minimalist ideational approaches, ideas do not have an independent impact on policy making. They are abstract expressions of interests. The argument is that it is not ideas but rather power relations that bring about policy change. As Gourevitch (1989: 87–8) says: 'To become policy, ideas must link up with politics—the mobilization of consent for policy. Politics involves power. Even a good idea cannot become policy if it meets certain kinds of opposition and a bad idea can become policy if it is able to obtain support.' This view on ideas is mainly found in pluralist and rational choice accounts of policy change (Walsh 2000: 487). However, some rational choice analysts have ascribed more prominent roles to ideas in explaining policy change. For instance, Goldstein and Keohane (1993: 6) incorporate ideas in rational choice analysis, arguing: 'Although we concede that the rationalist approach is often a valuable starting point for analysis, we challenge its explanatory power by suggesting the existence of empirical anomalies that can be resolved only when ideas are taken into account.' In their ideational approach ideas influence policy outcomes in three ways. First, ideas serve as road maps when actors are uncertain about the consequences of various means to obtain their goals. The choice of means is based on the *expected* effects of action. Ideas on causation 'help determine which of the many means will be used to reach desired goals and therefore help to provide actors with strategies with which to further their objectives' (1993: 13–14). Second, Goldstein and Keohane argue that ideas may even serve as guidelines for decision making when 'political actors must choose between sets of outcomes which all represent Pareto improvements for all and when there are no "objective" criteria on which to base choice' (1993: 18). Finally, ideas are institutionalized and may have impacts on future policy choices, even though the interest which an idea served is weakened over time. As they say (p. 21): 'the interests that promote some statute may fade away over time while the ideas encased in the statute nevertheless continue to influence politics. Thus at a later time, these institutionalized ideas continue to exert an effect: it is no longer possible to understand policy outcomes on the basis of contemporary configurations of interest and power alone'. However, according to rational choice theory it is questionable how long such a situation would prevail. When the costs of adhering to the idea (forgone benefits) exceed the costs of ideational change (the costs associated with the uncertainty of change), actors are likely to undertake an ideational shift.

Reviewing the rationalist literature on ideas in politics (including Goldstein and Keohane's work), Blyth (1997: 239) argues that rationalists define 'the utility of ideas simply as "helping" already existing forms of explanation... ideas merely supplement other forms of explanation'. In other words, ideas are incorporated in rational approaches to explain what cannot be explained by rationalistic accounts.

More sophisticated ideational approaches are developed by Hall (1993) and Blyth (2002). Both scholars attribute to ideas a prominent role in policy change. Challenging the traditional view that policy can be explained by analysing the pressures that various actors exert, Hall (1993: 289) argues:

> Politicians, officials, the spokesmen for social interests, and policy experts all operate within the terms of political discourse that are current in the nation at a given time, and the terms of political discourse generally have a specific configuration that lends representative legitimacy to some social interests more than others, delineates the accepted boundaries of state action, associates contemporary political developments with particular interpretations of national history, and defines the context within which many issues will be understood.

First component of a theoretical framework: ideational change

Criticizing Hall for paying too little attention to the process in which some ideas are accepted over others, Blyth (2002, see also 1997) develops an ideational approach in which ideas are given a dual role in institutional change in that they can be used to contest existing institutions and be blueprints for new institutions. Key to his hypotheses on the role of ideas in institutional change is the concept of 'Knightian uncertainty', which describes a situation in which 'agents have no conception as to what outcomes are likely, and hence what their interests in such a situation in fact are' (Blyth 2002: 32). This type of uncertainty is qualitatively different from a situation in which uncertainty is understood as complexity, meaning that 'agents are sure of their interests, but unsure of how to realize them' (p. 31). Ideas are narratives linking events in causal order and thereby providing meaning to certain situations. As Blyth (2002: 32) argues: 'Cognitive mechanisms, *pace* ideas, are important because without having ideas as to how the world is put together, it would be cognitively impossible for agents to act in a world in any meaningful sense.' If ideas provide meaning to a situation, then these ideas define the agent's interests in that situation (p. 32).

The first component of our framework suggests the factors bringing about ideational change in the international farm trade regime. Though Blyth's criticism of Hall's work points towards some deficiencies, Hall does highlight important factors leading to ideational change. For a new idea to gain force, arguments in favour of ideational change must link policy failure to the existing policy paradigm and thus the basic elite assumptions upon which it is based. As Hall (1993: 280) argues: 'a policy paradigm can be threatened by the appearance of anomalies ... As they accumulate, ad hoc attempts are generally made to stretch the terms of the paradigm to cover them, but this gradually undermines the intellectual coherence and precision of the original paradigm'. However, as pointed out by Skogstad (2007: 4), 'allegations of policy failure are rarely self-evident. They require a persuasive discourse to be compelling'. Further, policy failure has to be accompanied by an alternative paradigm that is both politically and economically viable (Hall 1989). If not, policy adjustments and experiments within the existing paradigm would simply continue. Arguments in favour of paradigm change can more forcefully be put forward if: first, there are available analytical tools to identify the problem and express it in quantitative terms; second, if a plausible theory which causally links the problem to the policy in question is available; third, if it can be persuasively argued that the problem cannot be solved by already known and tried solutions; and fourth, if it can be argued that paradigm change elsewhere has led to the desired outcomes. However, there are limitations to the force of argument, even if these tools are applied. For instance, policy failure is basically a social construct: when, for example, is a budgetary cost large enough to be perceived as an expression of policy failure? Those who pay the cost are likely to have a much lower crisis threshold than those who benefit from the budgetary outlay.

Finally, an important prerequisite for paradigm change is 'significant shifts in the locus of authority over policy' (Hall 1993: 280, see also Baumgartner and Jones 1993: 31–5). Policy paradigms are institutionally embedded and therefore are not likely to be changed by actors controlling existing policy institutions because it would question the institution's *raison d'être*, and actors privileged by the institutions risk losing powerful positions. Therefore successful attempts to bring about paradigm shift require that actors with a new idea, and with it a new policy paradigm, are brought into 'positions of authoritative decision making, or a new political coalition installed in existing decision-making bodies' (Skogstad 2008: 496; see also Hall 1993).

To some extent Hall's, but in particular Blyth's, model overcomes the problem of granting ideas an *ad hoc* role in attempts to explain institutional and policy change. However, to become applicable in relation to the subject matter of this book, they need refinement. Their models of ideational change are based on studies of macroeconomic policy reform. Such reforms are likely to result in political processes that are significantly different from those of sectorial policies, like agriculture. For instance they tend to mobilize different types of groups (Coleman et al. 1997: 276–7). Also, the institutional configuration in macro-political and sectorial policy reforms is different. Sectorial institutions are embedded in macro-political institutions and these have implications for sectorial processes (Daugbjerg 1999). In Hall's and Blyth's models, ideational change comes before institutional change in the sequence. However, *as well as ideas leading to change of institutions, change of institutions can lead to change of ideas*. This is particularly relevant in ideational change at the sectorial level. Macro-institutional change, even if brought about for reasons independent of sectorial conflict, may change the rules of the game in sectorial policy making and, as a consequence, alter sectorial actors' win-sets and power positions and thus the balance of power. Whilst macro-institutional change may empower advocates of paradigm shift in some circumstances, it may in others empower their *status quo*-oriented opponents. The specific impact on the balance of power depends upon the nature of macro-institutional change.

We suggest, as a hypothesis, that the erosion of agricultural exceptionalism in the global farm trade regime brought about by the URAA was caused by two main factors. First, significantly more forceful arguments for ideational change could be put forward than had been the case in earlier negotiations, and second, macro-institutional change within GATT altered the win-sets and hence the power balance within the farm trade talks.

Second component of a theoretical framework: implementing ideational change

There is a large number of studies demonstrating that implementation of public policy is not straightforward (see e.g. Winter 2006). In particular, the implementation of ideational change may be a troublesome process. Studies have shown that if ideational change is not accompanied by institutional reform there is a risk that ideational change will not be manifested in actual policy outcomes (see e.g. Marsh and Rhodes 1992: 185–6). Therefore, analysis of ideational change must also include the function and decision-making rules of institutions transforming ideational change into actual day-to-day policy decisions.

As they mature, institutions set up to implement policies are likely to become conservative factors. What made them useful in implementing the original policy may become *the* problem when policy makers attempt to implement policy change. As pointed out above, institutions provide certainty by setting standard operational procedures to structure implementation processes. However, by laying down certain interpretations of policy problems, and acceptable ways to deal with them, institutions privilege some interests at the expense of others. This means that there will be strong opposition to procedural change from those already privileged by the institution. Therefore, ideational change has to be accompanied by institutional change to achieve the new objectives.

To alter the direction of policy decisions in implementation, institutional reform must fulfil two requirements. First, the balance of power among the stakeholders must be changed. Those disadvantaged by the old institution must gain a power position in the new institution so that new concerns can prevail in implementation. Second, in politics, 'losers do not necessarily disappear' (Thelen 1999: 385) and therefore the interests of those previously privileged by the institution still have to be taken into consideration to ensure that it remains a broadly accepted and legitimate institution. Loss of legitimacy could lead to unwillingness to comply with decisions of the implementing institutions. This is particularly important for the WTO Dispute Settlement Body because it has no authority to force the losing defendant to comply with rulings, but instead must rely on legal persuasion and, if necessary, the ability of the winning party to adopt and implement effective retaliation.

We suggest, as a hypothesis, that the extent to which ideational change in global farm trade regulation is implemented depends on the WTO Dispute Settlement Body's ability to rule against the major trading powers and that the major powers accept these rulings as legitimate.

Third component of a theoretical framework: institutional and policy adjustment to ideational change

Hall (1993) and Blyth (2002) argued that ideational change leads to fundamental institutional and policy change over a relatively short period of time. The reformed policy would be based on new ideological foundations and new policy principles, and accordingly new policy instruments. However, ideational change need not be associated with rapid change of institutions and policy. It may also lead to gradual institutional and policy adjustment. For instance comparing policy reform processes in the Australian, Canadian, and US cereals and dairy sectors, Coleman et al. (1997) demonstrate that there may also be a 'cumulative, negotiated, problem-solving trajectory to paradigm change'. Thus, to cover a broader range of cases, ideational theory would benefit from importing gradualism into accounts of change. This can be done by devoting more attention to institutional adaptation and in particular to allow more room for variance in institutional response to ideational change.

Much of the work on institutional development within political science is premised on the notion of a punctuated equilibrium model (Thelen 2003: 209). However, in explaining institutional change, the punctuated equilibrium model is theoretically underdeveloped. Institutional change is usually explained by referring to exogenous alterations, in particular shocks, such as changes in socioeconomic and political contexts and/or in the balance of political power and the emergence of new ideas. However, these arguments on change are far too general because if we are to consider institutions as intervening variables, they must be able to neutralize exogenous changes in most cases. If every alteration in the context of the institution produced institutional change, the institutions themselves would be mere reflections of developments in broader contextual variables. What we need to know is when institutions neutralize change in context, and when they do not. In many historical institutionalist analyses, we are left with the problem that the 'institutions explain everything until they explain nothing' (Thelen and Steinmo 1992: 15). This is not the only problem associated with the punctuated equilibrium model when applied to explain institutional development. As Thelen (2003: 209) says: 'The implication is that institutions, once created, either persist or break down in the face of some kind of exogenous shock' (see also p. 212). She further argues (p. 211): 'From the perspective of a punctuated equilibrium model, there often seems to be too much continuity through putative breakpoints in history, but also often too much change beneath the surface of apparently stable formal institutional arrangements.' While she does not reject the notion that institutions may break down in critical moments, she argues that such instances are rare. Institutions do not only survive as a result of their reproduction mechanisms, but also as a result of 'a process of institutional transformation, to accommodate powerful new actors and to adapt the institutions to address new imperatives, both economic and political' (p. 225).

Thelen's critique of the notion of punctuated equilibrium must lead political scientists and policy analysts to devote more attention to the way an institution adapts to contextual change. Adjustments may not be the first best solution, but are nevertheless good enough to enable the institution to survive over long periods of time. In the institutionalist literature, important sources of institutional change are political, ideational, economic, or social change in the context within which the institution is embedded. Inability of institutions to adjust to changing environments is often seen as the source of outright institutional breakdown. However, as argued by Thelen, institutions often adapt to contextual change. Thelen (2003) distinguishes between two strategies of institutional adaptation: institutional conversion and institutional layering. The former is the more pervasive form of institutional adjustment and refers to a situation in which 'institutions designed with one set of goals in mind are redirected to other ends' (Thelen 2003: 228). New problems are addressed by 'using existing institutions in new ways or in the service of new goals' (p. 228). Examples of such transformations are many, for instance 'institutional arrangements developed under wartime conditions survive through their conversion to peacetime purposes' (p. 229).

The less pervasive type of survival strategy is institutional layering which refers to a 'process that preserves much of the core while adding amendments through which rules and structures inherited from the past can be brought into synch with changes in the normative, social, and political environments' (Thelen 2003: 228). Whilst fruitful, the concept of layering needs further clarification. We need to unpack what changes and what remains in the process of policy layering. In our reading of Thelen, 'core' would be the ideational foundation, or paradigm, under-pinning an institution while 'rules' and 'structures' would be decision rules and standard operating procedures for processing problems. Where an institutional layering strategy is chosen, the core of the existing policy would remain, but might be rephrased to legitimize policy. There would be a gradual shift of policy measures in order to respond to contextual pressure; however, basically, the institution serves the same purpose but by other means. In Hall's terminology (1993) it would be a second-order change in which policy instruments and their settings are altered, but the paradigm remains the same.

Institutions may also be able to neutralize the effects of new emerging ideas by: (*a*) ignoring them; (*b*) providing an enhanced defence of the existing policy; and/or (*c*) undertaking symbolic changes in policy which would not change the nature of policy and the way it operates. Of course, this conservative strategy involves greater risk of breakdown than the two types of institutional adjustments. At the other extreme, ideational

Table 2.1 Hypothesis on institutional reaction to ideational change and its policy consequences

Types of institutional change	Institutional breakdown	Institutional conversion	Institutional layering	Institutional stasis
Impacts of institutional change on policy	Rapid and funda-mental policy re-form. The new idea underpins the new policy measures intro-duced.	Gradual shift in policy. The new idea is adopted and sets the dir-ection for future policy evolution. Policy measures would gradually be changed to re-flect the new idea.	Existing ideational underpinning remains, but may be disguised through rephrasing. Policy measures are gradually changed to serve the original objective in new ways.	No policy change. Some symbolic acts may be undertaken. Significant effort to produce ana-lytical evidence and arguments in support of policy and to reject attacks on policy.

39

change may bring about institutional breakdown, which would produce rapid and radical policy reform. In Table 2.1 we suggest, as a *hypothesis*, the likely policy consequences of the different types of institutional reaction.

Fourth component of a theoretical framework: domestic feedback into the WTO

Since the theme of this book is the dynamic interrelationship between WTO farm trade negotiations and Common Agricultural Policy (CAP) reform, the fourth component of our analytical framework suggests how CAP reform, whilst driven by WTO concerns, feeds back into the WTO negotiations, setting limits to what can be agreed, but also providing opportunities for an agreement. Earlier we reviewed the two-level game model and presented the Schelling (1960: 19) conjecture which suggests that a negotiator in international negotiations can convert a small domestic win-set into bargaining power by referring to his/her inability to make concessions. Arguing that the Schelling conjecture cannot be universally applied, Meunier suggests that the circumstances in which it applies have to be more clearly specified. She is particularly concerned with international trade negotiations involving the EU.

She highlights *supranational competence* (the internal voting rules and the degree of competence delegated to the European Commission) and *negotiating context* as two key factors that influence the EU's bargaining power in trade negotiations. Voting rules within the Council of Ministers have an important impact on the formulation of the negotiating position and the bargaining power exercised by the EU's trade negotiator. When the unanimity voting rule applies the common position reached is the lowest common denominator, which 'enables the most conservative [EU member] state to set the terms of the collective message' (Meunier 2005: 55) sent to negotiation partners. Since trade negotiations 'are designed to achieve market liberalization' (p. 41), the unanimity rule means that member states reluctant to liberalize will carry great weight in the decision-making process because they have veto power. When rules on qualified majority voting apply, the most conservative state no longer holds *de jure* veto power and therefore the common position decided could diverge from the *status quo* and move towards liberalization. It must be said, however, that focusing on formal decision-making rules may miss important *informal* rules. There are many instances in EU decision making in which the formal rule is qualified majority voting, but the norm is to reach consensus (pp. 54–7), or to ensure that key member states are not outvoted. These informal norms apply to the CAP, particularly with respect to French sensitivities. In 2003, for example, the Fischler reforms were adopted by qualified majority vote (with Portugal the single dissenting voice) only after France had signalled its willingness to join the majority (Daugbjerg and Swinbank 2007: 17).

On many trade issues, the Commission negotiates on behalf of the EU. So doing requires that the Council of Ministers delegates competence to the Commission. This delegation can take various forms. Meunier (2005: 57–9) distinguishes between *restricted* and *extensive* delegation. In the former, the Council defines a fairly clear mandate to the Commission, leaving little room for manoeuvre, and it monitors intensively the Commission's actions during the negotiations. In particular, the *status quo*-oriented member states will closely watch the Commission's moves. Usually, restricted delegation is used when unanimity decision-making rules apply. Extensive delegation is often associated with situations where the decision-making rule is qualified majority voting (p. 59). This type of delegation grants more negotiating latitude to the Commission. In the extreme, the Council will simply ask the Commission to get the best possible deal.

The *nature of negotiating context* refers to 'the distribution of the policy preferences of the EU and of its negotiating opponent relative to the status quo' (Meunier 2005: 59). Meunier distinguishes between a conservative and a reformist configuration. The former refers to a situation in which the EU wants to defend the *status quo* and the opponent wants trade liberalization. A reformist configuration is a situation in which the opponent prefers the *status quo* and the EU prefers trade liberalization.

When the two variables, supranational competence and negotiating context, are combined, there is only one situation in which the Schelling conjecture applies. Bargaining power derived from a small win-set is most likely to result when a conservative configuration applies (the EU prefers the *status quo*) and the Council has granted a restricted competence to the Commission as a result of unanimity voting rules (Meunier 2005: 64–5). When such a situation applies, the Schelling conjecture suggests that the EU's negotiating position on agricultural trade policy would lead to limited commitments to reduce agricultural support and protection. As Meunier (2005: 17) suggests: 'In this "conservative" case, unanimity and restrictive delegation [of the negotiation mandate to the Commission] make the EU a tough bargainer: the negotiating opponent cannot obtain more than the most conservative EU state is willing to concede.' Thus, 'if the EU is blocked by the unanimity requirement, so will the WTO' (p. 186).

On the basis of these theoretical considerations we suggest, as a hypothesis, that the EU's internal voting rules and decision-making norms enable its international negotiators to obtain considerable bargaining power and thus set the limits for farm trade liberalization within the GATT/WTO.

A dynamic perspective

Our analytical framework enables a dynamic analysis of ideational, institutional, and policy change. In contrast to much theoretical work on ideational change, our framework sees this as a gradual process in which pressure on existing ideas gradually builds up and eventually leads to the acceptance of new ideas. Focusing on sectorial rather than macro-political ideational change, we suggest that macro-institutional change may be the decisive factor bringing about ideational change as a response to the pressures on existing ideas built up over a long period. Two-level analysis must be undertaken in situations in which such ideational change at the global level has to materialize in policy change at the domestic level.

Further, rather than undertaking a static 'snapshot' analysis, we approach our research questions from a dynamic perspective since ideational, institutional, and policy developments at one level influence the other. The direction of influence applies in *both* directions: changes at the WTO level lead to an EU policy response, which in turn feeds back into the WTO bringing about further change, and so forth. By distinguishing between the ideational and operational aspects of international trade agreements, we are able to analyse the interrelationship between changes taking place at the global and domestic levels, all of which are triggered by ideational change at the global level. Though ideational change signals a wish for fundamental and rapid change, changes of the operational aspect may be gradual and longer term. In subsequent chapters this framework provides a focus for our analysis of the evolution of farm trade rules within the GATT/WTO and the EU.

Chapter 3

WTO Rules for Agricultural Trade: GATT 1947 and the URAA

In Chapter 1, we introduced the concept of agricultural exceptionalism, and suggested this idea had been embedded in GATT 1947. The exceptional treatment of agriculture in the multilateral trade regime was eroded as a result of the Uruguay Round (UR) agreements, notably the *Agreement on Agriculture* (which we refer to as the URAA in this text) with agricultural normalism as its ideational underpinning. The purpose of this chapter is to explain *how* agriculture has been afforded exceptional treatment in the GATT, and to what extent this changed in the WTO.

Broadly speaking, two periods in the development of global farm trade rules can be identified. First, from 1948 to 1994 when GATT's basic provisions applied to trade in agricultural products. Second, from 1995 when, under the WTO, the URAA supplemented the basic GATT Provisions.[1] A third period would begin with the implementation of a revised Agreement on Agriculture following conclusion of the *Doha Round*. This chapter deals with those GATT/WTO rules that impinge directly on the Common Agricultural Policy's (CAP's) market price and income support mechanisms. It does not deal with the WTO Agreements on the Application of Sanitary and Phytosanitary Measures or on Technical Barriers to Trade—the SPS and TBT Agreements, respectively—although both impact on trade in farm and food products. Nor does it discuss Geographical Indications of origin, or other issues covered by the Trade-Related Aspects of Intellectual Property Rights (TRIPS) Agreement, or the General Agreement on Trade in Services (GATS) (see Josling et al. 2004 for a wider discussion of WTO regulation of food trade). Nor does the chapter attempt to detail *all* GATT provisions and their implications for trade in agricultural and food products; instead it indicates where exceptional treatment applies.

The GATT/WTO legal system is outlined in a large number of scholarly works, ranging from Oxford University Press's *Very Short Introduction* (Narlikar 2004) to the more bulky tomes of Jackson (1997) and Hoekman and Kostecki (2001). The WTO website has a vast amount of material, easily accessible and logically arranged; and, to celebrate 60 years of the GATT/WTO, its *World Trade Report* for 2007 (subtitled 'Six decades of multilateral trade cooperation: What have we learnt?') included several chapters, prepared by the Secretariat, outlining its history and the theory and practice of international trade cooperation (WTO 2007*e*). Provisions relevant to agriculture are discussed extensively by Desta (2002).

The GATT

GATT—the General Agreement on Tariffs and Trade—was salvaged from the *Havana Charter* which was to have created an *International Trade Organization* (ITO) to work alongside the International Monetary Fund (IMF) and the International Bank for Reconstruction and Development (now known as the World Bank) that had been agreed at Bretton Woods in July 1944 (Scammell 1983: 17). The draft charter for the ITO was very much based on US ideas, with some British involvement. Negotiations began in London in October 1946, and were concluded in March 1948 in Havana, Cuba, when the draft was signed by 53 countries. However, the charter was never ratified: late in 1950 the US president deferred his attempts to secure Congressional approval of the charter, in effect consigning the text to the waste bin of history (Diebold 1952: 1–5; Scammell 1983: 45).[2]

The draft charter was wide ranging and had chapters dealing with: 'Employment and Economic Activity', 'Economic Development and Reconstruction', 'Commercial Policy', 'Restrictive Business Practices', and 'Inter-governmental Commodity Agreements', as well as rules and procedures for the ITO itself.[3] Diebold (1952: 27–8) notes that GATT was conceived 'as an interim measure, . . . a kind of advance instalment of the Charter. It put into effect temporarily most of the provisions of the Charter's chapter on commercial policy and provided for multilateral negotiations to reduce tariffs, which were carried out at Geneva in 1947 . . .'. In practice GATT was applied on a 'provisional' basis—under the *Protocol of Provisional Application*—from 1948 to 1994, and never itself had the status of an international treaty: 'GATT was not originally intended to be an international organization but . . . evolved into one by necessity' (Jackson 1983: 164, 180).[4]

Contemporary American authors were clearly of the view that, although based on free-trade principles, the charter (and consequently, to a large extent, GATT) contained a number of provisions that made agriculture special. For example, Johnson (1950: 44) wrote: 'In fact many... feel that trade policy has been modified all too much to meet the presumed needs of agriculture. In order to protect agricultural interests, exceptions were provided in the American proposals for the ITO charter for import quotas, export subsidies, domestic subsidies to producers, and restrictive commodity agreements. The final provisions on these matters did not differ significantly from the American proposals.'

GATT's basic provisions

A basic premise of the GATT is that the removal (or reduction) of trade barriers will increase world trade and global economic welfare. The pure theory of international trade would suggest that a country could itself capture most of the benefits of trade liberalization by the unilateral elimination of its own trade barriers (although a country large enough to influence its terms of trade through its policy actions could, in theory, increase its welfare at the expense of others by applying an optimum tariff). But the reality is that the gains from trade liberalization are widely spread, and it is difficult to link policy to effect, whereas the costs of trade liberalization are concentrated and highly visible. Textile, steel or farm workers, and mill, foundry and farm owners, might be expected to contest vociferously the reduction of trade barriers, whereas consumers are un-likely to lobby strongly in favour. Thus a *modus operandi* of GATT is the negotiated bilateral or multilateral reduction of trade barriers, in which countries (and industries) trade off 'gains' and 'losses'. For example, Dam (1967: 256), referring to the reluctance of the European Economic Community (EEC) to enter substantive negotiations on agriculture in the Kennedy Round, noted: 'the United States has made progress on agricul-ture the *sine qua non* of reductions on industrial products. Those reduc-tions are of vital importance to Germany, a major industrial exporter, and to the Netherlands...'. We will return to this theme later in the book.

Since 1948, GATT (and then the WTO) has engaged in a series of major trade negotiations (known as Rounds) that have progressively reduced—and made more transparent—trade barriers, and tried to create a more coherent and rules-based system of international trade. The Dispute Settle-ment Understanding (DSU), discussed in Chapter 5, is an important, if sometimes controversial, element in this.

For the reader's guidance, Box 3.1 lists the more important GATT Articles referred to in this book. Two basic principles are the Most-Favoured-Nation (MFN) treatment of 'like' products (GATT Article I), and the 'National Treatment' of 'like' products (Article III). MFN treatment basically implies that products originating in all GATT members (known as *Contracting Parties* in the agreement) should be treated equally—no GATT signatory should be given less favourable treatment than that afforded the most favoured nation. National treatment basically means that—once imported, and apart from the imposition of the import taxes that importing states are allowed to retain—the subsequent imposition of rules, regulations, taxes, etc. should not differ from those applied to the home-produced good. However, it is important to note that two exceptions to the MFN principle apply: first, if subsets of GATT members combine together to form free-trade areas or customs unions in conformity with GATT Article XXIV, then they are free to remove all trade barriers *within* the free-trade area or customs union whilst retaining MFN trade restrictions against other GATT members. The European Union (EU) is itself a customs union, and it has in place a complex web of regional trade agreements with countries around the world. The extent to which the

---

Box 3.1 A LISTING OF SELECTED GATT ARTICLES

Article	Content
I	Most-Favoured-Nation (MFN) Treatment
II	Tariff schedules (bindings)
III	National Treatment
VI	Anti-dumping and Countervailing Duties (augmented by the UR Anti-dumping and Subsidies Agreements)
XI	General Elimination of Quantitative Restrictions
XIII	Non-discriminatory Administration of Quantitative Restrictions
XVI	Subsidies (augmented by the URAA and the UR Subsidies Agreement)
XVII	State Trading Enterprises
XIX	Emergency Action on Imports
XX	General Exceptions to the free trade provisions (augmented by the SPS agreement)
XXII	Consultation, in case of dispute
XXIII	Nullification or Impairment of benefits, underpinning the Dispute Settlement Understanding
XXIV	Customs Unions and Free-trade Areas
XXVIII	Provides for the modification of tariff schedules
XXVIII bis	Provides for periodic *Rounds* of Trade Negotiations
Part IV	Trade and Development

Sources: GATT and Hoekman and Kostecki (2001: 146).

agricultural sector is, or is not, included in Regional Trade Agreements (RTAs) is an issue that has led to some discussion (see, e.g., Josling 1993 and Swinbank and Tanner 2001).[5]

The second exception to the MFN rule is that GATT members are allowed to differentiate between developed and developing countries (see Box 3.2). Thus, under the Generalized System of Preferences (GSP), countries are allowed to offer more favourable access to their home market than would be the case for a 'like' product originating in a developed GATT member. In the EU the GSP scheme includes the *Everything but Arms* (EBA) initiative for the 50 Least Developed Countries (LDCs).

In both GATT Articles I and III—and indeed throughout GATT and other WTO agreements—reference is made to 'like' products; but the definition of 'like' products has proved problematic. As Picciotto (2003: 378) provocatively asks: 'Should a tomato which has been genetically modified

---

Box 3.2 DEVELOPING COUNTRIES AND THE ENABLING CLAUSE

The bulk of the WTO's 153 (as of July 2008) members have declared themselves to be developing countries: for an attempt to count the developing country membership see WTO (2007e: 289). As a briefing note points out: 'There is no WTO definition of "developed" or "developing" countries. Developing countries in the WTO are designated on the basis of self-selection although this is not necessarily automatically accepted in all WTO bodies' (WTO 2007f: 3). A subgroup of developing countries, the LDCs, are officially recognized by the WTO as they meet specific criteria established by UNCTAD and appear on an UNCTAD list. Of the 50 LDCs recognized by UNCTAD in July 2007, 32 were members of the WTO.[a]

Developing countries, as opposed to developed countries, are treated differently in the WTO in two important respects. First the UR Agreements incorporated *Special and Differential Treatment* to a greater or lesser extent: thus the URAA imposed lower reduction commitments, and allowed longer implementation periods, with no reduction commitments imposed on LDCs. The Doha Development Agenda pursued this theme.

Second, as a major departure from the MFN principle, developed countries are allowed to offer preferential access to developing countries under a GSP scheme: subject to the provision that there is no discrimination between developing countries (or the subgroup of LDCs). The GSP grew out of discussions in UNCTAD, and was implemented in GATT in 1971 by means of a 'waiver' (i.e. an agreement to relax the rules), of 10 years' duration, to the MFN principle of GATT Article I (WTO 2007e: 185). In the Tokyo Round this was codified in the so-called *Enabling Clause*, described by the WTO as 'a permanent waiver from the MFN clause' (WTO 2007e: 187).[b]

[a]http://www.wto.org/english/thewto_e/whatis_e/tif_e/org7_e.htm (accessed March 2008)
[b]The official title of this decision (L/4903) of 28 November 1979 is 'Differential and more favourable treatment reciprocity and fuller participation of developing countries'. It is available at: http://www.wto.org/english/docs_e/legal_e/enabling1979_e.htm

be treated like other tomatoes (some of which may have been bred by traditional selection techniques)? Is beef or milk from cows which have been fed growth-promoting hormones like the beef or milk from other cows? Are building materials made from asbestos fibre like those made from other materials?' Although these are pertinent questions that clearly impact on the EU's farm and food policies, and hence on the relations between the EU and its trading partners in the WTO, they are not directly addressed in this book (but see Swinbank 2006*a*).

Agricultural exceptionalism in GATT 1947: import quotas and export subsidies

The GATT agreement had two provisions that meant that trade in agricultural products was treated differently from trade in other goods. These provisions became the cornerstones of agricultural exceptionalism in the GATT. Both were prompted by US concerns.

The first provision, which is found in GATT Article XI, outlaws the general use of quantitative trade restrictions ('quotas, import or export licences or other measures'). But this is subject to three exceptions: temporary 'export prohibitions or restrictions' to 'relieve critical shortages of foodstuffs' or other essential products are allowed; 'standards or regulations for the classification, grading or marketing of commodities' are permitted; and in paragraph 2(c), import restrictions 'on any agricultural or fisheries product' are sanctioned if they are *necessary* to enforce government measures which: (*a*) apply a marketing or production quota to 'like' domestic products, or (*b*) remove temporary surpluses of the domestic product. The Sub-Committee of the Havana Conference that considered these provisions noted, however, 'that paragraph 2(c) was not intended to provide a means of protecting domestic producers against foreign competition, but simply to permit, in appropriate cases, the enforcement of domestic governmental measures necessitated by the special problems relating to the production and marketing of agricultural and fisheries products' (WTO 1995: 328).

The US *Agricultural Adjustment Act* of 1933, as amended, provided price support to producers who participated in supply control programmes through the Commodity Credit Corporation, and authorized the use of import taxes or quotas to sustain the integrity of the price support programme. Thus a key negotiating aim of the United States had been to ensure that these measures could remain in the post-war world (Josling et al. 1996: 12). In 1950, with the new GATT regime in place, the United States imposed

quantitative restrictions on dairy product imports, but there were no controls on domestic production. Subsequently, the import controls were found
to be in breach of Article XI. The Executive sought to change US domestic
policies, but Congress could not be persuaded to comply (Hudec 1998: 13).
Instead the United States sought a waiver to the provisions of Article II and
Article XI to allow it to restrict trade to the extent 'necessary to prevent a
conflict' with Section 22 of the *Agricultural Adjustment Act.* Josling et al.
(1996: 28) report: 'The other member countries had no choice but to accede
to this request, for the alternative might have been the withdrawal of the
United States from the GATT.' But with the United States benefiting from a
broadly based waiver of unlimited duration, 'no other major country was
prepared to abide by the GATT rules' (p. 28).

Until such time as Contracting Parties were willing to 'bind' tariffs they
were, arguably, free to vary those tariffs on a regular basis without restric-
tion, as the EU did with its variable import levy system that was a characteristic feature of the CAP until 1995.[6] The widespread unwillingness of
GATT Contracting Parties to bind agricultural tariffs was a major weakness
of the old GATT system. According to GATT Secretariat figures, only 35 per
cent of tariff lines for agricultural products were bound prior to 1994. As a
result of the UR the figure became almost 100 per cent, compared to 83 per
cent for industrial products (cited in Tangermann 2001: 6).

The second provision providing for agricultural exceptionalism in GATT
1947 is Article XVI, allowing the use of export subsidies. Dating from 1935,
Section 32 of the *Agricultural Adjustment Act* had made provision for export
subsidies, and US negotiators for the ITO were understandably eager to
retain the possibility of export subsidies as an integral part of farm price
support (Cohn 1993: 21). Thus the *Havana Charter* would have permitted the
use of export subsidies on primary products, provided they were not applied
'in such a way as to have the effect of maintaining or acquiring for that
Member more than an equitable share of world trade in that commodity'
(Article 28.1 of the *Havana Charter*), whilst outlawing them on manufactured goods (Article 26). Wilcox (1949: 130), the chief American negotiator,
commented subsequently: 'Here, as elsewhere, the *Charter* accommodates
itself to American agricultural policy.' These provisions, however, were not
replicated in the GATT agreement and, at the outset, Article XVI did little
more than impose a notification and consultation procedure on subsidy
schemes that acted 'directly or indirectly' to increase exports or reduce
imports (the existing paragraph 1 of Article XVI, derived from Article 25 of
the *Havana Charter*) (WTO 1995: 465). Export subsidies, whether on manufactured or primary products, were not prohibited.

By the early 1950s, with the collapse in commodity prices following the Korean War, international attention refocused on this issue. The international response, in the 1954/5 Review Session, was to strengthen the provisions on export disciplines, by re-inserting in the GATT some of the text that had not carried over from the Havana Charter. Thus Contracting Parties were now exhorted 'to avoid the use of subsidies on the export of primary products . . .',[7] and export subsidies on manufactured goods were to be eliminated. If subsidies were to be paid on primary products then this should not result in the country capturing 'more than an equitable share of world export trade in that product, account being taken of the shares of the contracting parties in such trade in the product during a previous representative period' (Article XVI:3).

As many authors have noted, the 'equitable share' rule of Article XVI:3 was almost impossible to implement. It was applied successfully once—by Australia against France in 1958 with respect to wheat—but subsequent attempts failed; for example by Australia and Brazil in 1978 on export subsidies for sugar, where 'the panel said it was unable to find that the EC had taken more than an equitable share' (Hudec 1998: 9).[8]

The subsidies code in the Tokyo Round

In the Tokyo Round an attempt was made to tighten the provisions of GATT Article XVI; but this did not take the form of an amendment to the GATT, or even an additional agreement, integrated into the GATT agreement, to which all GATT members adhered. Instead, as Jackson (1983: 165) notes, the result was a series of stand-alone side agreements, or *codes*, which legally could 'continue to exist even in the absence of GATT' (p. 172). One of these codes was the *Agreement on interpretation and application of Articles VI, XVI, and XXIII of the General Agreement on Tariffs and Trade*.[9] Not all GATT members were signatories of the Subsidies Code, but the EU, the United States, and some other important members were (Hufbauer 1983: 333).[10]

Article 10 of the Subsidies Code attempted to clarify the provisions of GATT Article XVI:3. For example, it explained that 'more than an equitable share' could include 'any case in which the effect of a subsidy granted by a signatory is to displace the exports of another signatory bearing in mind the developments on world markets'; and that 'a previous representative period' should 'normally be the three most recent calendar years in which normal market conditions existed'. Furthermore, signatories of the Subsidies Code (but not of course other GATT members who had not signed the code) agreed 'not to grant export subsidies on exports ... to a particular market which results in prices materially below those of other suppliers to the same market'.

However, these provisions were still insufficiently tightly drawn. Hufbauer (1983: 338) comments that 'when GATT Article XVI was drafted in 1955, US farm interests were too powerful to be disciplined; when code Article 10 was drafted in 1979, European farm interests were too powerful'. Nonetheless, the United States immediately brought a case alleging the incompatibility with the Subsidies Code of the EU's export subsidies on wheat flour, but 'once again, despite another large increase in the volume of EC exports, the panel was unable to find that EC exports had "displaced", "undercut" or taken "more than an equitable share"' (Hudec 1998: 10). The 'most heated controversy' at the GATT Ministerial meeting of November 1982 was the dispute over export subsidies on agricultural products, with the EU resisting requests for tighter controls. By 1983 the United States and the EU were engaged in a subsidy war, particularly over the subsidized sales of wheat flour to Egypt (Bergsten and Cline 1983: 761–3). As Desta (2002: 292) noted: 'Until the end of the Uruguay Round, an unfortunate combination of vaguely formulated rules backed only by an ineffective dispute resolution mechanism prevailed in the sphere of agricultural export subsidies.' Effective control over the use of export subsidies on agricultural products would have to wait until 1995, and the implementation of the UR agreements.

The UR package of agreements and understandings

The outcome of the UR, and the *Marrakesh Agreement Establishing the World Trade Organization*, was: (*a*) a series of *Multilateral Agreements on Trade in Goods*, at the heart of which remained GATT; (*b*) a new *General Agreement on Trade in Services*; (*c*) an *Agreement on Trade-Related Aspects of Intellectual Property Rights*; and (*d*) a new *Understanding on Rules and Procedures Governing the Settlement of Disputes* that applies across all the WTO agreements. This was all the result of a Single Undertaking, which we explain and discuss in Chapter 4.

The UR agreements did not alter the wording of GATT 1947, although it was re-enacted as part of a new legal instrument, the *GATT 1994* that also includes six *Understandings* on the interpretation of various GATT articles. In addition to GATT 1994, there are a further 12 multilateral agreements on trade in goods, most of which have relevance to agriculture. The two discussed in this chapter are the *Agreement on Agriculture* (referred to as the URAA in this text) and the *Agreement on Subsidies and Countervailing Measures* (commonly referred to as the Subsidies Agreement).

There was also a sector-specific *Agreement on Textiles and Clothing*, which can be traced back to an Arrangement on Cotton Textiles first agreed in the Dillon Round. But, unlike the URAA, this UR agreement 'brought to an end the exceptional treatment of this sector' (WTO 2007e: Box 19, 229–31) because, in its Article 9, it provided for the phasing out, over a 10-year period, of the remaining quantitative restrictions after which 'the textiles and clothing sector shall be fully integrated into GATT 1994'.

The multiplicity of agreements in trade in goods can cause complications. Article 21 of the URAA states that: 'The provisions of GATT 1994 and of the other [*Multilateral Agreements on Trade in Goods*] shall apply subject to the provisions of this Agreement'. Thus, for example, GATT Article XVI on subsidies remains in force. As a general rule Article XVI is augmented (and in effect replaced) by the UR Subsidies Agreement, except where the URAA prevails (Desta 2002). However, the special protection afforded agricultural subsidies by the URAA was not unconditional: Article 13 of the URAA (commonly known as the Peace Clause) set out the conditions under which the URAA would prevail over GATT Article XVI and the Subsidies Agreement during an 'implementation period' that expired at the end of 2003 (see Box 3.3).

Box 3.3 WHAT WAS THE PEACE CLAUSE?

Article 13, headed 'Due Restraint', was popularly known as the Peace Clause. It was added to the URAA by the US and EU negotiators in the Blair House Accord of November 1992, considerably enhancing the provisions that had been included in the Dunkel draft of December 1991 (see Chapter 7 for further discussion of the Dunkel draft and Blair House). At the time the European Commission said of the Blair House Accord: 'The draft agreement brings an essential innovation: the CAP is "safe" under the legal rules of GATT because of the adoption of the "peace clause"' (Commission 1992a: 10). However, this European optimism was perhaps a little overblown. First, the Peace Clause was not of unlimited duration, for it had a life of nine years, which has now expired. Second, it was not a *carte blanche* for the CAP: it dealt only with domestic support and export competition, and even then only on a qualified basis.

The basic idea, although heavily nuanced, was that if domestic support and export subsidies were in full conformity with the provisions of the URAA, then the URAA rather than the *Agreement on Subsidies and Countervailing Measures* (and GATT Article XVI) would prevail. However, the provisions were not entirely clear, which led to

---

some discussion (see e.g. Steinberg and Josling 2003), and were never tested in a dispute settlement proceeding. Some authors argued that the pending demise of the Peace Clause would be a powerful lever encouraging the EU (and other countries with protected agricultures) to the negotiating table for the further round of negotiations on agricultural trade liberalization mandated by Article 20 of the URAA, or else face 'a succession of hostile panel reports which will progressively limit the EU's ability to grant export subsidies and provide domestic support to the farm sector, over and above the bound tariffs' (Swinbank 1999*a*: 47).

Although the EU's policies have been challenged (see Chapter 5), the protective effect of the Peace Clause seems to have prevailed throughout the Doha Round. If the Doha Round were to be declared dead, then Swinbank's earlier concerns would return.

The Uruguay Round Agreement on Agriculture (URAA)

As suggested in Chapter 1, the URAA is characterized by ambivalence. For many observers, particularly amongst agricultural exporters, there was a disharmony between the URAA's long-term objective of 'substantial and progressive reductions in agricultural support and protection' and the rather limited reductions actually achieved.

At the ideational level, the URAA sent a message about the future direction of WTO negotiations on agricultural trade. It had a built-in agenda to continue the reform process in order to liberalize farm trade, and mechanisms to ensure that WTO members would enter into such negotiations. In the opening paragraphs of the Agreement it is stated that the 'long term objective . . . is to establish a fair and market oriented trading system', with 'substantial progressive reductions in agricultural support and protection' which would result in 'correcting and preventing restrictions and distortions in world agricultural markets'. The legal expressions of agricultural exceptionalism, Articles XI and XVI of GATT 1947, were overridden by the URAA: its Article 21, as we have seen, declaring 'The provisions of GATT 1994 and of other Multilateral Trade Agreements in Annex 1A to the WTO Agreement shall apply subject to the provisions of this Agreement.' Most importantly, the URAA was not the final stage in reducing agricultural border protection and support. Article 20 of the URAA stated that farm trade liberalization was 'an ongoing process' and that 'negotiations for continuing the process will be initiated one year before the end of the implementation process', that is, before the end of 1999. All this signalled a desire to end agricultural exceptionalism in global farm trade. The Peace Clause prohibited most WTO dispute settlement challenges against countries complying with the URAA (see Box 3.3). But as it would expire by the end of 2003 the protection it offered was time limited. This, it was widely assumed, would then make US and EU agricultural support schemes more vulnerable to legal challenge under the WTO Agreement on Subsidies and Countervailing Measures and therefore impose on them strong motives to engage in the new round of negotiations. Furthermore, as we shall suggest in Chapter 5, the ideational foundation of the URAA may also have had implications for the WTO Dispute Settlement Body's interpretation of the Agreement in trade disputes.

However, while some of the specific provisions of the URAA and the other UR agreements weakened agricultural exceptionalism, others went in the opposite direction and reinforced it. Nevertheless, the overall trend of the Agreement's provisions was to discipline agricultural support and protection. In the remainder of the chapter we analyse the specific provisions of the URAA to establish how they impact on agricultural exceptionalism.

Table 3.1 sets out the main provisions of the URAA for *developed* countries.[11] As explained earlier in this chapter, the WTO Agreements

Table 3.1 The main provisions of the URAA for developed countries

Three 'pillars'	Commitment
Market access	• 'Tariffication' of non-tariff barriers
	• Special safeguard provisions for tariff lines that underwent tariffication
	• Tariff reduction of 36% over the implementation period 1995–2000 (a simple average over all tariff lines) with a minimum reduction of 15% per tariff line
	• Current access and minimum access TRQs sanctioned
Domestic support	• It is commonly suggested that domestic support measures (for developed countries) fall into three categories: *green box* (with 'no, or at most minimal, trade-distorting effects or effects on production'), *blue box* ('direct payments under production-limiting programmes') or, by default, *amber box* (all other 'domestic support measures in favour of domestic producers')
	• No limits on green or blue box support
	• A *de minimis* exemption for amber box support (equal to 5% of production for product-specific support and 5% of the total value of agricultural output for non-product-specific support)
	• Otherwise a binding on the overall 1986–8 level of amber box support (known as the Aggregate Measurement of Support, or AMS) with a 20% reduction over the implementation period (1995–2000)
Export competition	• Bindings, on a commodity-specific basis, on the 1986–90 levels of export subsidy expenditure and volume of subsidized exports
	• Reduction of 36% in the expenditure bindings, and of 21% in the volume bindings, over the period (1995–2000)
	• Subsidies on the 'incorporated agricultural primary product' permitted
	• Disciplines on the 'circumvention of export subsidy commitments'

distinguish between developed and developing countries, allowing the latter—in the case of the URAA—longer implementation periods, lower reduction commitments, and other *special and differential treatment*; and, in the case of the LDCs, exemption from the reduction commitments. It should also be emphasized that the detail in Table 3.1 goes beyond the actual content of the legal text of the URAA, and includes the 'modalities' of the agreement: that is, the numerical targets that countries were expected to respect in drawing up their new tariff schedules, and domestic and export subsidy commitments. These details, together with the methodologies to be adopted (to undertake tariffication, for example), were specified in a document entitled *Modalities for the Establishment of Specific Binding Commitments Under the Reform Programme* (GATT 1993).

The objective of the URAA was to set 'specific binding commitments' in three areas (now referred to as 'pillars'): market access, domestic support, and export competition. Reduction commitments were applied in six equal steps by developed nations, the first in 1995 and then through to 2000.

Market access

On market access, tariffs were to be reduced by a simple arithmetical average (over all tariff lines) of 36 per cent over the implementation period, with no tariff line subject to a reduction of less than 15 per cent. But first, if 'ordinary customs duties' did not apply, countries were expected to convert their existing non-tariff barriers (e.g. the EU's old variable import levy mechanism) into tariffs—a process dubbed 'tariffication'—by comparing a representative internal price with an appropriate external price for a base period 1986–8. And so, for example, the EU declared its internal price for white sugar to be 719 ecu/tonne, compared to an external price of 195 ecu/tonne, resulting in a tariff equivalent of 524 ecu/tonne, and then committed itself to a 20 per cent reduction of this tariff to a new bound rate of 419 ecu/tonne in 2000 (Swinbank 2004: 59, 65). This process was undertaken by the GATT members concerned between the December 1993 closure of the URAA negotiations in Geneva[12] and the formal signing of the agreements in Marrakesh in April 1994, and appears to have been subject to relatively little external verification. Subsequently some commentators have talked about 'dirty tariffication', implying that some GATT members manipulated either the internal price, or the external price, or both, to produce an artificially high tariff equivalent. The EU's tariffication of sugar has been cited as an example (see e.g. Ingco 1996), but Swinbank (2004) found no evidence to suggest that the EU had engaged in dirty tariffication on sugar. What is true is that world market prices for many agricultural products were at an historic low in the base period (1986–8) chosen by GATT members, meaning that tariffication locked in historically high levels of border protection.

In some respects tariffication reduced the extent to which agriculture differed from other sectors in the GATT/WTO. First tariffication overrode GATT Article XI: Article 4 of the URAA says that 'Members shall not maintain, resort to, or revert to any measures of the kind which have been required to be converted into ordinary customs duties', and a footnote explains that this includes 'quantitative import restrictions . . .'.

Second, most tariffs were now bound, although many tariffs determined as a result of tariffication were *specific*—a fixed monetary amount per unit of import, as in the EU sugar example earlier—rather than *ad valorem* tariffs.

However, the creation of *Special Safeguard Provisions* for agriculture (Article 5 of the URAA) pulled in the opposite direction and reinforced agricultural exceptionalism. GATT Article VI deals with anti-dumping measures and allows WTO members to apply countervailing duties (see Box 3.4). But the Special Safeguard Provisions for agriculture go beyond this. They allow importers, under specified circumstances, to charge an *additional duty* on imports without the need to show either that the product was dumped or that the domestic industry suffered damage. However, two conditions must first be met. First, the provisions can only apply to a tariff line that underwent tariffication, and second the WTO member concerned must have had the foresight to insert the letters SSG against that tariff line in the tariff schedule lodged in Marrakesh in 1994. Thus the measure was skewed in favour of developed countries—as most developing countries opted for a simpler version of determining their UR tariff bindings[13]—and those countries that made most use of non-tariff barriers pre-Uruguay. The WTO Secretariat has reported that 39 members wrote SSG into their tariff schedules, in the EU's case covering 31 per cent of its agricultural tariff lines compared to 9 per cent for the United States, and that between 1995 and 2004 12 members had actually made use of this facility (WTO 2004*b*: 1, 6).

Box 3.4 TRADE DEFENCE INSTRUMENTS

GATT 1947 included two important articles that allowed contracting parties to restrict trade when certain criteria were met. First, Article VI allowed *anti-dumping duties* to be charged when foreign firms could be shown to be 'dumping' their product in the import market *and* causing material injury to the firms in the import market; or for a *countervailing duty* to be imposed to offset any subsidy granted by the exporting country. Post 1995, the anti-dumping provisions have been covered by the UR *Agreement on the Implementation of Article VI of the General Agreement on Tariffs and Trade 1994* (sometimes referred to as the Anti-dumping Agreement); and the countervailing duty provisions are regulated by Part V ('Countervailing Measures') of the UR Subsidies Agreement.

Second, GATT Article XIX ('Emergency Action on Imports of Particular Products') allowed countries that, as a result of 'unforeseen developments', experienced imports 'in such increased quantities and under such conditions as to cause or threaten serious injury to domestic producers . . . of like or directly competitive products', to suspend, withdraw, or modify GATT concessions. Post 1995 this is regulated by the UR *Agreement on Safeguards*.

Various authors have suggested that anti-dumping activity has increased markedly since the 1980s, and that the number of WTO members that have put in place anti-dumping legislation 'has been proliferating' (Blonigen 2004: 568). Blonigen comments that 'The most frequent filers in agricultural products correspond to the most frequent filers generally, *with the curious exception of the EU*. Since 1987, the EU has initiated only two AD [anti-dumping] cases, both against Atlantic salmon from Norway' (2004: 577–8, emphasis added). The EU's non-use of anti-dumping against agricultural imports continued until China joined the WTO: in January 2006 it did launch an anti-dumping enquiry into frozen strawberries from China following a complaint from the Polish Freezing Industry Union (Commission 2006).

Given that the EU is one of the major users of anti-dumping measures in the WTO, why this reticence to use them in agriculture? Part of the explanation may lie in the protective mechanisms of the CAP. Prior to 1995, and the implementation of tariffication, the CAP's variable import levies and minimum import price regimes insulated the internal market from low-priced imports: dumping simply triggered an increase in the variable import levy. Post 1995, it may be that there was so much 'water' in the tariffs of most agricultural products that, combined with the Special Safeguard provisions of the URAA, 'dumped' imports would still be uncompetitive.[a] If so, we might expect to see the EU make more use of the anti-dumping provisions against agricultural products following any further cut in tariffs in the Doha Round.

In contrast to products covered by the URAA, the EU has used all three trade defence instruments to limit imports of farmed salmon from Norway. For example, in October 2004 the EU began an anti-dumping investigation into Norwegian farmed salmon, following a complaint by the EU Salmon Producers' Group. A provisional anti-dumping duty was imposed in April 2005. In June 2005 these anti-dumping duties were replaced by a minimum import price (MIP) regime, which—if not respected—triggered an additional import charge to bring the landed price up to the MIP. These provisional arrangements were replaced by a definitive regime in January 2006. In March 2006 Norway launched a dispute settlement proceeding, and the panel reported in November 2007 (WTO 2007c: 1–3).

[a] When tariffs are prohibitively high—that is, higher than need be to eliminate the possibility of all imports—trade policy analysts talk about *water* in the tariff. The water is the tariff reduction that could be conceded without allowing imports to become price competitive on, and thus capture a share of, the domestic market.

There are two instances in which the special agricultural safeguard can be invoked. First, if countries experience an import surge (according to a complex formula), then all imports of that product from that source can be subject to an additional duty for the remainder of the year. Alternatively a price trigger can be set. Again the arrangements are complex, but if on a consignment basis the import price is found to be below an historic trigger price, then an additional duty is charged (see Swinbank and Tanner 1996: 123). The trigger price is equal to the country's average import price in the base period. Note that this may be well in excess of the 'world price' in the base period, if the bulk of the country's imports came in under preferential arrangements. This was the case with sugar into the EU: the bulk of its sugar imports came from a group of ACP (African, Caribbean, and Pacific) states under a sugar protocol annexed to the Lomé Convention. Consequently, the EU declared a trigger price of 531 ecu/tonne for white sugar for the base period 1986–8, even though—as we saw earlier—the 'world price' it had used for tariffication was only 195 ecu/tonne. This has meant that, for sugar imports into the EU, the special agricultural safeguard has been permanently invoked (Swinbank 2004: 65).

The import access arrangements of the URAA provided exceptional treatment of agriculture in the WTO in another way as well, namely in the large number of tariff rate quotas (TRQs) it created. Strictly speaking, TRQs are not an absolute limit on the volume of product that can be imported (which would fall foul of GATT Article XI, as discussed earlier), but instead allow a controlled quantity of a product to be imported at a low or zero duty, and additional imports (over and above the TRQ) at the full MFN tariff.

The URAA modalities document (GATT 1993: 11) provided for the codification of two types of TRQs: those to preserve *current access* opportunities, and those to provide new *minimum access* openings. Current access TRQs would usually be allocated to specified overseas suppliers (e.g. the EU opened a current access TRQ for butter from New Zealand), and were designed to preserve market access provisions that had been in place in the base period 1986–8. If current access TRQs were subsequently to be expanded, the modalities document said that this should be done on an MFN basis.

Minimum access TRQs were a clear case of exceptional treatment of agriculture, but they were not designed to restrict trade, rather the intention was to liberalize at least a minimum of trade. Recognizing that, even after tariffication and the URAA reduction in tariffs, many agricultural tariffs would remain prohibitively high, it was agreed that some market access should be allowed, in the form of a TRQ, on an MFN basis. By the end of the implementation period, minimum access TRQs were to be set at a level corresponding to 5 per cent of 'domestic consumption in the base period 1986–88', less any imports in the base period (and current access TRQs). Thus the EU opened a minimum access TRQ for cheddar cheese, in addition to current access TRQs for cheddar benefiting Australia, New Zealand, and Canada (*Agra Europe*, 21 January 1994: E/1). Japan and the Republic of Korea originally took advantage of a special provision set out in Annex 5 of the URAA (referred to by Josling et al. 1996: 180–1 as the 'rice clause') to delay tariffication for rice, reflecting the high political sensitivity of rice in their economies, but in return had to open larger minimum access TRQs for rice.

However, economists are critical of TRQs because they confer tariff quota *rents* (i.e. additional unearned profits on imports) on lucky recipients, giving rise to questions about the transparency (and honesty) of allocation mechanisms of TRQ entitlements (for a discussion see de Gorter 2004: 151–4).

Domestic support

Although GATT Article XVI, and the UR Subsidies Agreement, provides a general framework for domestic subsidies, the structure of the URAA's domestic support commitments is quite unique and sets agriculture aside from other sectors of the economy. The URAA does not do away with domestic support—indeed in many countries the agricultural sector continued to receive exceptionally high levels of domestic support—but it did impose some disciplines on agricultural exceptionalism by setting limits for the level of domestic support.

'Domestic support measures in favour of agricultural producers' (in developed countries) are allocated into one of three categories although, as Brink (2007) points out, the provisions are complex and difficult to summarize, leading to incomplete and sometimes misleading accounts.

Those that have 'no, or at most minimal, trade-distorting effects or effects on production', and meet the policy-specific criteria set out in Annex 2 to the URAA are commonly referred to as *green box* policies, and are subject to no expenditure limits.

Blue box policies are partially decoupled (on decoupling, see Box 3.5). They might have a trade-distorting effect, but provided they formed part of a 'production-limiting' programme and met the other criteria set out in Article 6(5) of the URAA, they too were subject to no expenditure limit.

Box 3.5 WHAT ARE DECOUPLED POLICIES?

During the UR a lot of emphasis was placed on decoupling. If farm support pro-grammes encourage farmers to produce more (and consumers to consume less) they affect a country's net trade in the product, and hence impact upon the interests of other trading partners. However, if some system of *decoupled* support could be devised that would benefit farmers without impacting upon production, this domes-tic policy would be of no international concern. Devising policies that truly have no impact on production is not an easy task, but the green box was an attempt to define an internationally recognized set of policies that were deemed to meet this requirement.

In practice a number of stages in decoupling can be identified; and the history of the CAP is illustrative. Prior to 1992 and the MacSharry reforms, CAP support typically involved guaranteed market prices well in excess of those prevailing on world markets, and no supply control. Farmers were encouraged to increase supply to make best use of the price guarantees. This was amber box policy. The 1992 reforms in the cereals sector involved a partial decoupling. Guaranteed prices were reduced significantly, and in compensation farmers were entitled to receive a pay-ment based on the area of land they had planted. Thus the price incentive to increase crop yields had been reduced, but the policy was still partly coupled in that farmers had to keep land in production (or set-aside) to receive the payment. This was blue box policy. In 2003, in the Fischler reforms, a further step was taken when the *Single Payment Scheme* was introduced. The planting requirement was now eliminated (and similarly livestock no longer had to be kept), and so no production was required, but the recipient had to remain a farmer, and the land had to be main-tained in good agricultural condition. The EU believes this meets the green box requirements, but Swinbank and Tranter (2005) suggested that because of the annual nature of the claim, and the link with *farm*land, the matter could be con-tested. A further step in decoupling would be to break altogether the link between compensation payments and agriculture: With a *bond scheme* recipients of compen-sation payments would no longer have to maintain their link with farming, and the farm's assets (e.g. its land) could be put to other uses (Swinbank and Tangermann 2004). However, even this, it might be argued, gave farmers increased financial resources (at least during the transition period) which could potentially impact upon their business behaviour. Thus a policy would only be fully decoupled when all price and income support had been eliminated, and all compensation payments too.

A significant literature has developed which tries to access how decoupled various schemes are (see e.g. Anton and Cahill 2005).

Furthermore, they benefited from limited protection under the Peace Clause, provided the measures did 'not grant support to a specific com-modity in excess of that decided during the 1992 marketing year'. This was an unsubtle reference to the CAP's MacSharry reforms of 1992, when support prices for cereals and beef were reduced, and farmers received 'compensation' in the form of area and livestock payments: payments the EU declared in the blue box. The blue box was written into the URAA by the EU and the United States at the November 1992 'Blair House' meeting, discussed in Chapter 7, and was designed to accommodate both the 1990 Farm Bill's deficiency payments in the United States, and the area and headage payments stemming from the 1992 MacSharry reform of the CAP (Orden et al. 1999: 107).

Developing country members can also exclude 'investment subsidies... generally available to agriculture... and agricultural input subsidies generally available to low-income or resource poor producers in developing countr[ies]' and measures to encourage diversification away 'from growing illicit narcotic crops'; but this Article 6.2 exemption has not been accorded a colour code.

Any residual support to the farm sector is subject to reduction commitments, and many authors refer to this as *amber box* support (see Figure 3.1).

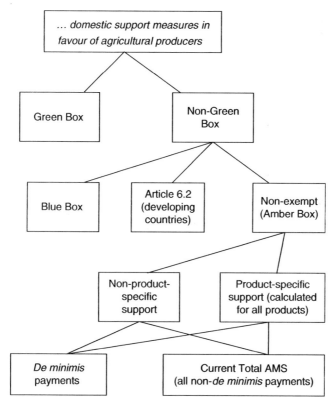

Figure 3.1 Classification of domestic support measures
Source: Adapted from Brink (2007: Figure 1).

No other sector of the economy faces an equivalent WTO-imposed constraint. Support consists of both direct subsidies paid by government not otherwise exempted, and an estimate of the gross financial benefit of market price support programmes based upon the difference between an 'applied administered price' and a 'fixed external price' (from the 1986–8 base period). For each 'basic agricultural product' an Aggregate Measurement of Support (AMS) was calculated for the base period, as was any 'non-product-specific' support (e.g. fertilizer subsidies). These were all added together to produce a Total Aggregate Measurement of Support. It is this Total AMS for the base period that had to be reduced by 20 per cent. Subsequently, on an annual basis, a corresponding calculation is undertaken (with the same 'fixed external price') to produce the Current total AMS, and this has to comply with the bound commitment levels.

However, in the annual calculation of the *Current* total AMS, a *de minimis* provision applies. Each product-specific AMS will only be included in the Current total AMS if it exceeds 5 per cent of the value of production of that product, and similarly (and in addition) the non-product-specific AMS will only count if it exceeds 5 per cent of the total value of agricultural production. Thus, even if a country declared a zero-base period AMS, it could still support its agricultural sector provided it remained within the *de minimis* provisions.

Box-shifting

WTO members make annual notifications (sometimes belatedly) to the Committee on Agriculture of their use of the amber, blue, and green boxes. There is a mass of data to be found in those submissions, and from time to time the WTO Secretariat prepares summary documents. Table 3.2 makes use of a tiny proportion of the data set, but helps illustrate the concerns of some members about *box-shifting*.

Thirty-five members (counting EU15 as one) had declared AMS base commitments that exceeded zero. Table 3.2 shows, for three important players, that proportion of their AMS commitment that has been used in subsequent years. Clearly the countries selected show contrasting experiences, but delving beneath the data illustrates the fungible nature of the AMS limit.

Japan in the early period was utilizing 70 per cent of its AMS commitment, and this suddenly dropped below 20 per cent. What was the change in Japanese policy? Japan's Current AMS went from 3.2 trillion (thousand

Table 3.2 Use of AMS commitments by selected WTO members, 1995–2001 (% utilization)

Country	1995	1996	1997	1998	1999	2000	2001
EU15	64	67	68	65	69	65	58
Japan	73	72	71	18	18	18	
US	27	26	29	50	85	88	75

Note: Blanks indicate that the WTO Secretariat had not received notifications by 14 January 2005.

Source: WTO (2005c: Table 2).

billion) yen in 1997 to 0.8 trillion in 1998, and this entire reduction is accounted for by the elimination of a 2.4 trillion yen AMS for rice (WTO 2005*b*: Table 3.1). Was support for the rice sector removed? The simple answer is no; but Japan did change its policy mechanisms with the introduction of its *Rice Farming Income Stabilization* programme (Fukuda et al. 2003: 11). Although actual expenditure on direct government support payments is directly included in the AMS, the bulk of the AMS for many countries is computed: As noted earlier it is based on the volume of production of the supported commodity, and the difference between a fixed external reference price and an 'applied administered price'. The latter could be an intervention price, or some other price that triggered domestic support. It would appear that Japan believes that the changes it made to its support arrangements for rice eliminated its 'applied administered price' for rice, and hence a large chunk of its AMS (Fukuda et al. 2003: 11).

The United States, by contrast, started with a low level of utilization that had increased markedly by 1999. What was the story there? Over the period there has been a number of changes to US farm policy. The base period (1986–8) AMS was calculated at a time when US farm programmes were rather different than they were in the mid 1990s, and what in the 1980s had been amber box support had in the 1990 Farm Bill been switched to a deficiency payments regime paid on 85 per cent of eligible land (Orden et al. 1999: 102–3). The United States classified these deficiency payments as blue box support, and so they fell out of the Current AMS calculation.

The 1996 FAIR Act introduced Production Flexibility Contract (PFC) payments for the period 1996–2000, which were paid to farmers on the basis of past plantings of feed grains, cotton, and rice provided the land remained in agricultural production, but not planted to fruits and vegetables (Orden et al. 1999: 237). These authors refer to the United States having 'unilaterally adopted fully decoupled support payments'; and that as a consequence the United States 'no longer needs the blue box exemption' (p. 168). Believing the PFC payments to be genuine green box support, they were declared as such. However, as we shall see in Chapter 5, in 2005 the WTO's Dispute Settlement Body ruled in *Upland Cotton* that the PFC payments did not meet the strict criteria of the green box, and were therefore—by default—amber box support. Table 3.2 does not reflect the impact of this ruling.

In 1998 commodity prices fell, and the United States introduced emergency measures in the form of *market loss assistance* payments to PFC recipients. These were not green box payments, because they were linked to market price movements, but—it was argued—they were not product-specific, and they accounted for less than 5 per cent of the overall value of US farm production. Thus, somewhat controversially, they were declared *de minimis* support, and were not included in the Current AMS calculations.

The EU too has engaged in box-shifting, as Figure 3.2 confirms. Between the base period and the 1995 implementation of the agreement, the MacSharry reforms of 1992 had shifted €21 billion out of the AMS and into the blue box, for cereals, oilseeds, beef, and sheep. According to our very rough calculations, the Fischler reforms of 2003/4, and subsequent changes (including the sugar reform), would shift about €12.4 billion from the Current AMS and about €18.6 billion from the blue box, whilst increasing green box expenditure by about €31 billion, for EU15, based on the EU's 2003/4 submission (Swinbank 2008*b*: Annex).[14]

Export competition

As we saw earlier in this chapter, GATT Article XVI:3 allowed members to subsidize the export of primary products. The URAA severely constrained that freedom in that only 25 members (counting the EU15 as one) notified export subsidy reduction commitments (WTO 2002*b*: 1), and they could only subsidize products on their original list, and within the limits determined. All other WTO members were now committed to forgo the use of export subsidies. This provision was clearly aimed at eroding agricultural exceptionalism in export competition and, as we shall see, in the Doha Round negotiations WTO members agreed to phase out export subsidization and thus normalize export competition.

On a product-specific basis members had to notify both the expenditure on export subsidies and the volume of subsidized exports in a base

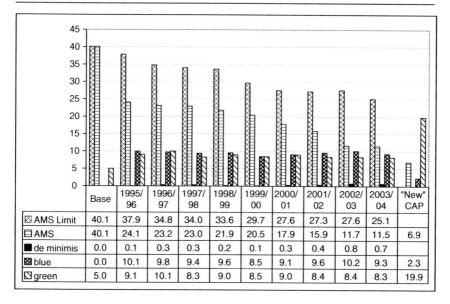

	Base	1995/ 96	1996/ 97	1997/ 98	1998/ 99	1999/ 00	2000/ 01	2001/ 02	2002/ 03	2003/ 04	"New" CAP
▨ AMS Limit	40.1	37.9	34.8	34.0	33.6	29.7	27.6	27.3	27.6	25.1	
⊟ AMS	40.1	24.1	23.2	23.0	21.9	20.5	17.9	15.9	11.7	11.5	6.9
■ de minimis	0.0	0.1	0.3	0.3	0.2	0.1	0.3	0.4	0.8	0.7	
▨ blue	0.0	10.1	9.8	9.4	9.6	8.5	9.1	9.6	10.2	9.3	2.3
▨ green	5.0	9.1	10.1	8.3	9.0	8.5	9.0	8.4	8.4	8.3	19.9

Figure 3.2 EU domestic support expressed as a percentage of the value of agricultural production

Sources: Derived from:

Base period (1986–88), for EU12, EU's notification of 1994. Only EU-funded (and not Member State-funded) green box measures were notified.

Subsequent data (EU15) from the EU's periodic submissions to the WTO in the document series G/AG/N/EEC/... For each year after the base period the first of the five columns shows the maximum level AMS allowed in that year (expressed here as a percentage of the value of agricultural production, rather than in ecu/euro); the second column shows the actual Current Total AMS declared for the year; third the *de minimis* amount of amber box support that was excluded from the actual AMS declared; fourth blue box expenditure; and fifth green box expenditure. The EU's 2003/04 notification was for an EU of 25 member states: thus the AMS calculations are, apparently, based on production data for EU25. However, area payments in the new member states were not charged against the budget in this period.

'New' CAP: authors' back-of-the-envelope calculation of the effect of the Fischler and subsequent reforms. Details are shown in the annex to Swinbank (2008b).

period 1986–90. By the end of the implementation period, for developed countries, the annual level of budgetary outlays was not to exceed 64 per cent, and the volume of subsidized exports 79 per cent, of these base levels.

The URAA attempted a list of export subsidies subject to the agreement (Article 9), and in Article 10 it went on to say that 'Export subsidies not listed in... Article 9 shall not be applied in a manner which results in, or which threatens to lead to, circumvention of export subsidy commitments'. Article 9 made clear that producer-funded export subsidies ('payments that are funded from the proceeds of a levy imposed on the agricultural product concerned') fell within the export subsidy commitment. In earlier times the EU had argued that this should not be so: for example, in 1982 in the Working Party set up to examine trade in sugar, the EU had 'stated that since the introduction of the new sugar regime in 1981, the European Communities were no longer subsidizing exports of sugar produced within the European Communities, as the entire losses on the exports of such sugar were covered by levies on production' (GATT 1982b: 4). However, there was less clarity over export credits, and dual price systems where no explicit subsidy was paid. In a dual price system domestic producers achieve a price above the world market price for produce sold in the domestic market whilst receiving the world market price for exported quantities. The inflated domestic price can be viewed as an indirect export subsidy because it compensates indirectly for a lower world market price and thus enables exports that would not otherwise have been possible. Subsequently, in *Upland Cotton*, the Dispute Settlement process determined that export credits were export subsidies subject to the URAA constraints (Benitah 2005) and, in *Canada Dairy* and *EU Sugar*, that dual-price systems did in effect confer a subsidy on exports which was also subject to the URAA constraints (on *Canada Dairy* see van Vliet 2000: 228–9). The EU sugar case is briefly discussed in Chapter 5.

Although the URAA places much tighter limits on export subsidies compared to GATT Article XVI:3, Article 11 of the URAA at first sight appears to have extended the range of products on which export subsidies can be granted, in that it provides for export subsidies on 'incorporated' (e.g. processed food) products, provided the 'per-unit subsidy on an incorporated product' does not 'exceed the per-unit subsidy on exports of the primary product as such'. Thus there is a potential conflict between GATT Article XVI, which prohibits the use of export subsidies on processed products (such as pasta), and the URAA that sanctions their use (Swinbank 2006b).

The EU has been by far the most important player, accounting for 89 per cent of export subsidy *expenditure* of all WTO members in 1995, for example (WTO 2002c: Table 3.1). Neither Japan nor South Korea, countries that wished to retain significant flexibility to protect their farm sectors in the Doha Round, had the right to subsidize exports. Some of the 25 countries on the export subsidy list, for example Australia and Brazil, had made very limited use of export subsidies. Consequently, in the Doha Round, the EU was relatively exposed, and—as we shall see in

Chapter 7—in May 2004 it agreed that, subject to a satisfactory overall agreement, it would be willing to outlaw their future use.

Although the EU is the dominant user of URAA export subsidy entitlements, and has found some of the product-specific limits to be binding, in aggregate it has not used its full entitlement. Figure 3.3 reports two data series: the percentage utilization of the expenditure limit aggregated across all product groups, and that for incorporated products. What the former shows is that in 2001/2 it used only 35 per cent, and in 2002/3 only 42 per cent, of its overall expenditure limit. This leeway would have allowed the EU to avoid any further cuts in export subsidies had its original January 2003 suggestion of 'an average 45 per cent cut in the level of budgetary outlays', with the elimination of export subsidies for 'certain products' (European Union 2003: 3), been accepted as the basis for a Doha Round agreement. In some instances policy had changed since the 1988–90 base period. For instance, the MacSharry reforms of 1992, reinforced by those of Agenda 2000 in 1999, reduced substantially the EU's internal support price for cereals, and hence the export subsidy per tonne of exported product, but—depending on world market prices—did not eliminate the need for export subsidies altogether.

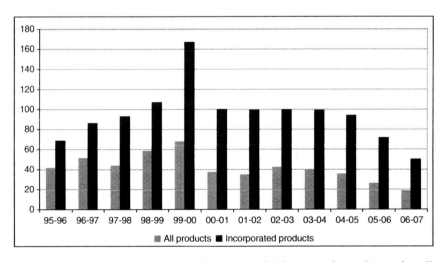

Figure 3.3 EU's percentage usage of export subsidy expenditure limits for all products and incorporated products (annual data: 1995/6 to 2006/7)

Note: EU15, 25, or 27 as appropriate. Excludes exports of C and ACP sugar until 22 May 2006. EU25 commitments from 2006/7.

Source: EU's periodic submissions in WTO document series G/AG/N/EEC/.

What the latter data series (expenditure on incorporated products) shows is that in the first three years of implementation of the URAA, the expenditure limits were not breached, whereas in 1998/9 and 1999/2000 they apparently were. This reflects a provision of Article 9 of the URAA which, the EU claimed, allowed members in years two through five of the implementation period to carry forward unutilized entitlements from earlier years (see, however, Desta 2002: 267–71, for a strongly expressed contrary view). From 2000/1 on, however, each product-specific expenditure and volume limit applied on an annual basis, and in Figure 3.3 expenditure on export refunds on incorporated products can be seen hovering at just under 100 per cent of the limit until EU enlargement in 2004 relaxed this constraint (as the EU15 was no longer subsidizing its exports to the new member states). With rising commodity prices, particularly in 2007 and 2008, export subsidies were of less importance to the CAP.

Non-trade concerns

Although Article 20 of the URAA committed WTO members to a continuation of the reform process, it did so taking into account '*non-trade concerns*, special and differential treatment to developing country members, and the objective to establish a fair and market-oriented trading system' (emphasis added). The preamble to the agreement had also noted, in part, that 'commitments under the reform programme should be made in an equitable way among all members, having regard to *non-trade concerns*, including food security and the need to protect the environment' (emphasis added). This reference to non-trade concerns is not repeated elsewhere in the WTO agreements, and it again marks agriculture as being different from other sectors of the economy. However, we leave a discussion of what these non-trade concerns might be until Chapters 6 and 7.

Concluding comments

Our objective in this chapter was to explain how, first, GATT 1947 provided for exceptional treatment of agriculture, and second how that changed after 1995. Despite the introduction of agricultural normalism as its ideational foundation, the URAA is ambivalent in that its specific provisions for reductions of agricultural support and protection point in a different direction. Whilst some URAA provisions weaken the exceptional treatment of agriculture, others reinforce it. However, the overall trend is a move towards more normalized conditions for farm trade, though it may take decades before farm trade is fully integrated, if ever, into the GATT/WTO legal system.

Throughout, the focus of the chapter, and indeed of the book, has been the interaction between GATT/WTO provisions and the traditional price and income support measures of the CAP. In 1995 agriculture was not the only economic sector that had a sector-specific agreement, derogating from the more general GATT/WTO provisions. Following on from the Multi-fibre Agreement, there was also a Uruguay Round Agreement on Textiles and Clothing; but that had a 10-year lifespan which has now lapsed, thereby integrating trade in textiles and clothing fully into the GATT/WTO (although, admittedly, with high tariff protection). There is no such specific plan for agriculture: the Doha Round negotiations, which we discuss in Chapters 7 and 8, envisaged a revised URAA with tighter constraints on support and protection, but with no expiry clause built into the provisions. Whilst an Agreement on Agriculture remains part of the family of WTO Agreements, agriculture will be different.

When the URAA was agreed, its Peace Clause was seen as an important provision, ensuring that the URAA agreement could not be challenged under other WTO agreements. When the Peace Clause expired, that protection presumably did so too, suggesting that the agriculture sector now had somewhat less exceptional treatment in the WTO than it did whilst the Peace Clause was in force.

Chapter 4

Explaining the Erosion of Agricultural Exceptionalism in the Uruguay Round

In this chapter we identify the factors which enabled free-trade advocates to erode agricultural exceptionalism as the ideational foundation of WTO farm trade rules. From the early 1960s the United States had attempted unsuccessfully to align trade rules for farm products with those applied to other industries. This chapter analyses the circumstances that allowed the United States, supported by the Cairns Group, to force through a new trade regime for agriculture founded on a new ideational underpinning. We begin with an analysis of the most important reasons why attempts up until the 1980s to erode agricultural exceptionalism were unsuccessful. Further we briefly account for the meagre outcomes of the negotiations on farm trade during the Dillon, Kennedy, and Tokyo Rounds. Then the chapter concentrates on identifying and examining the circumstances enabling change. As set out in the first component of our analytical framework, to understand ideational change one should ask whether and how new circumstances affected the *force of argument*. We show that developments in agricultural economics in the 1970s and 1980s produced new insights into the costs and trade impacts of agricultural policies, how research findings interacted with changes in the broader economic and political contexts, and how this interaction influenced the force of the arguments for ideational change put forward. The first component of our analytical framework also highlights *macro-institutional change* in the GATT as an important factor influencing win-sets and power balances in the farm trade negotiations. We demonstrate that it was *macro-institutional change*, the UR being negotiated and concluded as a *Single Undertaking*, that forced the European Union (EU) to accept an erosion of agricultural exceptionalism in the WTO.

Eroding the idea of agricultural exceptionalism

This section analyses the pre-UR period, focusing on the critique of agricultural exceptionalism which gradually gained strength and became a forceful argument in favour of ideational change in the GATT/WTO farm trade regime. First, we identify the early sources of this criticism and the failed attempts to use it in the trade rounds of the 1960s and 1970s. Second, we analyse the development of support measures to reveal the magnitude of agricultural support and how these played an important role in questioning the need for agricultural support among politicians and government officials. Finally we show how the growing criticism of agricultural exceptionalism coincided with changes in the political and economic context in the 1980s.

Pre-UR criticisms of domestic farm policies

Although agricultural exceptionalism remained embedded in GATT from 1948 until the start of the new WTO legal system in 1995, this is not to say it did not have its critics, or that there were no attempts to expunge agricultural exceptionalism from the system. Academic economists were especially critical: David Ricardo's classic exposition of comparative advantage, *On the Principles of Political Economy, and Taxation*, published in 1817, did after all use the example of an agricultural good—wine— in discussing the relative costs of production of wine and cloth in Portugal and England, and the 'significance of the theory to Ricardo was to strengthen greatly the arguments against the Corn Laws' (Hartwell 1971: 21).

However, in the aftermath of the Second World War and during the Korean War, strong counter-arguments that emphasized agricultural exceptionalism (or 'agrarian fundamentalism'), and the need for food security, prevailed. Rau was certainly of the view that agrarian fundamentalism—'the doctrine that agriculture is the foundation of national prosperity more than any other industry or occupation'—was rife (Rau 1957: 21).

Agricultural policies were criticized, but it is telling that GATT rules often found no place in the discourse. McCrone's careful economic critique (1962) of British farm policy, for example, which devotes considerable space to trade issues (including agriculture's potential contribution to solving a balance of payments constraint, a particular British problem of the time) appears not to mention GATT at all.

In 1957 academics were given a fairly unique opportunity to contribute to GATT deliberations when a group of experts was asked to draw up a report on *Trends in International Trade* for presentation to the Thirteenth Session of GATT's Contracting Parties. The team of four comprised Dr. Roberto de Oliveira Campos (Director of the Brazilian National Bank for Economic Development) and Professors Gottfried Haberler (of Harvard University, who chaired the panel), James Meade (of the University of Cambridge), and Jan Tinbergen (of the Netherlands Institute for Advanced Economic Studies, Rotterdam) (GATT 1958a: i). GATT's Executive Secretary, Eric Wyndham White, in his foreword to the Haberler Report, noted it had been commissioned because of 'some disturbing elements' in world trade: 'the prevalence of agricultural protectionism, expressed in restrictive measures in international trade in agricultural and food products, and the building up of large stocks of these products which have no outlet through the normal channels of trade; sharp variations in the prices of primary products, accompanied by wide fluctuations in the export earnings of primary producers; and finally the failure of the export trade of the under-developed countries to expand at a rate commensurate with their growing import needs' (GATT 1958a: i).

The Haberler Report pointed out that many agricultural policies had both a price-stabilizing effect ('they ensure to the farmer a return that varies less than the free market price would vary'), and a protective effect ('a return which, over the average of years, is higher than the free market price would be') (GATT 1958a: 81), both of which had adverse consequences for world trade. Domestic price stabilization policies tended to destabilize world market prices, whilst agricultural protection depressed world market prices and reduced the exports of competitive producers. However, Haberler and his colleagues found it impossible, on the evidence then available, 'to conclude whether or not there has been an increase in agricultural protection in industrial countries in recent years'; but believed it was an 'incontrovertible fact' that 'agricultural protectionism exists at a high level in most of the highly industrialized countries' (GATT 1958a: 6, 87). Accordingly the Expert Group, in addition to its cautious recommendation 'that there should be some gradual moderation of the degree of agricultural protection in exporting and importing countries', also suggested that 'the FAO [Food and Agriculture Organization of the United Nations] and the GATT should make a joint study of the possibility of measuring degrees of agricultural protectionism' based on 'a comparison between the total return actually received by the domestic farmer for his production and the return which would correspond to the ruling world market price' (GATT 1958a: 9, 102). As we shall see later, the FAO embarked on just such a study in the 1970s.

Discussions on the Haberler Report at the 1958 GATT Ministerial Meeting led to the creation of three committees, drawn from GATT's Contracting Parties, with a view to expanding international trade. Committee I's task was to discuss 'the proposal for a fresh round of negotiations to reduce general tariff levels' (which became the Dillon Round), the remit of Committee II was 'obstacles to the expansion of trade which arise from national agricultural policies', whilst Committee III was concerned with 'other obstacles to the expansion of the export trade of under-developed countries' (GATT 1958b; see also Curzon and Curzon 1976: 149, 166, 169). Committee II's second report (actually its first substantive report) in May 1960 gave an account of consultations held with 24 countries, including all six members of the European Economic Community (EEC), reaching broadly the same conclusions as the Haberler Report (GATT 1960).

In its third report Committee II was still unable to 'make quantitative assessments of the effect of non-tariff protective measures on international trade', although 'an expert group has been set up to look into the question of measuring the degree of agricultural protection' (GATT 1961: 2). Nonetheless, in its concluding paragraph, it was bold enough to suggest that:

> there has been extensive resort to the use of non-tariff devices [*including variable import levies*], whether or not in conformity with the General Agreement, which, in many cases, has impaired or nullified tariff concessions or other benefits which agricultural exporting countries expect to receive from the General Agreement. Hence, the Committee concludes that the balance which countries consider they had a right to receive under the General Agreement has been disturbed. These developments are of such a character that either they have weakened or threatened to weaken the operation of the General Agreement as an instrument for the promotion of mutually advantageous trade. This situation raised the question as to the extent to which the GATT is an effective instrument for the promotion of such trade. (GATT 1961: 10)

In the 1960s and early 1970s, as Britain discussed the merits of EEC membership, the trade policy concerns arising from a protectionist Common Agricultural Policy (CAP) came frequently to the fore. Economists had long since recognized that the creation or expansion of a customs union could give rise to trade creation or trade diversion (terms popularized by Viner in 1950): trade creation when high-cost domestic production was displaced by lower-cost imports from a customs union partner (though not necessarily the world's lowest-cost supplier), and trade diversion when lower-cost imports from another trading partner were displaced by higher-cost imports from a customs union partner.[1] Thus Harry Johnson, a leading trade theorist of the time, in a collection of essays hostile to the United Kingdom's application to join the EEC, wrote: 'Acceptance by Britain of the EEC's Common Agricultural Policy... would aggravate enormously the already serious problem of trade in temperate-zone agricultural products—apart entirely from the extra costs it would impose on the British economy. The British market would be pre-empted for the support of Continental farmers, and violently closed or virtually closed to the food-surplus countries; in the course of time, Europe would emerge as yet another surplus country attempting to press unwanted surplus grain on a reluctant world market' (Johnson 1971: 169).

These concerns had also been expressed in Committee II. One outcome of the Dillon Round (1960–2) was that Committee II was given the task of undertaking consultations with GATT members that had made 'substantial changes' to their agricultural policies (GATT 1962: 3). Thus in its 1962 consultations with the EEC, as the first elements of the CAP were put in place, it was noted that:

> Exporting members of the Committee felt that a closed market system in which a high level of price support exists, could not fail to generate increased levels of production which in turn were protected by the levy system ... Combined with the element of Community preference to promote a higher level of intra-Community trade, such a situation could only result in eventual displacement of imports from third countries, who could further be penalized by fiercer competition in price in non-European Economic Community markets to the extent that the European Economic Community exported its surpluses with the aid of the refund system. Efficient producers in third countries could not possibly protect themselves against these effects by lowering their own costs. This adverse impact on world trade assumed even greater importance if and as the Six became an enlarged Community [*this referred to the United Kingdom's bid for EEC membership*]. The very size of such a Community as an economic unit, could enable it to dictate the terms of trade in agricultural products to the outside world. The effects on third country producers could be alleviated by the adoption of a low price policy. (GATT 1962: 43)

These early critical investigations into the trade effects of domestic agricultural policies failed to develop analytical tools to measure the magnitude of agricultural support and its impact on trade. They lacked the data to underpin their conclusions empirically. Hence opponents of trade liberalization could easily defend their position by arguing that the criticism lacked substance, or that the effects were inconsequential.

Ideational theory suggests that to undermine the idea of agricultural exceptionalism, it must be forcefully argued that the idea with its state-assisted policy paradigm underpinning is dysfunctional and produces undesired outcomes. This requires both a theory causally connecting the policy paradigm with the undesired outcomes, and systematic empirical analysis to underpin the theoretical claim. Furthermore, a politically and economically viable alternative idea and policy paradigm must be available. Up until the 1980s, no Western country in post-war history had embarked upon agricultural policy reform, dismantling agricultural support and protection. Consequently, there was no evidence that market liberalism *would* work in agriculture.

Failed attempts to end agricultural exceptionalism in the GATT

GATT was an international regime in which trade liberalization could be achieved by negotiating on several issues simultaneously, as concessions in one field could be balanced by gains in others, but this was difficult to achieve in agriculture. Although issue linkage was *talked* about in the Dillon and Kennedy Rounds—linking progress in other sectors to a deal on agriculture—this never took hold. The first phase of the Dillon Round (1960–2) was a negotiation under GATT Article XXIV:6 designed to compensate the EEC's trading partners for trading losses stemming from the recent formation of the common market: but as yet there was no common agricultural policy, hence there was no agreement on EEC border protection for most agricultural tariff lines, and consequently no basis for negotiations on agriculture (Curzon and Curzon 1976: 170). On a few products of little interest to European agriculture, unlikely at the time to be a key part of the CAP, the EEC did however enter upon tariff bindings: for example, a zero duty on soybeans with the United States as the principal supplier (Warley 1976: 379). It was this zero binding that subsequently led to the oilseeds dispute, which we discuss in Chapter 7. In the 'reciprocal phase' of the Dillon Round, a traditional offer and request negotiation with the initiative being taken by the principal supplier to a particular market, little progress was made on agriculture, as the CAP was still undeveloped. Thus at the closure of the round, other Contracting Parties still had 'unsatisfied negotiating rights'. In particular, Germany's import duty on poultry had previously been bound at 15 per cent; the new CAP arrangements for poultry that came into force in July 1962 included a variable import levy mechanism, which was applied at treble the bound rate. Thus the 'chicken war' began (see Curzon and Curzon 1976: 210–13). But the chicken war was no threat to international security, unlike the Cold War. In August 1961 construction of the Berlin Wall began. The EEC was seen as an important bastion against a Soviet threat, and in the larger scheme the EEC's attachment to agricultural exceptionalism could be tolerated.

At the launch of the Kennedy Round (1964–7) the US chief negotiator, Christian A. Herter, told agricultural ministers: 'my Government will not be prepared to conclude the negotiations until equitable tariff and trade arrangements have been developed for agricultural products' (as quoted in Warley 1976: 290). President Kennedy had been keen to launch a new round, but as the Curzons (1976: 182) note, it 'came before the EEC was ready for it'. At the outset, the CAP was still in embryonic form; the EEC's institutions (and hence its ability to negotiate) were paralysed by the 'empty chair' crisis which persisted from June 1965 when France absented itself from the Council chamber until January 1966 when France secured a *de facto* right of veto as a result of the Luxembourg compromise (see Chapter 1); and the United States rejected the EEC's one initiative on agriculture, its offer to bind its margin of support in the 'montant de soutien' proposal.[2] For the Curzons, this was the end of issue linkage. They comment: 'Having rashly rejected the Community's offer to negotiate over the "montant de soutien" . . . , the United States was thus left to face the totally unnegotiable variable levies. Hence . . . it abandoned its attempt to link progress in industrial trade liberalization with similar progress in agricultural trade liberalization . . . The United States held out as long as was useful (in terms of negotiating tactics) . . . , but was clearly not prepared to sacrifice the industrial side simply because the agricultural talks had failed' (Curzon and Curzon 1976: 180).

The Tokyo Round—referred to at the time as the Multilateral Trade Negotiation, or MTN—was formally launched in September 1973, but not concluded until April 1979. As Paemen and Bensch (1995: 28) note, it quickly 'became bogged down in the morass of agriculture'. The Deputy United States Trade Representative (USTR), Clayton K. Yeutter,[3] pressed strongly for concessions on agriculture, which the EEC resisted and stressed the exceptional characteristics of the agricultural sector. As the Vice-President of the Commission of the European Communities, Sir

Christopher Soames, stated at the GATT Ministerial Meeting in Tokyo in September 1973:

> while we accept that the general objective of the negotiations should apply in this sector as in others, we believe nevertheless that account must also be taken of the special characteristics of agriculture and agricultural products. In our view the main objective in the agricultural fields should be to achieve the expansion of trade in stable world markets in conformity with existing agricultural policies. To achieve this expansion in the stability which is an essential prerequisite for it, we consider that appropriate international arrangements should be negotiated to organize trade on a more orderly basis. Such arrangements could be concluded, for example, for cereals, rice, sugar and for certain homogeneous milk products. For other products where such arrangements are less appropriate a system of joint discipline could be negotiated to ensure that exports on the world market would be organized on a more smooth-running basis. But I must make it very clear that in stating the Community's willingness to negotiate seriously on agriculture I am not suggesting an intention to negotiate about the principles of our Common Agricultural Policy. These principles and the mechanism which support them we consider to be a matter of internal policy and we do not consider them to be the object of international negotiation. (Soames 1973)

Thus the discussion between the EEC and the United States resulted in a 'dialogue of the deaf' (Paemen and Bensch 1995: 29). For the EEC 'the CAP was inviolable, and neither its principles nor its mechanisms could be subject to negotiation', whereas the United States 'sought to negotiate agriculture identically with other products' (Winham 1986: 156). This impasse on agriculture impacted on the talks as a whole, and was only broken when President Gerald Ford failed to win the November 1976 presidential election, and gave way to Jimmy Carter, a Democrat with a different perspective on agricultural trade liberalization. The Democrats were less critical of farm subsidies, and the Carter administration 'took a more multilateral approach to world politics than its predecessor' (Winham 1986: 165). In May 1977, in London, Carter committed to a successful conclusion of the round, and in July 1977 his USTR, Robert Strauss, agreed on a new approach with his European partners, which in effect separated the agricultural negotiations from those on industrial tariffs (Winham 1986: 165; Paemen and Bensch 1995: 29). For industrial goods a formula approach (actually the Swiss formula[4]) would subsequently be the basis for the tariff negotiations, whereas agricultural tariffs would be negotiated in the agriculture negotiating group, on a traditional offer–request basis. Winham (1986: 166–7) is of no doubt that this 'fundamental change from the posture of the United States for the previous two years of the negotiation . . . was in effect an American concession'. Without it the Tokyo Round might have failed. However, the Tokyo Round did result in a new code on subsidies and countervailing duties, which in part was designed to strengthen the disciplines applied to export subsidies on agricultural products (as noted in Chapter 3); and the United States had high hopes that this could be used to curb the CAP.

Towards the end of the Tokyo Round, the then EEC Farm Commissioner Finn Olav Gundelach, addressing a mixed audience of academics and policy practitioners, gave somewhat mixed messages when he first stated 'We cannot have a free-trading philosophy with regard to industry, and when we come to agriculture suddenly become self-sufficient, and refuse to accept the concept of division of labour'; and yet later in the same speech suggested that subsidized EEC exports of cereals, in the face of a 'world shortage of foodstuffs', met a real need, so that the EEC 'should not be overly concerned by the cost, because the latter is an investment justified by politics and ethics, towards peace in the world' (Gundelach 1979: 424, 426). He also commented on the outcome of the Tokyo Round negotiations on agriculture, saying: 'Countries like Australia, which have felt it their duty to attack the common agricultural policy with increasing vehemence for the last five years, have turned around and accepted it—that is, accepted that this policy is politically, economically and socially absolutely necessary for Europe, their only demand being that it be conducted in such a way that they can live with it as well' (p. 425).[5]

If this optimistic interpretation of the views of the EEC's trading partners represented the genuine Brussels view in 1979, it must have been brusquely overturned by events in the early 1980s. Hudec (1993: 145), noting that 'Problems with the EC, particularly in agriculture, had been at the head of the US agenda for the Tokyo Round, and no Tokyo Round legal reforms could claim success without achieving some visible change in EC policy', goes on to document the US assault on the CAP in the *Wheat Flour* (1981–3), *Pasta* (1981–3), *Canned Fruit* (1982–5) and *Citrus* (1982–5) disputes. 'If successful, the sum of the US legal complaints would have made it impossible to continue the CAP in its present form. No change of this magnitude had been agreed to in the Tokyo Round. . . . And so the Community resisted the US legal assault' (p. 146).[6] The United States failed to convince the *Wheat Flour* panel that the EEC's export subsidies had earned it more than an equitable market share (which would have contravened the Tokyo Round subsidies code), and so the United States blocked adoption of the report; but—to preserve the integrity of the CAP—the EEC was forced to block adoption of the other three (pp. 146–61).[7]

Developing methodologies to measure farm support

The Kennedy, Dillon, and Tokyo Rounds were big disappointments for those in favour of farm trade liberalization. The failures highlighted the need to develop a better methodology to measure farm support and its impact on trade. D. Gale Johnson, in his compelling *World Agriculture in Disarray*, was sceptical about the prospects of a renegotiation of GATT rules on agriculture in the context of a new round of trade negotiations focused on trade barriers (Johnson 1973: 256–61)—as indeed proved to be the case in the Tokyo Round. Instead he advocated, first, an empirical phase, 'under the auspices of a responsible international group' (p. 261) to assemble comparable data across countries of the effects of farm support; and second international negotiations in GATT in which limits on the overall scope of support to agriculture be determined. Johnson's blueprint was not followed in detail, but the work on Producer Support Estimates (PSEs) undertaken first in the FAO and then the Organisation for Economic Co-operation and Development (OECD) (discussed later), and the negotiation of an Agreement on Agriculture in the UR, reflect the thrust of his advocacy. However, GATT Contracting Parties had first to experience the frustrations of the Tokyo Round, and of implementing the Tokyo Round accords, before embarking upon the UR.

The FAO published its first document outlining a PSE methodology, with PSE calculations for five countries (Canada, France, Germany, the United Kingdom, and the United States) covering five products, in 1973 (FAO 1973), the same year in which Johnson's book was published. The *Producer Subsidy Equivalent* (later *Support Estimate*) measures the share of farmers' gross farm receipts attributable to direct or indirect support. Tim Josling had been commissioned to produce the report (Legg 2003: 180) as a contribution to FAO's work in monitoring International Agricultural Adjustment. As Josling and Valdés (2004: 5) subsequently explained: 'The project was motivated by the realization that these [*agricultural*] policies were having a profound impact on world markets for agricultural goods. The 1973 paper lays out the rationale for monitoring such policies and the links with the issues of trade liberalization in the GATT. Two main indicators were developed: the Producer Subsidy Equivalent (PSE), and the Consumer Tax Equivalent (CTE).' The methodology was revised in 1975, and regular updates were presented to a series of FAO conferences, but eventually the methodology was displaced by the OECD's PSE calculations. Legg (2003: 180), an OECD official, concludes that the impact of the FAO's work 'was muted'.

In May 1982, the Council of the OECD (meeting as Ministers of Economics, Trade, and Foreign Affairs) had discussed various 'trade issues of the 1980s', including agricultural trade, and had 'agreed that agricultural trade should be more fully integrated within the open and multilateral trading system' (OECD 1982, paragraph 33). Accordingly it decided that the OECD 'should study the various possible ways' such an objective could be achieved 'as a contribution to progress in strengthening cooperation on agricultural trade issues and as a contribution to the development of practical multilateral and other solutions'. Legg (2003: 176) suggests that New Zealand's prime minister, Robert Muldoon, 'facing severe economic pressures at home and decreasing revenue from agricultural exports (partly the result of the United Kingdom joining the European Community in 1973)' was particularly influential in securing this outcome. Later that year, in November, the GATT Ministerial Conference degenerated into a hostile confrontation between the EEC and its critics over the CAP, but it did at least start the process of consultation that led to the launch of the UR in 1986 (Croome 1999: 8–10). Specifically, it established a Committee on Trade in Agriculture, with a mandate to report two years later, and committed Contracting Parties themselves 'to bring agriculture more fully into the multilateral trading system' (GATT 1982*a*: 4).

The OECD, and its predecessor the OEEC (Organisation for European Economic Co-operation), had a long track record of reviewing and discussing farm policies. Its Secretariat played a professional role in undertaking and publishing research (after clearance by the member states), unlike the small GATT Secretariat whose main role was to service the meetings of a member-driven organization. But, as Legg (2003: 176–7) comments, the challenge the Secretariat faced in 1982 was that of developing 'a consistent and comparable way to measure agricultural subsidies' to fulfil its mandate. Eventually it decided to adopt a modified version of the PSE methodology developed by the FAO in the 1970s. The outcome of this work was publicly reported in 1987 (OECD 1987), as a joint report of the Trade and Agriculture Committees, although OECD Member Governments had of course participated in earlier committee meetings that had discussed the report before giving it clearance.

This 1987 report was considered by the May 1987 OECD Council, meeting again as Ministers of Economics, Trade, and Foreign Affairs, who stated:

> This important work clearly highlights the serious imbalances that prevail in the markets for the main agricultural products. Boosted by policies which have prevented an adequate transmission of market signals to farmers, supply substantially exceeds effective demand. The cost of agricultural policies is considerable, for government budgets, for consumers and for the economy as a whole. Moreover, excessive support policies entail an increasing distortion of competition on world markets; run counter to the principle of comparative advantage which is at the root of international trade and severely damage the situation of many developing countries. (OECD, 'Communiqué', PRESS/A(87)27, 13 May 1987; paragraph 19, as reported in OECD 1992: 213)

A statement that Ministers recognized the principle of comparative advantage is particularly noteworthy! They went on to outline a reform programme, based upon a number of principles including measures to reduce guaranteed prices, and farm income support measures based upon direct payments, rather 'than being provided through price guarantees or other measures linked to production or to factors of production'. However, they also said: 'In considering the long-term objective of agricultural reform, consideration may be given to social and other concerns, such as food security, environmental protection or overall employment, which are not purely economic' (paragraph 21). These so-called *non-economic* concerns became the *non-trade* concerns of the UR.

The UR was said to be of 'decisive importance', and that it would 'furnish a framework for most of the measures necessary to give effect to the principles of agricultural reform agreed upon by OECD Ministers, including a progressive reduction in assistance to and protection of agriculture on a multi-country and multi-commodity basis' (paragraph 22). Thus GATT was the forum for the negotiations, not the OECD. However, the OECD Secretariat was given a new mandate: *to update and improve the analytical tools* it had begun to develop, and to monitor developments in agricultural policy (paragraph 25). Thus the OECD continued to produce and publish PSE (and other) estimates as part of its regular monitoring and outlook activities. Methodologies and terminology have changed, and the range of indices has been extended (see, e.g., Legg 2003). PSE and other support estimates are not unambiguous measures of support, and certainly do not measure the trade impact of intervention in agricultural markets, as various critics (e.g. Peters

1988; Oskam and Meester 2006) have emphasized; but the numbers and the terminology have been part of the international policy-making landscape ever since. As pointed out by Josling et al. (1996: 110), during the early phases of the UR the tools for aggregate measurement of agricultural support and protection developed by the OECD 'helped to focus the minds of the negotiators on the need to adopt an all-embracing and across-the-board approach rather than slipping back to the traditional approach of engaging in requests and offers on specific border measures for particular products in individual countries'.

Markets in crisis

The work of OECD developed in parallel with a mounting crisis in the world market for farm products. During the World Food Crisis of the early 1970s it had been soaring world prices and depleted world stocks of food grains that had caused concern. By the 1980s, however, depressed prices and soaring stocks were the focus of attention. Thus world stocks of wheat were increasing year-on-year throughout the 1980s, until peaking in 1987, with a corresponding drop in price (see Figure 4.1). In many parts of the world this resulted in depressed farm incomes and land values (for a discussion see Swinbank and Tanner 1996: chapter 2). In the United States this was further compounded by the increasing strength of the dollar on world markets, as discussed later in this chapter.

Although the CAP's policy mechanisms, and through to 1985 the growing weakness of the European currency unit (ecu) against the US dollar, shielded European farmers from these adverse developments on world markets, budget expenditure on the CAP continued to rise, doubling (in nominal terms) in the 1980s. Figure 4.2 clearly shows an increase in CAP expenditure as a percentage of the EU's GDP, both for EU9 in the late 1970s, and for EU10 in the 1980s following accession of Greece in 1981. However, these figures underplay the real budgetary cost of the CAP, because from 1983 until the system was reformed in 1988, with EU budget resources exhausted, a variety of strategies was deployed to push expenditure onto the member states or into later accounting periods (Tanner and Swinbank 1987). The EU's budget crisis, which played through the 1980s, was in large part related to the growth of surpluses. This is clearly seen in the emergence of the EU as a net exporter of cereals from the turn of the 1980s (Figure 4.3).

As a *net* importer of cereals, the EU's budget benefited from the import taxes (variable import levies) collected. As the EU became a net exporter of cereals, the budget was called upon to pay the export subsidies (or to fund

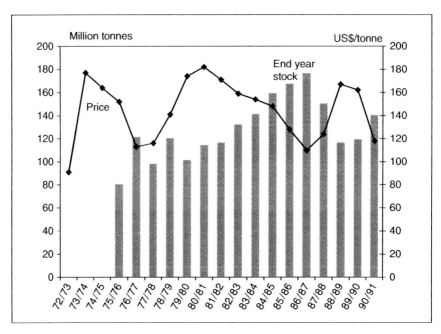

Figure 4.1 World wheat stocks (1975/6–1990/1) and prices (1972/3–1990/1)
Price: US$/tonne, No. 2 Hard Red Winter, fob, Gulf ports.
Source: International Wheat Council, *World Grain Statistics 1991*, Table 1.

an increase in intervention stocks), and so this growth in production in the face of more or less static demand (common to many other commodity sectors) contributed to the EU's budgetary crises. These developments were a direct consequence of high price support under the CAP. As the EU's level of self-sufficiency increased, not just for cereals but for other commodities too, other suppliers were, *first*, squeezed out of the EU market, and then faced subsidized competition in third country markets, as had been predicted by the Exporting Countries in Committee II in 1962. A particular bone of contention was the EU's payment of export subsidies on wheat flour which, in 1981 as noted earlier, the United States attempted to challenge using the new subsidies code agreed in the Tokyo Round, but without success (Hudec 1998: 10).

With the analytical tools and databases developed by the OECD, these developments in the world market could be better explained and understood. In particular, the 'PSE as an all-embracing common denominator for the widely varying forms of agricultural protection and support' pointed to the fact that it was the 'totality of agricultural policies' rather

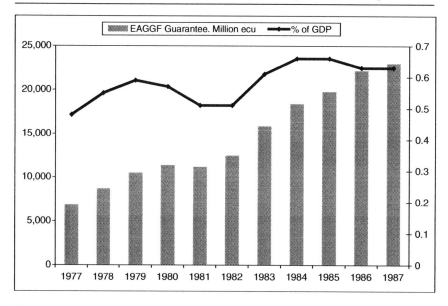

Figure 4.2 CAP budget expenditure: million ecu, and expressed as a percentage of EU GDP (EU9 [1977–80], EU10 [1981–7])

Note: EAGGF Guarantee: expenditure on market price and farm income support under the European Agricultural Guidance and Guarantee Fund.

Source: Extracted from various editions of Commission of the European Communities, *The Agricultural Situation in the Community*, Office of Official Publications of the European Communities: Luxembourg.

than border measures alone which was causing distortion in the world market (Josling et al. 1996: 110). Though the OECD's findings held no surprises for agricultural economists, they had an important impact on governments. Since the findings were the result of an intergovernmental institution, rather than academics, and had been discussed by government officials before publication, the OECD succeeded in establishing 'a number of insights among governments which academics had not sufficiently managed to get across to that audience' (p. 109).

The lesson from the OECD studies was that distortions produced by farm support policies were disproportionate in relation to any likely improvement in the incomes of farmers, a key objective of farm policies in most Western countries. The budgetary costs of agricultural policies had soared, but with limited positive impact on farm incomes. The OECD's study suggested that cutting support would increase world prices. For instance, a 10 per cent cut in global dairy support would increase world prices for dairy products by 4.4 per cent (OECD 1987: 32), as a result of

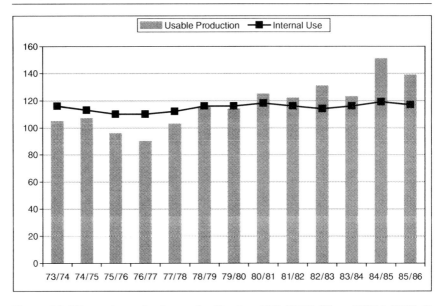

Figure 4.3 EU cereals production and utilization, EU9 (1974–80) and EU10 (1981–5) (million tonnes)

Source: Eurostat and European Commission data.

'the high level of assistance granted to the dairy sector almost everywhere' (p. 30). The work of the OECD provided persuasive arguments for people inside and outside government who were questioning whether farm policies based on the state-assisted paradigm delivered what they promised, and whether the costs of such policies were acceptable. Although it would be an exaggeration to claim that farm policies were a failure, the work of the OECD did seriously question their impact and suggested that state assistance was not a necessity in the farm sector. Leaving more space for market forces would improve not only the market situation but also state budgets. Indeed, the whole idea of agricultural exceptionalism was questioned: perhaps the farm sector was not that different from other economic sectors after all.

Changes in the global economic policy environment

Ideational change, and with it policy paradigm change, also requires a belief among policy makers that the new policy paradigm underpinned by a new idea is both economically and politically viable. These beliefs are partly shaped by the economic and political contexts within which a new idea and paradigm emerge. Furthermore, policy experiments with paradigm change elsewhere will also influence policy makers, making them more amenable to engage in paradigm shift.

A major concern of policy makers in the 1940s was that, with the cessation of hostilities and armaments production, and the demobilization of the armed forces, unemployment would return because of a lack of effective demand. In fact Keynesian demand-management policies drove Western economics forward in the 1950s and 1960s, with full employment and high rates of economic growth. The economic challenges of the 1970s, however, led some economists and politicians to confront the dominant Keynesian orthodoxy, emphasizing instead the role of markets (and hence 'supply-side' policies) and monetary policies ('monetarism'). In 1979 Margaret Thatcher's election success put her in power as Britain's prime minister for the next decade and in January 1981 Ronald Reagan took over as US president for the first of two four-year terms. Both Thatcher and Reagan shared similar economic perceptions. 'Privatization' became a buzzword. In Christopher Johnson's opinion it 'was a master-stroke of public relations on the part of the Thatcher Government to coin and put into worldwide circulation the concept of "privatization"'. Privatization was motivated in part by the perceived need 'to reduce the role of the state in the economy', 'to improve productive efficiency by promoting better management of public assets', and 'to introduce allocative efficiency by substituting competitive free-market pricing for administered pricing and controlled rents' (Johnson 1991: 144–5). There was much talk of the *Washington Consensus*: the collective view of the Washington-based IMF and World Bank, together with that of the US Treasury, that 'market fundamentalist ideas', 'predicated on the conservative free market ideology of Reagan and Thatcher', should be reflected in strategies for development (Stiglitz 2004: 229, 352).

The first challenges to agricultural exceptionalism took place in Australia in the late 1970s and 1980s, and most dramatically in New Zealand in 1984. In the United States, President Reagan challenged agricultural exceptionalism, and with it the state-assisted policy paradigm, in the mid 1980s. Australia (together with Canada and New Zealand) had 'traditionally attempted industrialization behind formidably high tariff barriers' (Warley 1976: 325). This placed it at a disadvantage in early rounds of tariff negotiations, based on countries entering into bilateral bargains in which they 'offered' tariff concessions in exchange for improved access to protected markets. If they were unwilling to open up their markets for industrial products they were unlikely to secure reciprocal market openings in return.

Under the premiership of Malcolm Fraser (1975–83) Australia suffered a rather unfruitful relationship with the EEC over the CAP (Benvenuti 1999). The United Kingdom's accession to the EEC impacted severely on exports of Australia's agricultural products, but the EEC was stoic in defence of the CAP and unwilling to grant concessions to Australia. Moreover, 'Australia's political and economic leverage [was] too limited to allow its government to exert fruitful diplomatic pressure on the EC' (Benvenunti 1999: 196). But this once highly protected economy embarked upon a programme of policy reforms, and by the UR it had emerged as a champion of freer trade, and was advocating farm policy reform with missionary zeal.[8] An iconic development was the creation of the *Industries Assistance Commission* (IAC) in 1974, with a mandate to scrutinize the support given to all industries including agriculture. About the same time there was a 25 per cent across-the-board cut in industrial tariffs (Harris 1990: 356), and the publication of a Green Paper commissioned by the Commonwealth Government on *The Principles of Rural Policy in Australia* (Mauldon 1990: 321). The complicated mechanisms of industrial and agricultural protection came under increased scrutiny: the IAC reported on the wheat stabilization scheme, for example, in 1978 (p. 324). But a more rapid process of economic reform took hold after the change of government in February 1983: a devaluation and later flotation of the Australian dollar, a 'general deregulation of the financial system' in 1984, and reductions in assistance to the farm sector, including elimination of the fertilizer subsidy, in 1988 for example (pp. 325–6).

Internationally, Australia (together with Canada and New Zealand) took the lead in creating an international alliance of fair trading nations that would lobby within the GATT for the liberalization of agricultural markets when it hosted a conference in Cairns (in Northern Australia) in August 1986 prior to the launch of the UR.[9] Alan Oxley (1990: 118), Australia's GATT Ambassador at the time, argues that a 'coalition of interests was needed' to 'ensure that agriculture was a central part' of the agenda for the new trade round.

Before the mid 1980s the New Zealand economy had been based on an export-oriented agricultural sector, and a highly protected and regulated manufacturing sector supplying the domestic market (Rayner 1990: 15–16). For industry, the average protection level was estimated to be as high as 60–70 per cent (Wooding 1987: 91). Consequently farmers faced high input and consumer prices; and therefore the basic rationale behind the agricultural subsidies was to compensate the farm sector for these costs. The Supplementary Minimum Price Scheme was the most important agricultural support mechanism, guaranteeing farmers a minimum price for beef, lamb, wool, and dairy products. In addition there were a number of input subsidies: fertilizer, interest rate, irrigation, and electricity. Furthermore, the government supported the sector through investment allowances and development schemes (Cloke 1989: 36–7). Although these agricultural subsidies were raised over time, they never fully compensated farmers for the costs imposed by the protection of domestic industry (Evans 1987: 107; Rayner 1990: 18). Artificially high input costs hurt New Zealand's export sector, decreasing the international competitiveness of its agriculture whilst other countries were increasing their farm subsidies and border protection.

New Zealand's Labour government, elected in July 1984, had to make drastic decisions right from the beginning of its term in office. Following an exchange rate crisis triggered by the election, the currency was devalued by 20 per cent, financial markets were deregulated, and a neo-liberal reform programme was initiated. Agricultural policies were among the government's first targets. Already, in June 1984, the outgoing government had announced that it would abolish the Supplementary Minimum Price Scheme, which absorbed the lion's share of agricultural subsidies (Evans et al. 1996: 1895). In November 1984, the new government announced that input subsidies for farmers would be dismantled. The fertilizer subsidy, the most important, was phased out over a two-year period (Cloke 1989: 38). Interest rate subsidies were also abolished: consequently the real interest rate rose by five percentage points, a significant increase (Johnston and Sandrey 1990: 190–1). Subsidies to irrigation, and special tax deductions for investments in agriculture, were brought to an end in 1985 (Cloke 1989: 38). The impact of the reforms was significant. The PSE percentage decreased from almost 30 per cent in 1984 to 5 per cent in 1989, and fell to as low as 2 per cent in 1994 (Sandrey and Scobie 1994: 1044). The reforms had almost totally abolished agricultural support in New Zealand.

In the United States, Reagan's attempt in the 1981 farm bill to reduce farm spending was largely rebuffed, but he had some success in that the increase in target prices (at 6 per cent per annum) looked like a *real* decrease as inflation had been 13.5 per cent the previous year (Orden et al. 1999: 72). However, economic circumstances quickly changed: inflation fell, and the dollar's exchange rate soared. This priced US farm products out of world markets, as the combination of a high exchange rate and the loan rate—the price at which farmers could deliver their product to the Commodity Credit Corporation, the CCC—meant that farmers sold to the CCC rather than for export.[10] According to Orden et al. (1999: 73), 'the US farm sector slumped into its worst financial crisis since the Great Depression' despite a sharp increase in costs to the Federal budget. Consequently, the Reagan administration tried again, in the 1985 farm bill, to cut farm subsidies. However, as Orden et al. (1999: 74) note, the Reagan administration's proposal was 'dead on arrival' in Congress, and was ignored. Congress nonetheless did agree to lower loan, but not target, rates, which meant that American farm products could recapture international markets, but at the cost of yet larger deficiency payments to farmers. This was not enough for the Reagan administration and consequently it changed strategy by attempting to internationalize the problem (Rapp 1988: 19–26, 39–43). Thus Orden et al. (1999: 85) claim that: 'By 1986, reform advocates had grown weary of seeking policy change unilaterally through congressional channels dominated by the farm lobby . . . For some, this proved that US farm support entitlements were impervious to significant reform. For a cohort of more visionary . . . reformers, a different conclusion was drawn: perhaps farm policy reform could never advance at home without the prior negotiation of an international agreement imposing parallel reforms on competitors and trade partners abroad.' This could be done by bringing agricultural support into the new round of multilateral trade negotiations. Consequently the United States 'took an early lead in insisting that negotiations on domestic agricultural policy reform become a key component of the larger Uruguay Round' (Paarlberg 1993: 41). As the then Undersecretary of Agriculture and later top US agricultural negotiator in the GATT, Daniel G. Amstutz, wrote in 1986: 'we must reject the "go it alone" approach, and move toward a global solution. The new round of trade negotiations is a major opportunity for making that move . . . [T]he international bargaining table is where the solution lies' (quoted in Orden et al. 1999: 85).

The overall change from Keynesianism to neo-liberalism in the 1980s had provided more fertile ground for ideational change in global farm trade rules. Agricultural policy reforms in Australia and New Zealand had involved a shift from the state-assisted paradigm to the market-liberal paradigm. However, what really mattered was the Reagan administration's decision to 'go international' in its attempt to reform agricultural policy.

Institutional change in the GATT: the Single Undertaking

Several factors had developed in favour of an ideational shift in GATT farm trade rules. The economic policy context had changed favourably, the market crisis of the 1980s was severe and had sharply increased the budget costs of farm policies, and new methodologies and research findings in agricultural economics had improved understanding of the costs and trade impacts of farm support and border protection. However, earlier trade rounds in the GATT had demonstrated that farm trade liberalization was a difficult issue on which to agree. Earlier GATT rounds had been characterized by a separation of issues into discrete negotiating groups, because some GATT members wished to avoid cross-linkages in the negotiations, and by the *ad hoc* acceptance of the codes negotiated. Thus the implementation of the Tokyo Round has been characterized as 'GATT à la carte', with participants allowed to choose whether they would, or would not, sign up to the various codes negotiated (Paemen and Bensch 1995: 52; Jackson 1997: 47).

By contrast, the Punta del Este declaration proclaimed: 'The launching, the conduct and the implementation of the outcome of the negotiations shall be treated as parts of a single undertaking.'[11] Strictly speaking, this related to the launch of negotiations on trade in goods, and not to the parallel negotiations on trade in services, but trade in goods did embrace agriculture (including 'the adverse effects that sanitary and phytosanitary regulations and barriers can have on trade in agriculture'), GATT's dispute settlement provisions, and trade-related aspects of intellectual property rights. Croome (1999: 26) comments that the Single Undertaking was a rule on which the EU had 'laid particular stress', and led to the oft-repeated assertion throughout the round that 'nothing is agreed until everything is agreed'. France in particular had been very reluctant to include agriculture in the negotiations unless there was potential for offsetting gains in other sectors: to 'rebalance' trade with Japan, and to ensure that the newly industrializing countries, especially in Asia, met 'in full their obligations under the GATT', for example (Paemen and Bensch 1995: 49, 50). Despite the creation of a Single Undertaking, the Punta del Este declaration went on to say: 'Balanced concessions should be sought within broad trading areas and subjects to be negotiated in order to avoid unwarranted cross-sectoral demands'. But, in the words of Paemen and Bensch (1995: 60), the 'history of international trade was about to enter a new chapter', and the United States had achieved its ambition of including both agriculture and services in the new round.

Launching the round as a Single Undertaking did not, however, guarantee that it would be *closed* in the same fashion. As Croome (1999: 277) notes, as the negotiations proceeded, 'crucial questions' arose as to how the new agreements were to be applied. 'Should the post-Round institutional structure include . . . a new multilateral trade organization to administer all or some of the agreements? What was to be the relationship between the GATT agreements and the agreements reached on the "new subjects"? Could governments pick and choose among the agreements, or must the whole outcome of the Round be accepted as a single undertaking?' These issues were being discussed by mid 1989, 'and in early 1990, Canada put forward the first official government-tabled proposal for a new institution, which it called the "World Trade Organization"' (Jackson 1997: 45). Croome (1999: 233–4) reports that in February 1990 the EU began to voice the idea that a new organizational treaty—termed the 'Multilateral Trade Organization' (MTO)—would be needed to oversee the UR agreements, but claims that the United States was hostile. It was not until December 1991, on the eve of the presentation of Arthur Dunkel's *Draft Final Act*, that the negotiators accepted that there would be a MTO, and—by implication—that the agreements would be implemented as a Single Undertaking (Croome 1999: 282).

In particular this procedural arrangement meant that GATT 1947 did not have to be amended. An amendment to GATT would have meant that the revised agreement could only come into force when a minimum number of countries had ratified the revisions (Jackson 1997: 47). Instead, those countries that definitely wanted the new world trading order, as a Single Undertaking, to replace the old, could withdraw from the old arrangements and (once ratified) immediately apply the new. This, 'exit tactic', according to Steinberg (2002: 349), was the plan hatched by the United States and the EU in 1990. As the round had progressed, the United States and the EU had become concerned that a large number of developing countries were reluctant to sign the emerging agreements on trade-related aspects of intellectual property rights (TRIPS) and investment measures (TRIMS) (Steinberg 2002: 359), despite their acceptance of the Single Undertaking in the Punta del Este declaration, or of the General Agreement on Trade in Services. Furthermore, if these were to be adopted on an *ad hoc* basis (like the Tokyo Round codes), the concessions would have to be granted on a most-favoured-nation (MFN) basis to *all* GATT Contracting Parties, and not just those that had accepted the new disciplines (Steinberg 2002: 360). Based on a series of unpublished US documents, Steinberg (2002: 359–60) traces the evolution of the US initiative from December 1989, through EU acceptance of the plan in October 1990, and its incorporation into the *Draft Final Act* of December 1991.[12] This 'single undertaking to closing the round' created a new collection of 'agreements and associated legal instruments' that would be 'integral parts' of the *Marrakesh Agreement Establishing the World Trade Organization* and 'binding on all Members' (Article II.2). GATT 1947 was re-enacted as part of GATT 1994, one of the *Multilateral Agreements on Trade in Goods* listed in Annex 1 of the WTO agreement (Jackson 1997: 48). With the WTO in place, both the United States and EU 'withdrew from the GATT 1947 and thereby terminated their GATT 1947 obligations (including its MFN guarantee) to countries that did not accept the Final Act and join the WTO' (Steinberg 2002: 360).[13]

The ploy paid off, and the GATT membership switched *en bloc* to the WTO. GATT, as an institutional agency, was terminated on 30 August 1995 (Jackson 1997: 64). But, by its acceptance of this strategy in October 1990, the EU had signalled its willingness to make concessions on agriculture: a *Single Undertaking* without an agreement on agriculture was inconceivable. This was eventually recognized by EU farm ministers after the UR had broken down at the Heysel ministerial in December 1990. As outlined in Chapter 6, ministers then embarked on a lengthy reform process in which some EU farm subsidies were switched from price support to direct payments.

Having agreed upon the MacSharry reform in May 1992, the EU was better prepared for bilateral negotiations with the United States, culminating in the Blair House Accord in November 1992, although it was not until December 1993 that the final deal was struck (see Chapter 7). The Uruguay Round Agreement on Agriculture (URAA) package was a compromise. On the ideational level of the agreement, the EU had accepted a fundamental shift; but in relation to its specific provisions (the operational level) the United States had retreated from its earlier positions (Daugbjerg 2008). The MacSharry reforms severely constrained the shape of the final URAA package, resulting in little additional trade liberalization; but the URAA did displace GATT Articles XI and XVI, which had been the institutional expression of agricultural exceptionalism in international trade.

Conclusion

In this chapter we have demonstrated that economists' critiques of agricultural protectionism were well known, and debated, by trade diplomats throughout the period 1948–94, but that the failure to quantify the alleged adverse impact of protectionist agricultural policies until the 1980s facilitated an obscurantist defence that allowed criticisms to be deflected. By the 1980s, however, the FAO and the OECD's PSE calculations had helped clarify the level of support to the farm sector. The fact that this coincided with a severe crisis in global markets for farm products focused political attention on the costs and trade distortions caused by agricultural policies and improved understanding of the consequences of farm support outside academia. Mirroring a more general retreat from the Keynesian policies of the 1950s and 1960s, farm policy reforms in Australia and New Zealand, and aborted reforms in the United States, refocused the *international* debate on farm policy reform. However, it was institutional change in the GATT that was the crucial factor that made possible the meaningful inclusion of agriculture in the UR, and the conclusion of the URAA: these negotiations were launched and concluded as a *Single Undertaking*. The URAA eroded agricultural exceptionalism in the GATT/WTO legal system; but the Single Undertaking could only be concluded by consensus, which meant that reluctant liberalizers (such as the EU) could only be pushed so far.

Chapter 5

Dispute Settlement and Its Implication for Agricultural Exceptionalism

In Chapters 1 and 3 we demonstrated that the Uruguay Round Agreement on Agriculture (URAA) laid down a new ideational underpinning for international rules governing farm trade, even though it was widely acknowledged that the specific commitments agreed upon at the time to reduce agricultural support and protection would have limited consequences.

This would not, however, be the only consequence of the agreement. There are good reasons to believe that the ideational shift would also influence WTO panels, and the Appellate Body, when interpreting and applying the rules of the URAA. With the *completion* of the Uruguay Round (UR) as a Single Undertaking, the major players were determined to *implement* it as a Single Undertaking as well. This resolve was strengthened by the second major institutional change brought about by the UR: a revised *Understanding on Rules and Procedures Governing the Settlement of Disputes* (often referred to as the DSU, Dispute Settlement Understanding), which is applicable across all the UR Accords. Dispute settlement is now based upon a 'consensus to reject' rule, in contrast to the old GATT 'consensus to accept' provision. Whilst the WTO can only proceed on the basis of consensus in determining the rules (e.g. as in the Doha Round negotiations), once a dispute is launched it flips into a quasi-judicial mode for interpreting and applying the rules. Furthermore, as in most judicial systems, there seems to have been a certain evolution of the rules as a result of panel and Appellate Body rulings: 'judicial lawmaking' according to Barton et al. (2006: 61).

In this chapter we consider whether the rules of the URAA allow effective policing by the WTO. That is, are rules formulated in ways that allow the dispute settlement system to establish whether or not URAA rules have been broken, and do the panels effectively use their powers to rule against WTO members that do not comply with the rules? Under the old GATT, some rules were difficult to police. For instance, as seen in Chapter 3, the GATT rule stating that export subsidies on primary products were not allowed to result in the country capturing 'more than an equitable share of world export trade in that product' (GATT 1947: Article XVI:3) was almost impossible to implement.

No judicial system can be effective if its rulings are considered illegitimate. This problem is particularly relevant for the WTO dispute settlement system because, unlike in nation states, there is no global authority that can force the losing defendant to comply. This problem is particularly relevant when rulings go against major trading powers like the United States and the European Union (EU). Thus, the effectiveness and legitimacy of the dispute settlement system relies upon the major trading powers accepting the legitimacy of WTO rulings, and then complying with them. The extent to which the EU and the United States consider the rulings of the dispute settlement system to be legitimate can be indicated by assessing how they react to rulings on sensitive products which go against them.

We demonstrated in the introductory chapter that the EU was a major player in international farm trade, with an uncompetitive farm sector, applying a highly protective agricultural policy. In this chapter we now analyse the extent to which the EU has complied with rulings in cases against the Common Agricultural Policy (CAP). There have only been a limited number of such cases since 1995. We present an overview of these, and provide more detailed analyses of three high-profile cases: bananas, beef hormones, and sugar. We find evidence to suggest that the EU has tried to comply, particularly in the context of the Doha Round's Single Undertaking. Compliance may vary across cases and if so a key question is what has then determined the extent of compliance. Interestingly, the degree of EU compliance varied across the three cases. We suggest that this variance is to a large extent explained by different EU decision-making rules applied to *farm* as opposed to *food safety* policy. We then ask whether other aspects of the current CAP are vulnerable to challenge. Finally, we briefly review the instances in which the EU has used dispute settlement proceedings to complain about the farm policies of other WTO members. We begin the chapter with an outline of the dispute settlement process.

Dispute settlement and the consensus to reject rule

The overarching institutional innovation of the UR, discussed in Chapter 4, was the Single Undertaking. The second innovation, which put pressure on agricultural exceptionalism, was the new dispute settlement system. In particular, consensus was replaced by automaticity.

There was a dispute settlement procedure in the GATT prior to 1995, which had evolved over the years (Hudec 1993). If two GATT Contracting Parties differed in their interpretation of GATT provisions, a *panel* of three (possibly five) experts could be established to adjudicate the matter. However, countries that were reluctant to have their trade policies challenged in this way could block proceedings at several points, because all decisions were taken by consensus: in establishing the panel, in adopting a panel report, and in authorizing retaliation if the recommendations of a panel report had not been implemented. Unsurprisingly, panels tended to be rather cautious, and conciliatory, in their interpretation of GATT provisions.

This 'consensus to accept' provision was replaced by a 'consensus to reject' rule in the new WTO legal system, which had the effect of displacing the old GATT 'diplomatic' mode of dispute settlement by a new 'legalistic' mode in the WTO (Srinivasan 2007: 1056). Quite why major GATT players such as the EU and the United States were willing to accept this external discipline is a question that goes beyond the scope of the present volume. However, we might note in passing that Barton et al. (2006: 71) suggest that the EU and the United States had decided in 1990 that a revamped dispute settlement system should be an integral part of the Single Undertaking. The major players wanted 'the contract enforced'. In particular, the United States had become frustrated with the old GATT system that had failed to deal with 'unfair trade practices abroad' (p. 69) and believed that the new arrangements 'represented . . . an Americanization of the GATT/WTO dispute settlement process' (p. 74). The new procedures meshed very well with (indeed were modelled on) US legislation. Paradoxically, others viewed 'the increased legalization of GATT/WTO dispute settlement as constraining the United States's unilateral determination of the terms of the contract' (p. 74). The principal US negotiator during the UR, noting 'the United States's frustration with the lack of progress in settling agricultural trade disputes, as well as with the inability of GATT to deal with counterfeiting and other intellectual property rights violations', suggested that this had led the USTR to threaten unilateral trade sanctions, causing the other main players to agree 'on a central objective:... to produce a result that tied the US' hands with respect to the threat and use of unilateral trade sanctions' (Stoler 2004: 102–3).[1]

The DSU applies to all the UR Agreements (the *covered* agreements, to use WTO terminology). Figure 5.1 sets out the process schematically, together with indicative time frames.[2] Although the DSU applies to all the WTO agreements, some of the agreements do provide for slightly different procedures (e.g. for non-violation cases under the Subsidies Agreement).[3]

Procedures revolve around the *Dispute Settlement Body* (DSB), which is basically the General Council, the highest decision-making body within the WTO short of the Ministerial Council, and made up of representatives of all WTO members. If two (or more) WTO members are in dispute over any provision in the covered agreements they are expected to consult. At issue might be an allegation that rules have been violated, or it might be a *non-violation* dispute challenging a policy that supposedly nullifies or impairs the expected benefits of a previously agreed concession. The consultation phase is an important part of the process, and many disputes are amicably settled, but if the consultation fails to resolve the problem the complainant can ask the DSB to establish a panel. This request can be deflected on the first time of asking but at the next meeting of the DSB a panel (of three, exceptionally five) will be authorized. Panellists are independent experts, and do not necessarily have a legal training. Normally they are appointed in consultation with the parties to the dispute, but if the parties cannot agree they are chosen by the WTO's Director-General.

The panel is serviced by the WTO Secretariat. It receives written submissions from the parties to the dispute, followed by a hearing when both parties, and other WTO members with an interest in the dispute, can present their case. This is followed by rebuttals, and a second hearing. The general procedure is that 'WTO Members, as sovereign entities, can be *presumed* to act in conformity with their WTO obligations. A party claiming that a Member has acted *inconsistently* with WTO rules bears the burden of proving that inconsistency' (WTO 1999*b*: paragraph 9).

The panel can consult experts. Since 1997, it has been possible for private lawyers to form part of a WTO member's team at panel hearings; and since 1998 panels have been allowed to receive submissions from other interested parties (typically NGOs), so-called *amicus curiae* briefs (Barton et al. 2006: 75–6). This Latin phrase (meaning literally 'friend of the court') refers to submissions from groups that have no *direct* interest in the case (in this instance they are not themselves WTO member states), but who nonetheless want their views to be considered. The issue was

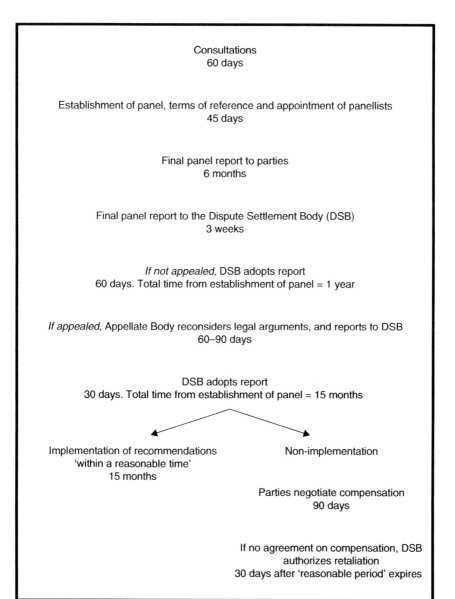

Figure 5.1 The dispute settlement process

Source: http://www.wto.org/english/thewto_e/whatis_e/tif_e/disp1_e.htm, accessed 19 February 2007, and Narlikar (2004: 88).

forced onto the WTO's agenda by various environmental groups seeking to express their views over the shrimp-turtle case. Two *amicus curiae* briefs were submitted to the panel by environmental NGOs broadly supportive of the US import ban. The complainants—India, Malaysia, Pakistan, and Thailand—protested; and the panel decided it did not have the authority to accept unsolicited submissions. It did, however, allow the United States to include the NGOs' material in the US submission. The Appellate Body ruled that a panel could accept unsolicited *amicus curiae* briefs, but was not obliged to (WTO 1998: paragraphs 99–110).

The panel produces a first draft of the factual components of its likely report, but excluding its findings and conclusions, for comment by the parties. This is followed by an Interim Report for the two sides to consider: they have one week to ask for a review of the panel's conclusions, and if they do so this review should not take more than two weeks before the Final Report is submitted to the two parties (and three weeks later to all WTO members). The report is automatically accepted by the DSB within 60 days, unless it is rejected by consensus, or one of the parties appeals. The whole process should have taken less than a year. Appeals must challenge the panel's interpretation of WTO provisions, or procedures, and not the facts of the case.

Appeals are common: indeed, sometimes both parties appeal some aspect of WTO law as interpreted by the panel. From 1995 to 2006 inclusive, 68 per cent of panel reports were appealed (WTO 2007*a*: 4). Appeals are considered by three members of the *Appellate Body*, which is a permanent grouping of seven individuals each serving a (renewable) four-year term: they are 'persons of recognized authority, with demonstrated expertise in law, international trade and the subject matter of the covered agreements generally...unaffiliated with any government...broadly representative of membership in the WTO' (Article 17 of the *Understanding on Rules and Procedures Governing the Settlement of Disputes*).

The appeal process should not normally take more than 60 days. The Appellate Body produces a report that upholds, rejects, or modifies a panel's legal findings and conclusions, which is then automatically accepted by the DSB unless it is rejected by consensus. In its determinations, the Appellate Body usually supports the thrust of a panel's findings, but frequently reverses particular findings and legal reasoning. For example, there were six Appellate Body reports circulated in 2006. In its Annual Report for 2006, which contains short summaries of these six cases, the Appellate Body records that it reversed some aspect of the original panel's findings in five of the six cases: Indeed, in three cases the opening sentence reads 'The Appellate Body reversed the Panel's finding(s)...' (WTO 2007a: 6–10). In one instance, 'several aspects of the Appellate Body's reasoning differed from the Panel's own reasoning' (p. 7); and in another instance 'The Appellate Body was unable to complete the analysis and determine whether [x] is consistent or inconsistent with... obligations...due to the absence of pertinent factual findings by the Panel...' (p. 8).

As Barton et al. (2006: 82) point out, it is the WTO's Ministerial Council that has 'exclusive authority to adopt interpretations of the Agreement and the Multilateral Trade Agreements' (WTO Article IX:2), not the Appellate Body through the dispute settlement procedures. In practice however, precedents do lead to the definition of legal principles that guide subsequent panels in their determinations: We would not expect two panels to come to different conclusions when faced with the same set of facts. But a number of provisions in the UR Agreements suffer from ambiguity or procedural gaps. Barton et al. (2006: 75) suggest that the procedural gaps were often left there deliberately as a result of 'sharp disagreement among members'. Negotiators could not agree on appropriate procedures. Ambiguity has often served the purpose of papering over differences that emerged in the negotiation phase when agreement proved elusive. However, ambiguity is problematic in a quasi-judicial procedure. Thus panel and Appellate Body reports have clarified ambiguity in the UR Agreements, and filled procedural gaps. On several occasions this has caused negative reactions from WTO member states and non-governmental stakeholders, in particular when they had 'engaged in behavior that was within a range of possible meanings, given the ambiguity' (Barton et al. 2006: 76). Under the old GATT dispute settlement proceedings, an 'interpretation' of GATT law that was not acceptable to a GATT member would have been blocked: thus 'GATT panels had to be somewhat deferential to disputants' interpretation of law if they wanted consent to adoption of their reports' (Barton et al. 2006: 83). With the WTO's 'consensus to reject rule', the same constraints do not apply, potentially permitting panels and the Appellate Body to reach more ambitious conclusions than might have prevailed under the pre-1995 arrangements. As Josling et al. (2006: 2) remark: 'In such circumstances, it is predictable that [the] WTO dispute settlement mechanism on occasion will be subject to criticisms of overreaching its mandate or role'. In national legal systems, judicial interpretations of the law that do not meet with the approval of the body politic can subsequently be overturned by the legislature: in the WTO the procedure is much more cumbersome, in that revisions to WTO rules can in effect only be agreed by consensus in the context of a negotiating round, such as Uruguay or Doha.

Following adoption of a report by the DSB, the question of implementation then arises. The country whose policies have been found contrary to WTO obligations is expected to comply 'within a reasonable period of time' (Article 21:3 of the *Understanding*). This might lead to arbitration; the guideline to the arbitrator being 'that the reasonable period of time to implement panel or Appellate Body recommendations should not exceed 15 months from the date of adoption of a panel or Appellate Body report' (Article 21:3). A country may change its policy, claiming it is now in conformity with WTO rules, but face further challenge from the complainants. Under Article 21:5 this can result in the original panel being reconvened to consider whether or not the failed defendant is now in compliance, and this too can lead to a further reference to the Appellate Body.

If the losing defendant is unable or unwilling to comply (e.g. because of public opinion, parliamentary procedures, etc.) it can instead offer 'compensation' to the victors. This is seen as a 'temporary' outcome, although it is not clear how long this temporary outcome could prevail. Compensation could take the form of enhanced market openings through Tariff Rate Quotas (TRQs) for the victors, 'consistent with the covered agreements' (Article 22:1).

However, the victors are not obliged to accept compensation, and if they cannot be induced to do so by a sufficiently generous offer they can seek the DSB's permission to apply sanctions. This would usually take the form of cancelling the loser's Most-Favoured-Nation (MFN) concessions on selected products on import into the victor's market, and the application of punitive import duties. This too may result in arbitration. Sanctions are usually applied within the framework of the particular agreement, but occasionally the DSB may allow a suspension of concessions across agreements. Thus Ecuador was allowed to engage in 'cross-retaliation' in the bananas dispute, for example. As a small economy, of little consequence to EU exporters, and importing mainly capital equipment and raw material from Europe, there was nothing to be gained from a suspension of MFN tariffs on goods from the EU because this would be a self-inflicted penalty on Ecuadorian industries whilst imposing little pain on the EU. Thus Ecuador sought, and obtained, permission to retaliate by withdrawing concessions under the Trade-Related Aspects of Intellectual Property Rights (TRIPS) agreement (McCall Smith 2006: 269).

'Economic' tests and dispute settlement

As in national judicial systems, the WTO dispute settlement mechanism often struggles with rules that made sense as political compromises, but leave room for interpretation on when they are breached and when they are not. Although no dispute is easy to resolve—one presumes it would not have become a dispute if it were—a broad distinction can be drawn between those instances in which the material facts lead to a binary outcome—the contested policy is either in conformity, or not, with the WTO provision—and those that potentially involve a continuum, and only beyond a threshold does the policy fall foul of WTO provisions. In this latter instance some sort of 'economic' test might have to be applied. In this section we discuss some of the difficulties in establishing whether national trade policy conforms to WTO rules.

An example of a binary outcome is export subsidies. These are prohibited under the Subsidies Agreement, unless provided for under the URAA. In challenging an alleged export subsidy, the complainant does not have to show that the subsidy has had an adverse impact on any market. It is sufficient to show that the subsidy exists.[4] This is in marked contrast to the 'equitable shares' rule for export subsidies on primary products that applied prior to 1995: with this it was virtually impossible to prove a breach of the provisions.

Similarly there are various criteria laid down that must be met if a policy is to qualify for inclusion in the green box (Annex 2 of the URAA). As well as some overarching criteria, to which we will return in a moment, certain policy-specific criteria must be met. For example, paragraph 6 on *Decoupled Income Support* includes the condition that: 'The amount of such payments in any given year shall not be related to, or based on, the type or volume of production (including livestock units) undertaken by the producer in any year after the base period.' In *US–Upland Cotton* the panel found that this criterion had not been met, and consequently that the subsidy payments in question did not qualify for inclusion in the green box (Swinbank and Tranter 2005). In this instance this did not mean that these payments were illegal: simply that they were by default amber box payments, and as such could potentially have pushed the United States over its domestic subsidy commitments. If so, this in effect would be a violation of its Aggregate Measurement of Support (AMS) limit (Sumner 2005: 10).

But as well as these policy-specific criteria, a valid green box policy must satisfy some overarching criteria, one of which is 'the fundamental requirement that they have no, or at most minimal, trade-distorting effects or effects on production' (extract from paragraph 2). Clearly this does involve an economic test: is there a trade-distorting effect or effect on production, and if so is it *minimal* (whatever calibration might be applied to the word minimal)?[5] In *US–Upland Cotton*, Brazil claimed that US payments infringed this fundamental requirement (WTO 2004*d*: paragraph 7.355). However, the panel concluded that, as it had already decided that paragraph 6 had not been satisfied, it was unnecessary to determine whether or not this fundamental requirement was met (paragraph 7.412).

But in addition to arbitrating on whether or not a member has violated a WTO provision, the DSU (and the old GATT Article XXIII dispute settlement proceedings it displaced) also deals with *non-violation* disputes. Here the measure is not illegal *per se*, but the complaining party 'considers that any benefit accruing to it directly or indirectly under the relevant covered agreement is being nullified or impaired or the attainment of any objective of that Agreement is being impeded as a result of the application by a member of any measure, whether or not it conflicts with the provisions of that Agreement' (Article 26(1) of the DSU). If it is found that a measure does nullify, impair, or impede, 'the panel or the Appellate Body shall recommend that the Member concerned make a mutually satisfactory adjustment' to its policies, but the defendant is not obliged to withdraw the measure. At the request of either party, an arbitrator can 'include a determination of the level of benefits which have been nullified or impaired, and may also suggest ways and means of reaching a mutually satisfactory adjustment'; but this is not a binding recommendation.

As noted earlier in this section, Part II of the Subsidies Code does prohibit certain subsidies: export subsidies, and domestic subsidies contingent upon the use of domestically produced raw materials, except as provided for in the URAA. Part III of the Subsidies Code, on the other hand, deals with subsidies that are not prohibited, but are *actionable*. Here members are enjoined that they *should not* cause, through the use of such a subsidy, 'adverse effects to the interests of another Member' (Article 5, SCM). Adverse effects are: (*a*) 'injury to the domestic industry of another Member'; (*b*) nullification or impairment of expected benefits stemming from tariff concessions; and (*c*) 'serious prejudice to the interests of another Member'. Serious prejudice includes effects such as: 'to displace or impede the exports of a like product of another Member from a third country market'; or 'a significant price undercutting by the subsidized product as compared with the price of a like product of another member in the same market or significant price suppression, price depression or lost sales in the same market'. Clearly, such effects must be established to the satisfaction of the panel, and this may require detailed economic modelling of the market in question.

Thus in *US–Upland Cotton*, as well as complaining that the United States had used prohibited subsidies, Brazil also alleged that other policies supporting US cotton production 'contributed to serious prejudice of Brazil's interests, mainly by causing world cotton prices to be lower than they would otherwise have been and by causing the US world market share to be higher than otherwise' (Sumner 2005: 7). In fact Sumner was retained by Brazil as an economic expert in this case, and produced 'A Quantitative Simulation Analysis of the Impacts of US Cotton Policies on Cotton Prices and Quantities' for presentation to the panel (Sumner 2005: 29). For this he was portrayed as a traitor by some US farm groups (Blustein 2004).

Participation

The new DSU has dealt with far more cases than the old GATT dispute settlement system it displaced: in its first five years the number of requests for consultations was running at three times the annual rate in the old GATT (Hoekman and Kostecki 2001: 78). The WTO Secretariat claims that 'More cases can be good news.' It believes there are 'strong grounds for arguing that the increasing number of disputes is simply the result of expanding world trade and the stricter rules negotiated in the Uruguay Round; and that the fact that more are coming to the WTO reflects a growing faith in the system'.[6]

It is often claimed that the WTO dispute settlement system is biased against the interests of developing countries, but developing countries have been actively involved, either contesting policies or as defendants, and in challenging each other's policies. Later we will take a brief look at Argentina's attack on Chile's 'price band' system regulating imports of cereals, for example. Ecuador, as we saw earlier, has forced the EU to change its import regime for bananas; and in 2005 Brazil achieved two successful outcomes against, first, the United States (in *US–Upland Cotton*) and then the EU (in *EC–Export Subsidies on Sugar*) demonstrating that developing countries can hold the major powers to account through the dispute settlement process, though admittedly Brazil is a substantial developing country. Small low-income economies can find that the whole process of active participation in the WTO, including the DSU, overwhelms their limited resource base.

DSU challenges are launched by WTO *members* against other WTO members: the process cannot be accessed by private individuals or organizations, although they will of course try to persuade their home governments to initiate DSU proceedings in pursuit of their own economic interests.[7] There might be a number of reasons why a government might decide not to pursue (or delay pursuit of) a legitimate claim. The government (particularly a small economy) might not have the resources to prosecute the case, or it may be waiting for a more opportune time to intervene. The URAA's Peace Clause, for example, probably led to the deferral of a number of cases that might otherwise have been brought against US and EU farm policies, with the ceasefire prolonged into the negotiation phase of the Doha Round.

A number of analysts did suggest that, should the Doha Round ultimately fail, this phoney peace would collapse, and a new round of litigation would begin. For example, Pedro de Camargo Neto, former Secretary of Production and Trade for the Brazilian Ministry of Agriculture when he was heavily involved in both the sugar and cotton cases, was quoted by the *Financial Times* (28 July 2005: 12) as saying: 'Negotiation is better than litigation, but the fact that the US is not moving on domestic agricultural subsidies in the Doha round means that bringing a WTO case may help to push the talks along.' In the run-up to the Hong Kong Ministerial in December 2005, Anania and Bureau (2005: 548) suggested that for some WTO members the possibility of securing trade liberalization through the DSU meant that a negotiated outcome was less urgent than it was for those members whose highly protected farm sectors were vulnerable to disputes, such as the United States and EU. For the latter, a new agreement was 'needed to re-classify their domestic policies under new rules, and to introduce "interpretations" and "clarifications" of existing rules to shield their policies from challenge in the WTO dispute settlement system'.

Even though the WTO is a rules-based, rather than a power-based, system, with the DSU theoretically accessible to all WTO members, an element of power diplomacy still remains. As Hoekman and Kostecki (2001: 87) note, some governments might be deterred from bringing cases 'if they fear this will have detrimental consequences in nontrade areas (e.g. continued aid flows or defence cooperation)'; and in other instances they may be deterred because of their fear of counter-claims. There is certainly circumstantial evidence to suggest that the EU and the United States on occasion have engaged in tit-for-tat retaliatory action.

But do governments comply with WTO rulings, and if not what can be done? In the next section we examine the EU's post-1995 record on DSU challenges to the CAP. Here we adopt a more general discursive approach.

Analysts come to conflicting conclusions in assessing the success of the old GATT dispute settlement procedure. Hoekman and Kostecki (2001: 74–5) seem to endorse the 'conventional wisdom . . . that the GATT dispute mechanism worked much better than generally recognised'; but they note that after 1980 'the rate of nonadoption increased significantly, reflecting the fact that many of the contested issues were in areas where the rules were not clear or that were the subject of ongoing negotiations during the Uruguay Round'. By contrast, Busch and Reinhardt (2002: 473) point out that, between 1948 and 1994, in nearly a third of cases examined, 'defendants fail[ed] to comply at all, effectively spurning panel rulings'. Davis (2007: 2–3) has been particularly critical of the EU in its defence of the CAP, saying it was 'notorious for delaying tactics', that it 'established a pattern of non-cooperation', and claiming that this 'recalcitrance in adjudication of agricultural polices has continued under the new rules of the WTO'.

One factor pressuring governments to comply is their shared interest in a rules-based system: the WTO is a 'repeated game', with interaction 'over an indefinite time horizon', in which failure to comply with an adverse adjudication sets a bad precedent for others to follow later (Hoekman and Kostecki 2001: 75). Similarly, Davis (2003: 52) emphasizes the role that reputation plays for countries that favour trade liberalization: 'a record of cheating makes it more difficult to credibly commit to abide by future agreements . . . As a result . . . trade partners . . . will bargain harder to extract additional concessions as a risk premium for the uncertain compliance'. She suggests that 'if negotiators want to protect their reputation, then they are better off to settle following the public complaint in order to avoid a lengthy, public dispute and possible violation ruling'. Thus the Single Undertaking extends to enforcement of rules too. Trade officials and diplomats are likely to feel shared ownership of the rules they helped craft and be inclined to press their governments to comply, even when lobbyists and politicians—more distant from the WTO arena—might express defiance. Thus the institutional context of the decision to comply with, or defy, the adjudication may be significant.

If countries cannot or will not comply, by bringing their laws into conformity with WTO provisions, finally one is left with retaliation. But big trading entities have more muscle than do the small, and therefore in economic terms retaliation is an inefficient remedy for small economies.

For Ecuador, as noted earlier, the EU is an important market for its bananas; but to EU exporters Ecuador is of little significance. Thus there were few *trade* sanctions that Ecuador could bring to bear to cause the EU to think again about complying with the banana ruling; and in any case it made little economic sense for Ecuador to raise trade barriers against EU imports.

The EU's response to challenges to the CAP

Hudec (1998), writing soon after the inauguration of the new WTO system, was by no means convinced that WTO members would adhere to the new commitments. Referring to the 'shallow' UR commitments, he noted that 'signing an international commitment is usually just one of many steps along the road toward a government decision to adopt the behavior called for by the rule . . . it often requires a continued debate, and several more decisions, before governments actually deliver the promised behavior. During that continued debate, one usually finds that the forces that opposed the initial legal commitment have by no means been vanquished. To the contrary, one finds that they are both willing and able to do battle again and again—sometimes till Hell freezes over' (p. 24). And later:

> Any student of GATT's history with agricultural trade restrictions will know the strength of the political forces that resisted compliance were strong enough to have carried the United States and the European Community out of GATT before they would have complied. It is hard to believe that adjustments to an adjudication procedure in Geneva are going to make a significant difference in whether such forces prevail, especially since the adjustments do not really change things very much from the way they were under the old GATT procedure (p. 40).

Given Hudec's scepticism, it is relevant to enquire how well the EU has coped with this new situation. Table 5.1, compiled from information on the WTO web site in December 2008, summarizes the cases in which the EU's agricultural policies had been questioned, or challenged, through the dispute settlement process.[8] A couple of cases concerning coffee, and those on fish[9] and wood, are excluded; and some aggregation has been undertaken. In a number of instances consultations were requested, but no further action resulted. In other instances, mutually agreed solutions were subsequently notified to the WTO, in one instance after the panel had been convened (rice, in case DS210). In a number of instances EU

Table 5.1 WTO challenges to the CAP

Title	Complainants and DS number	Comments
Approval and marketing of biotech products	Argentina (293), Canada (292), the United States (291)	Dates from May 2003. In November 2006 the DSB adopted the panel's report that had found that the EU had delayed the approval process. The parties then struggled in trying to decide on a reasonable time for implementation.
Bananas III	Ecuador, Guatemala, Honduras, Mexico, the United States (27) (see also DS16, 105 and 158)	A continuation of old GATT squabbles. Process started February 1996. Panel reported May 1997 (Appellate Body September 1997). Found that the EU's import regime contravened WTO provisions. The Lomé waiver did cover tariff preferences, but not import quota mechanisms. Because of delays in changing the EU regime, an arbitration report allowed the complainants to retaliate against EU economic interests. Despite lodging the details of a mutually agreed solution with Ecuador and the United States in 2001, the complainants were still unhappy about the level of tariffs applied from 1 January 2006, arguing inter alia that the Doha waiver had, for bananas, expired; and there was recourse to a second Article 21.5 panel. DS16, 105 and 158 were requests for consultations that did not lead to the establishment of panels.
Butter	New Zealand (72)	Consultations requested March 1997. Mutually agreed solution notified in November 1999, days before the panel reported. The issue was whether or not spreadable butter could be included in the TRQ granted for New Zealand butter.
Cereals (9); and Duties on imports of grains (13)	Canada (9) and the United States (13)	June/July 1995, Canada and the United States were unhappy about the way import taxes on cereals were to be applied in the new regime. US complaint had potentially broader product coverage. Settled.
Chicken cuts	Brazil (269), Thailand (286)	Dates from October 2002. Panel report May 2005, Appellate Body September 2005. Issue was the EU's tariff classification of salted chicken pieces. EU found at fault, and Arbitrator set 27 June 2006 as the final date for implementing the ruling.
Export subsidies on sugar	Australia (265), Brazil (266), Thailand (283)	Dates from 2002. Panel report October 2004, supported by Appellate Body April 2005. Found that the EU's C sugar exports, and its 're-export' of ACP sugar, did infringe its export subsidy constraints. Arbitration panel set date of 22 May 2006 to bring EU exports into conformity with the ruling. EU sugar reform (agreed November 2005) more or less did this.

(continued)

Table 5.1 (Continued)

Title	Complainants and DS number	Comments
Hormones (and EU's counterclaim against continued suspension)	Canada (48), the United States (26); and counterclaims against Canada (321) and the United States (320)	The beef hormones case formally dates back to January 1996, but it had been an issue in the old GATT. The panel (August 1997) and Appellate Body (January 1998) found the EU's measures infringed the SPS Agreement. The EU was unable/unwilling to make its rules WTO compliant, and so trade sanctions against the EU were authorized from July 1999. The EU claimed that Directive 2003/74/EC did make the EU compliant, and so it launched counterclaims against Canada and the United States challenging the continued suspension of concessions. The Appellate Body's report on this second panel's ruling was delivered in November 2008.
Measures affecting the export-ation of processed cheese	The United States (104)	In October 1997 the United States requested con-sultations on the EU's grant of export subsidies on processed cheese. No action.
Measures affect-ing imports of wine	Argentina (263)	In September 2002 Argentina requested consulta-tions on various mandatory measures concerning oenological practices affecting imports of wine. No further action is recorded.
Poultry	Brazil (69)	In February 1997 Brazil requested consultations on the EU's implementation of a TRQ on poultry cuts. The panel report of March 1998 did not substanti-ate Brazil's claim. Brazil went to the Appellate Body, which reversed some of the findings. In October 1998 the parties announced they had reached a mutual agreement on the implementation of the Appellate Body's findings.
Rice: (a) Duties on imports of rice (17) and imple-mentation of the UR Commitments concerning rice (25); (b) Restric-tions on certain import duties on rice (134); and (c) Rice (against Belgium: 210)	Thailand (17), Uruguay (25), India (134), the United States (210)	17 and 25 were 1995 requests for consultations on the implementation of the UR agreements, which led nowhere. The issues were similar to those raised by Canada (9) and the United States (13) on the import of other cereals. The Indian complaint (134) of May 1998 concerned a 'so-called cumulative recovery system (CRS), for determining certain import duties on rice, with effect from 1 July 1997. India contended that the measures introduced through this new regulation will restrict the number of importers of rice from India'. Again, no further action is recorded. In Case DS210 the United States (in October 2000) requested consultations with Belgium over the latter's administration of import duties. A panel was established in June 2001, but the United States almost immediately requested a suspension of its activities, and in December 2001 the parties announced a mutually agreeable solution.

TRQ on corn gluten feed from the US	The United States (223)	January 2001 request for consultations on the EU's imposition of a TRQ. No action.
Trademarks and Geographical Indicators	Australia (290), the United States (174)	US complaint dates back to 1999 (Australia 2003). Panel reported March 2005. Found the EU's registration procedures infringed the WTO's national treatment provisions. EU amended its procedures from 31 March 2006; but both Australia and the United States claimed that the EU had not met their concerns, and invited the EU to make further revisions.

Source: Extracted from: http://www.wto.org/english/tratop_e/dispu_e/dispu_subjects_index_e.htm, accessed 15 December 2008 (see text for further details).

policy was amended: to allow imports of salted chicken pieces at lower tariff rates (DS269 and DS286), and to allow imported products the same registration rights for geographical indications of origin as those originating within the EU, for example (DS174 and DS290), although both these disputes are probably not yet fully resolved.[10] But three 'big' cases stand out: bananas, (beef) hormones, and export subsidies on sugar. Furthermore, the dispute over 'biotech' products was likely only the first skirmish in a long-drawn-out transatlantic trade war over genetically modified organisms (GMOs) (see e.g. Winham 2007).

Based on the period 1970 to 1999, Davis (2003: 106) claimed that: 'On the controversial cases, the EU has entirely disregarded both the reputational harm and international obligation arising from violation rulings'. Doubtless she had beef hormones and bananas in mind: the sugar case falls outside her period. We would argue that, *in the context of CAP decision making*, beef hormones and bananas were unrepresentative cases and that sugar (although special in its own ways) was more indicative of how the EU responds to WTO constraints (or how it did respond, whilst the Doha Round was in progress).

Both the beef and the banana disputes were of long standing: there had been skirmishes in the old GATT, and it was perhaps inevitable (but unfortunate) that they should re-emerge as early cases in the WTO. Table 5.2 summarizes some of the salient features of the political economy background to these three disputes.

Bananas involved a heady mixture: commitments to African, Caribbean and Pacific (ACP) states through the Lomé convention, derived from old colonial ties; commercial interests of transnational corporations; and conflicting views in the Council of Ministers, reflecting in part their historical perspective (Tangermann 2003)[11]. Alter and Meunier (2006: 378) assert:

Table 5.2 Political economy characteristics of three WTO disputes

	Bananas	Beef Hormones	Sugar
EU farm interest	Limited to specific islands and the French overseas departments	Beef production widespread	Important crop in some arable areas
EU processor/trade interest	Transnational corporations involved in shipping and ripening, but sources of supply are fungible	Abattoirs (and to a lesser extent meat-packing plants) reliant on local livestock	Capital-intensive, location-specific, sugar-beet processing industry
EU consumer interests	German consumers said to be very concerned about an increase in banana prices	Consumers very concerned about beef hormones	Dietary concerns, but no specific link to EU farm policy
ACP states (complicated by the extension of preferences to the LDCs through EBA)	A number of Caribbean economies were very dependent on the banana trade, and benefited from ACP preferences	Selected African states benefit from the beef protocol	Selected ACP states, often highly dependent on sugar, benefit from the sugar protocol. Also an EU-based industry processing raw cane sugar
Decision making	Qualified majority vote; but strong development interests in the European Parliament also took an interest	Joint decision of the European Parliament and the Council	Qualified majority vote in the Council

'The banana dispute was a specific dispute about a specific policy, but it was not an 'old-style' trade dispute about protecting the domestic losers from international competition... Rather the European protection of the Lomé guarantees was about development aid through off-budget measures.'

Alter and Meunier (2006: 374) also say: 'The creation of the WTO led to an immediate change in EU behavior... Anticipating a challenge to the banana regime under the new WTO system, the EU offered a deal to the Latin American countries that were party to the GATT case...' Thus the EU did make changes to its banana policy, although the new import regimes were also challenged, and the EU remained in breach of WTO rulings for some time. Knock-on effects were the realization that its Lomé Convention was incompatible with its WTO commitments, leading to the decision to negotiate a series of WTO-compatible free-trade area agreements (known as 'Economic Partnership Agreements') with its Lomé partners, which have not been easy to achieve; and, as part of its diplomatic offensive in the WTO, the decision to offer duty- and quota-free access to virtually all goods produced in least-developed countries (LDCs) (a policy later known as 'Everything but Arms', EBA), which we discuss in Chapter 7 (Pilegaard 2006). The latter, to be fully applied to sugar from 2009, was then a further pressure leading to the 2005 sugar 'reform'.

The long-standing and still ongoing dispute over beef hormones is complex and politically charged (for an overview see Davis 2003: Chapter 9, and Kerr and Hobbs 2005). The dispute pre-dates the negotiation of the Sanitary and Phytosanitary Measures (SPS) Agreement. Davis (2003: 329), on the evidence of an interview with a United States Department of Agriculture official, suggests that the EU was 'not a major player in these negotiations', and was 'never able to articulate a coherent position'. Skogstad (2001: 494), referring specifically to the EU's wish to see 'consumer concerns' incorporated into the SPS Agreement, suggests that the EU played a much more active role, but, recognizing it had few allies, it decided to abandon this line of action. She suggests the EU believed 'that the risk posed to the hormone ban could be managed', that it saw 'that the EC's interest in restricting SPS barriers to trade went beyond winning the hormone dispute with the [United States]', and that it responded to 'pressure not to hold up the protracted negotiations on agriculture'.

However, if the EU did believe it could 'manage' the hormone dispute, it miscalculated. A WTO panel (and the Appellate Body) ruled against the import ban, and the EU then failed to negotiate compensation in the form of increased TRQs for Canadian and US hormone-free beef: Kerr and Hobbs (2005: 203) claim that, as 'the EU had no intention of complying with its obligations', compensation 'was not acceptable and retaliation by Canada and the United States became the only option'. But that was only part of the story, because the form the retaliation should take was contested, involving yet again the DSU. The United States claimed that trade to the value of US$202 million a year was blocked by the import ban (with Canada claiming Canadian $75 million); but these estimates were disputed by the EU, which sought arbitration. Determining the volume of trade that would have taken place in the absence of the ban is no easy task, but the WTO arbitrators finally settled on $116.8 million and Canadian $11.3 million respectively, and it was on this volume of trade from the EU that the United States and Canada were authorized to suspend tariff concessions (see e.g. WTO 1999b: paragraph 84).

The EU, however, had changed its policy, in particular in the form of Directive 2003/74/EC of the European Parliament and of the Council, which entered into force on 14 October 2003. The EU claimed that this was in 'conformity with the recommendations and rulings' of the DSB, and in particular that it was 'based on a comprehensive risk assessment'. Canada and the United States disagreed and continued to apply trade sanctions. As a result another WTO panel was established in February 2005 to examine the EU's claim that these sanctions were not WTO compliant, but this was another complex case and it was not until March 2008 that the panel reported. Both parties felt their stance had been partly vindicated, and both appealed aspects of the ruling.[12]

The EU has struggled to legitimize its policy on beef hormones within the WTO, which for North American observers could well be seen as further evidence of the EU's recalcitrance and foot-dragging within the WTO (Ames 2001: 220). Why then was the EU willing to change its policy on sugar, one of the last bastions of the old CAP?

The EU's support regime for sugar was basically unchanged from 1968. The EU price was kept well above world market prices (often three times higher) by prohibitive import duties, export refunds (subsidies), and the possibility of intervention buying. However, the quantity of sugar that could (directly) benefit from price support was limited by quota. Any sugar produced in excess of this (known as C sugar) had to be exported from the EU without an export refund. Despite a structural surplus of sugar within the EU (in addition to the C sugar exports) the EU had a commitment to import 1.3 million tonnes of white sugar equivalent from selected ACP states, and India, stemming from its old colonial ties, and the 1986 and 1995 enlargements of the EU had added to the preferential import arrangements.

When establishing its export subsidy commitments in the UR, the EU chose to notify its commitments on sugar by excluding C sugar exports (on the grounds they were not subsidized) and after netting out its preferential imports from the ACP states and India.[13] As a consequence, after the scheduled reductions through to 2000, the maximum quantity of sugar that the EU was entitled to export annually with the aid of export subsidies was 1,273,500 tonnes (Hoekman and Howse 2008: 160).

The panel found that the EU's subsidized exports were well in excess of its bound commitments. This was because C sugar was effectively cross-subsidized, and the footnote excluding a quantity equivalent to the import of ACP sugar had no legal binding. And this despite the fact that, had the EU known this in 1994, it could have included both C and ACP sugar in its schedule of commitments, giving it a much bigger basic entitlement. From the EU's perspective, the rules had been changed by the DSB, and yet it chose to comply. After an appeal, and arbitration, the EU was obliged to curb its subsidized exports by 22 May 2006, which it more or less did. It had changed its policy.[14]

The change was not easy, and the process was long. In November 2005 the Council of Agricultural Ministers reached political agreement on the complex regime that was to apply from July 2006 (Noble 2006). Support prices were cut by 36 per cent in four unequal instalments, with compensation payable to farmers (through the Single Farm Payment Scheme), a restructuring scheme for processors involving a quota buyout, and some limited help for ACP states. This was expected in time to result in a substantial contraction in sugar production in the EU and in some ACP states. Indeed the sole Irish sugar-beet refiner (Irish Sugar, owned by Greencore) immediately announced it was ceasing production (*Agra Europe*, 24 March 2006: N/1). But the quota buyout failed initially to control production, and so the EU was forced to impose quota cuts of more than 2 million tonnes (about 12 per cent of total quota) for both 2006/7 and 2007/8 (*Agra Europe*, 23 February 2007: EP/2).

Why sugar and not beef hormones? The commercial impact on the sugar sector of the sugar reforms was likely more severe than any relaxation of the ban on growth hormones would have been to the beef sector; and industrial concentration in sugar-beet processing is more marked than it is for abattoirs. The ACP beneficiaries of the sugar protocol lobbied extensively against the reforms as they did with bananas, but with less success. We would suggest there were two differences between beef hormones and sugar.

First, the timing was different. If the EU was to be seen as a committed negotiator in the Doha Round, intent upon a Single Undertaking, it had to abide by the WTO ruling. It did not want to be locked in to the defence of the indefensible, as appeared to have been the case with bananas and beef.

Second, and most importantly, the institutional contexts within which the rulings are processed in the EU are different. Despite the interests of the ACP sugar suppliers, and the LDCs through EBA, this was a *farm* policy issue to be decided by the Council of Agricultural Ministers, without the direct involvement of the European Parliament, since the latter only has a consultative role in decisions on the CAP.[15] In contrast, the beef hormones case was a *food safety* policy issue with legislation jointly determined by the European Parliament and the Council under the co-decision procedure. Involving the European Parliament meant that policy making became more susceptible to public sentiment because of the intense public interest in food safety and Parliament's quest for an important policy-making role.

This suggests that, contrary to the negotiating phase, when the EU's negotiators argue that the EU member states are unwilling to accept externally imposed disciplines, during the implementation phase the EU is able to conform when the dispute relates to decisions on *farm* policy (as epitomized by the classic CAP price and income support mechanisms) that can be decided by the Council of Ministers; whereas those involving *food safety* policy (e.g. beef hormones, GMOs), which involve the European Parliament, are less acceptable of WTO-imposed policy changes. It is beyond the scope of this book to speculate on how an extension of the European Parliament's powers of co-decision to include EU *farm* policy (as proposed in the as yet unratified *Treaty of Lisbon*) might impact on future CAP decision making.

Other potential challenges to the CAP

In the period since 1995 the DSB has considered a number of cases involving the URAA, with litigants and defendants drawn from both developed and developing country members. As already noted, in 2005 important Appellate Body reports were delivered on Brazil's challenge to the US programme for *Upland Cotton*, and on Australia, Brazil, and Thailand's challenge to the EU's export subsidy regime for sugar. In both instances key aspects of the domestic farm policies of these major powers were under scrutiny, and yet both said they would bring their policies into conformity with WTO rules. Whilst the panel and Appellate Body reports referred to the particular details of these two specific cases, analysts suggest that other commodity regimes in both the EU and the United States were at risk if similar challenges were to be mounted. In addition to these cases involving both domestic and export subsidies, the third pillar of the URAA (its import access arrangements) was subject to scrutiny in the *Chile–Price Band System* case brought by Argentina (Bagwell and Sykes 2004; Josling et al. 2006: 15–17). Agricultural products have also been subject to DSU proceedings under WTO provisions other than the URAA, but these are not systematically discussed here. We discuss in turn rulings relating to the three 'pillars' of the URAA. Although many did not directly relate to the CAP, they signal to EU agricultural policy makers those features of the CAP that may be challenged in the future. Thus they provide input for considerations on future reform of the CAP.

On market access, Article 4.2 of the URAA states that 'Members shall not maintain, resort to, or revert to any measures of the kind that have been required to be converted into ordinary customs duties.' A footnote explains that such measures 'include quantitative import restrictions, variable import levies, minimum import prices', etc. Despite this a number of countries, particularly in South America, have maintained price band systems. Essentially, these mechanisms are designed to maintain domestic price stability in the face of fluctuating world market prices. If the world market price rises above the price band, the import tariff is reduced (or even eliminated). If it falls below the band, the tariff increases, but the maximum level is the rate bound in the country's tariff schedule. It is perhaps important to note that countries can have *applied* rates that are lower than their bound rates—indeed, this is a common feature of many countries' tariff schedules—and that applied rates can be changed provided they remain at or below the bound rate. What is problematic is the systematic variation in the applied rate, reflecting world market price movements.

Argentina challenged the Chilean system. The Appellate Body upheld the panel's ruling 'that Chile's price band system is a border measure that is similar to variable import levies and minimum import prices', and that the system was 'inconsistent with Article 4.2' (WTO 2002a: paragraph 288).[16] The Appellate Body was keen to clarify that it had reached its 'conclusion on the basis of the particular configuration and interaction of all ... specific features of Chile's price band system': no 'particular feature', on its own, had 'the effect of disconnecting Chile's market from international price developments in a way that insulates Chile's market from the transmission of international prices' (WTO 2002a: paragraph 261). Nonetheless it is interesting to speculate on whether other import regimes might be inconsistent with Article 4.2: the EU's minimum entry price system for fruit and vegetables for instance? (Swinbank and Ritson 1995).

Upland Cotton resulted in a number of interesting rulings on domestic subsidies. It determined, for example, that so-called Step 2 payments to United States-based users of United States-grown cotton (to enable them to pay a higher price to US cotton growers) constituted a prohibited subsidy under the Subsidies and Countervailing Measures (SCM) Agreement not sanctioned by the URAA (one 'contingent ... upon the use of domestic over imported goods') and required the United States to remove this subsidy by July 2005 (Sumner 2005: 7; Josling et al. 2006: 9). This ruling echoed the problems the EU had faced over oilseeds during the UR negotiations, when a GATT panel had ruled that payments to oilseed crushers, contingent on their use of EU-grown oilseeds, infringed the national treatment provisions of GATT Article II (see Chapter 7). A casual reading of the URAA, and a consideration of its amber, blue, and green boxes, would not highlight this problem: but the URAA read in conjunction with the SCM Agreement did. No doubt other countries are now re-examining their domestic subsidy provisions to forestall any future challenge. Indeed, the EU's decoupling of the processing aids paid on certain fruits and vegetables (for tomato paste, canned peaches, etc.) might be seen in this light (European Commission 2007).

The panel also concluded that various elements of the subsidy programme resulted in 'significant price suppression in the ... world market ... constituting serious prejudice to the interests of Brazil'. The United States was told to take steps to remove the adverse effects, but Brazil believes that the United States has not complied, and in August 2006 it launched a new complaint (WTO 2006). Despite this semi-victory in a non-violation dispute, the fact that the panel and Appellate Body were able to come to the ruling that domestic policies did result in price suppression, leading to serious prejudice, must give other 'large' WTO members cause for reflection. Canada, learning from *Upland Cotton*, initiated action against the US corn (maize) programme in January 2007, arguing not only that various programmes caused 'significant price depression and price suppression for corn in the Canadian market for marketing years 1996–2006', but also that the threat continued (WTO 2007*d*: 2).

The third domestic subsidy issue that *Upland Cotton* addressed, almost in passing, was that a large part of the US farm budget could not qualify as green box expenditure, as had previously been presumed. As we noted earlier in this chapter, this is because various planting restrictions on land that attracted what had been thought to be decoupled income support payments, violated green box criteria. US programmes did not mandate what farmers *had* to produce to receive subsidy: they were free to farm, except there were certain things they could not produce (e.g. fruit and vegetables). Thus, by default, the subsidies were amber box payments. At the time Brazil had not alleged that this would result in the United States breaching its AMS binding, although scholars have (e.g. Sumner 2005: 9). Canada, however, again learning from *Upland Cotton*, subsequently alleged that the United States exceeded its AMS limits in 'in each of 1999, 2000, 2001, 2004, and 2005' (WTO 2007*d*: 3).

This had implications for EU policy, particularly for the Single Payment Scheme that we introduce in Chapter 6.[17] Again, the 2007 reforms to the fruit and vegetable regime, making the land on which fruits and vegetables are grown eligible for these payments (European Commission 2007), presumably overcome the problem the United States encountered over

Upland Cotton. However, EU payments are still made to farmers, annually, on the basis of the land at their disposal, and cross-compliance applies, raising the question of whether the scheme fully meets the criteria of paragraph 6 of the green box, which in part reads, 'The amount of such payments in any given year shall not be related to, or based on, the factors of production employed in any year after the base period' (see Swinbank and Tranter 2005, McMahon 2007 for further discussion).

The third pillar of the URAA, relating to export subsidy commitments, has attracted a lot of attention from WTO litigants. To recap, an export subsidy is a prohibited subsidy under the SCM Agreement unless sanctioned by the URAA. Thus attention has, first, focused on identifying export subsidies that were not previously identified as such; and second on establishing that export subsidies have breached WTO members' export subsidy reduction commitments.

In *Upland Cotton* it was determined that the so-called Step 2 payments to United States-based cotton processors who subsequently exported the product were, in effect, export subsidies which were not included in the US schedule of export subsidy commitments, and were therefore prohibited subsidies that had to be removed within six months, or by 1 July 2005 at the latest. The United States did so as of 1 August 2006 (Josling et al. 2006: 10). Given the outcome in this particular case, what other domestic subsidies currently declared in the amber, blue, or even green, boxes might also be found to be export subsidies?

Upland Cotton also resulted in a determination that the US system for export credit guarantees (effectively a subsidized insurance scheme for exports to risky markets) was an export subsidy, which again was a prohibited subsidy because it too was not included in the US schedule of reduction commitments (Benitah 2005; Josling et al. 2006: 10). This came as a shock to the United States, because they thought (or at least they said they did!) that export credits were excluded from the purview of the URAA and SCM Agreement constraints by virtue of Article 10.2 of the URAA, which reads: 'Members undertake to work toward the development of internationally agreed disciplines to govern the provision of export credits, export credit guarantees or insurance programmes and, after agreement on such disciplines, to provide export credits, export credit guarantees or insurance programmes only in conformity therewith.' Negotiations had been ongoing in the OECD, but with no outcome, and in this lacuna the United States had argued there were no disciplines in place (WTO 2004*d*: paragraph 7.999).

In *Canada—Measures Affecting the Importation of Milk and the Exportation of Dairy Products*, a two-tier pricing system was scrutinized. The Canadian government had put in place a marketing system that allowed raw milk to be sold to domestic processors for sale in Canada at a higher price than the same raw material could be sold to processors for export. No explicit export subsidy was made, but the higher-priced domestic sales were deemed to cross-subsidize export sales, and this was found to be an export subsidy (van Vliet 2000: 229). Similar reasoning was used in *EC–Export Subsidies on Sugar*, discussed in the previous section, to determine that C sugar exports were in effect subsidized, breaching the EU's export subsidy commitments in sugar (Swinbank 2008a). What other two-tier pricing system might be viewed in the same light?

One outcome of the 2005 Hong Kong Ministerial was an agreement to phase out export subsidies by '2013', in the context of an overall agreement. In effect, all export subsidies would become prohibited subsidies under Part II of the SCM Agreement. Where market price support still forms an important component of the CAP, as with milk and sugar, this would not be a trivial commitment for the EU to undertake.[18]

Export surpluses of commodities might have disappeared by 2013, but processed products containing milk fat and sugar will presumably still be exported.[19] It is interesting to note that the Commission in its *Monitoring Agri-trade Policy* briefs made a virtue of the fact that 'the share of commodities in EU agricultural exports has dropped to just 8% of their total value', with a corresponding increase in semi-processed and processed exports (European Commission 2006: 6). This might cause some of the EU's trade partners to query the existing export 'refund' arrangements on processed products. Post 2013 the EU's food industries will not willingly pay high raw material prices for agricultural raw materials if they are denied access to export 'refunds' on processed goods, and they are likely to lobby for the elimination of the remaining elements of market price support.

If there is no outcome to the Doha Round, the existing export subsidy constraints should not prove too problematic for the enlarged EU in most sectors. Indeed, the EU could in a number of instances increase its subsidized exports. The EU's partners are no doubt scrutinizing its policies to see whether they can identify any more subsidy programmes that could be shown to be prohibited subsidies: export subsidies on processed products might be such a case if it could be shown that GATT Article XVI (which allows for export subsidies on primary but not processed products) prevailed over URAA provisions which do allow for export subsidies on primary products incorporated into processed goods (Swinbank 2006*b*).

The EU as complainant

Perhaps reflecting the old adage that people who live in glass houses should not throw stones, the EU has not actively challenged other members' farm policies through the Dispute Settlement System. The WTO website lists the EU as a complainant in 79 cases, and as a respondent in 63.[20] Cases explicitly involving agriculture (but not fish) in which the EU has been a complainant are listed in Table 5.3. Challenges to the tax regimes on alcoholic beverages in Chile, India, Japan, and Korea of importance to the EU's exporters of spirits (whisky, brandy, etc.) are excluded, as is a case involving Canadian taxes on wine and beer, and challenges to export restrictions on raw hides and skins (Argentina, India, and Pakistan) which impact on raw material supplies for the EU's tanning industry.

By contrast, the EU has challenged some members' use of trade remedies (trade defence instruments)—countervailing duties, anti-dumping duties and safeguard measures. In particular the United States's use of trade remedies across a number of sectors has attracted EU action, but only one case is reported in the table: *United States—Continued Dumping and Subsidy Offset Act of 2000* (but the Act is more commonly known as the Byrd Amendment). Under the Byrd Amendment, anti-dumping duties collected by the US authorities were distributed to the US industries competing with the imports. Thus over the four-year period 2001 to 2004 some $25.5 million of anti-dumping duties were collected on imports of pasta from Italy for distribution to United States-based pasta makers (Harris and Devadoss 2005: 229). The DSB found this system to be inconsistent with WTO provisions, and the United States struggled to comply.

The other 'big' United States–EU dispute reported in the table is *United States—Tax Treatment for 'Foreign Sales Corporations'*, which again crossed several sectors and caused much anguish to US lawmakers. The agricultural interest here is that the DSB found that the US tax concessions, when applied to trade in agricultural products, breached the URAA commitments on export subsidies (van Vliet 2000: 230–1).

Table 5.3 The EU as complainant in cases involving agriculture (selected cases)

Respondent and title	DS	Comments
Japan—Measures Affecting Imports of Pork	66	Problems with GATT provisions: no panel established or settlement notified
India—Quantitative Restrictions on Imports of Agricultural, Textile and Industrial Products	96	Mutually agreed solution
Korea—Definitive Safeguard Measure on Imports of Certain Dairy Products	98	Korean system found to be at fault
United States—Measures Affecting Imports of Poultry Products	100	GATT, SPS, and Technical Barriers to Trade (TBT): no panel established or settlement notified
United States—Tax Treatment for 'Foreign Sales Corporations'	108	*Inter alia* determined that the URAA export subsidy constraints were breached
Argentina—Countervailing Duties on Imports of Wheat Gluten from the European Communities	145	No panel established or settlement notified
United States—Definitive Safeguard Measures on Imports of Wheat Gluten from the European Communities	166	US system found to be at fault
United States—Continued Dumping and Subsidy Offset Act of 2000	217	Known as the Byrd amendment. US policy found to be at fault
Australia—Quarantine Regime for Imports	287	SPS restrictions on pig and poultry meat. Mutually acceptable agreement notified
Mexico—Provisional Countervailing Measures on Olive Oil from the European Communities	314	No panel established or settlement notified
United States and Canada—Continued Suspension of Obligations in the EC—Hormones Dispute	320 & 321	Follow-up to the beef hormones case. The Appellate Body's report was delivered in November 2008.
Argentina—Countervailing Duties on Olive Oil, Wheat Gluten and Peaches	330	No panel established or settlement notified
Mexico—Definitive Countervailing Measures on Olive Oil from the European Communities	341	Panel report circulated September 2008

Source: http://www.wto.org/english/tratop_e/dispu_e/dispu_by_country_e.htm, accessed 15 December 2008.

Conclusions

In this chapter we have seen the DSU in action. Developing country members have challenged the farm policies of developed country members, and prevailed. Panels (and the Appellate Body) have ruled against established policies, and in doing so have challenged both EU and the US perceptions of the balance of rights and obligations established by the UR agreements signed in Marrakesh in 1994. This has sometimes involved an interpretation of the URAA, and the other WTO agreements, not readily apparent to the negotiators at the time. The prevailing trend in farm trade disputes has been to strike down protectionist farm policies, not to support them, reflecting the URAA's basic ideational foundation—agricultural normalism.

Several rulings have been a challenge for those countries that believed their agricultural policies were in conformity with the WTO rule set. Our analysis demonstrated that rulings, even when they go against a member, are in general considered to be legitimate, and that they are often complied with even by the major trading powers, at least to some extent. Both the United States and the EU have tried to abide by DSB rulings, although the United States has had difficulty doing so with *Upland Cotton*, the Byrd Amendment, and Foreign Sales Tax Corporations, and the EU with beef hormones, bananas, and 'biotech' products. Nonetheless our review does support the notion that the DSU has progressed the liberalization of farm trade further than was envisaged when the URAA was negotiated and agreed; further eroding the exceptional treatment of agriculture in the WTO and prompting the defendants to move their agricultural policies in the direction of the liberal market paradigm. This trend can be expected to continue, as we discuss in Chapter 8.

Although the EU is not the only target of disputes over agricultural policies, it has faced serious challenges and has lost important cases. In contrast to the situation under the old GATT's diplomacy-based dispute settlement system, the EU does seem to be more willing to comply with judicial rulings under the new system. However, the extent of compliance is to a large degree determined by the EU's own institutional rules. Food safety legislation, for example, in contrast to agricultural policy, is in part determined by the European Parliament: an institution which seems to more heavily emphasize EU public concerns about food safety than it does WTO trade rules.

Chapter 6

EU Agricultural Institutions and the CAP: Coping with GATT/WTO

In previous chapters we analysed developments at the international level. We demonstrated that the Uruguay Round Agreement on Agriculture (URAA) changed the core ideational underpinning of global farm trade regulation, replacing agricultural exceptionalism with agricultural normalism. In this chapter we show how these developments influenced institutional and policy developments at EU level, demonstrating how *this revised ideational underpinning of the URAA influenced EU agricultural institutions and Common Agricultural Policy (CAP) reform.* Establishing the way EU agricultural policy institutions respond to the URAA, and how this influences CAP reforms, has wider implications for trade liberalization within the WTO since agricultural trade was a key political issue in the Doha Round as it had been in the Uruguay Round (UR). However, in this chapter we limit ourselves to analysing the way in which the URAA and Doha negotiations influenced the evolution of EU agricultural institutions and policy. Acknowledging that there is an interrelationship between EU agricultural policy evolution and WTO farm trade agreements, the following chapter analyses how EU agricultural policy then sets limits for WTO agreements.

In Chapter 2, we distinguished between four types of institutional adjustment to ideational change: institutional breakdown, institutional conversion, institutional layering, and institutional stasis, as set out in Table 2.1. We suggested that these types of institutional adjustment would result in different policy responses to ideational change at the global level. *Institutional breakdown* causes rapid and fundamental policy reform in which a new idea underpins the reformed policy. *Institutional conversion* leads to gradual shift in policy. A new idea is adopted and sets the direction for future policy evolution in which policy measures would gradually be changed to reflect the new idea. In *institutional layering* the existing ideational underpinning remains, but may be disguised through rephrasing. Policy measures are gradually changed to serve the original objectives in new ways. Finally, *institutional stasis* preserves the existing policy, but some symbolic adjustments may be undertaken. On the basis of these considerations, this chapter analyses how the EU has responded to the new ideational underpinning of global farm trade regulation as set out in the URAA.

Adjusting EU agricultural policy institutions

Prior to the URAA, the GATT played only a minor role in shaping the CAP. Instead, the policy concern was focused on domestic issues. The Commission often emphasized the need to protect farm incomes. For instance, in 1981, it pointed out that the Community had a large responsibility in making agricultural decisions because these had 'a direct effect on the incomes of 8 million persons employed in agriculture, who together with their families represent 40 million persons' (Commission 1981: 4). The 'green paper', *Perspectives for the Common Agricultural Policy*, repeatedly returned to the question of farmers' income (Commission 1985: 13, 49, 59, 60), arguing, for example, that the 'Community must ensure that the social and economic conditions of those working in agriculture are not prejudiced . . . ' (p. VI). Similar concerns were expressed in one of the Commission's reform papers in 1991 which emphasized that price cuts could not be undertaken unless the Community compensated farmers for their income losses. Further, it stressed that farmers' incomes should be safeguarded if the CAP was to be reformed (Commission 1991*a*: 8, 12). Agriculture Commissioner Ray MacSharry defended these positions, promising farmers that 'he would continue to protect the idea of compensation for price cuts' (*Agra Europe*, 8 May 1992: E/5). More or less officially, a major objective of the CAP has always been the commitment to maintain the family farm as the foundation of European agriculture. This goal was written into the Stresa declaration in 1958: 'Given the importance of the family structure in European agriculture, and the unanimous desire to preserve its family character, every means should be [employed] to increase the economic and competitive capacity of family farms' (as quoted in Commission 1985: 9). In its 1985 'green paper', the Commission had earlier raised the rhetorical question of whether the EU wished 'to maintain a substantial number of workers in agriculture', to which it responded: 'there can only be a positive reply'. The challenge, it continued, 'which must be faced is how to ensure the maintenance of a significant number of persons in agriculture by means which do not result in unacceptable waste of economic and financial resources' (Commission 1985: II). Similarly, in the introduction to its reform proposals in 1991, the Commission (1991a: 9–10) stated: 'Sufficient numbers of farmers must be kept on the land. There is no other way to preserve the natural environment, traditional landscapes and a model of agriculture based on the family farm as favoured by society generally.'

These traditional concerns of the CAP were gradually supplemented with others related to international trade as the UR approached its planned completion in late 1990, and in particular after it was brought to a halt that December. During the UR it had become more than ever apparent that farm trade was a contested issue. As the Round approached its planned conclusion in December 1990 there had been little progress on agriculture. Although an offer was eventually tabled by the EU, it was too late and insufficiently radical to salvage the ministerial talks scheduled for the Heysel conference centre in Brussels, as we explain in Chapter 7. This gave Farm Commissioner Ray MacSharry the opportunity to propose a new reform of the CAP early in 1991. The official motive for the proposed reform was said to be the increasing, and costly, surplus production which put pressure on the EU's agricultural budget. The international trade implications of surplus production were hardly mentioned in the reform paper of February 1991 (Commission 1991a), and Community spokespersons officially denied any link between the UR and the reform debate. MacSharry had an important incentive to keep the GATT talks and the reform process separate. He did not want to give the impression that the CAP reform was triggered by American pressure (*Agra Europe* no. 1424, 25 January 1991: E/3). The suggestion that the Americans were the root cause of reform would not help attempts to persuade farmers and member states, in particular France, to accept it. Nevertheless, the real concerns preoccupying decision makers slipped out. The Dutch minister of agriculture, who was the Agriculture Council president in the second half of 1991, made clear the link between a CAP reform and the GATT talks when telling the press: 'What is necessary for the Uruguay round is that . . . there is an indication of the direction in which the CAP will be adjusted and reformed' (*Agra Europe* no. 1448, 12 July 1991: E/6).

Though the linkage between the GATT farm trade talks and the MacSharry reform appears fairly clear, there is disagreement on the extent to which GATT concerns influenced the decision to undertake the reform.

Some argue that it had minor importance. Instead they suggest that domestic concerns, primarily budgetary, triggered the reform. Kay (1998: 165–6), for example, suggests that whilst the 'international dimension affected the start of the domestic policy reform process', it was the provisions of the 1988 stabilizer regime that 'forced' the Council of Agricultural Ministers 'to reach an outcome on the reform proposals and conclude the MacSharry reform process'. Rieger (2000: 193–6) makes a similar point, arguing that 'it was neither the state of international agricultural markets nor the pressure applied by the US government that convinced European policy makers to take the inclusion of agriculture in the Uruguay Round more seriously... Much more important... were the mounting budget costs of the CAP, and, even more so, the way that market support mechanisms had perversely redistributed incomes to farmers'.[1] Paarlberg (1997) concludes that international trade negotiations have limited impact on agricultural policy reforms in other political systems as well as in the EU. Comparing reforms undertaken in the EU and the United States during, or at the conclusion of, the UR he concludes that 'the reforms secured through international negotiation were modest at best. In many instances the modest reforms that were written into the final agreement [the URAA] reflected policy changes already undertaken unilaterally in response to internal budget pressures or in response to other pressures that did not derive specifically from the Uruguay Round negotiation...' (p. 441).

Others argue that the UR was indeed an important trigger for reform of the CAP. For instance, Grant (1997: 196) argues that the 'GATT negotiations provided the impetus for the MacSharry reforms because the consequences of a complete breakdown in the economic relationship with the United States were too serious to contemplate. What was needed was to get an agreement on agricultural trade which offered enough concessions to the US position to make it acceptable to the Americans, but still protected the essential objectives of the EU'. Coleman and Tangermann (1999: 386) 'strongly subscribe' to this hypothesis, arguing that 'the timing of the CAP reform and the very logic of the reforms introduced represent direct responses to international pressures emanating from the GATT negotiations'. Swinbank and Tanner (1996: 156–7) assert: 'The MacSharry reform proposals of 1991 were prompted by the struggles in the Council to adopt a credible negotiating mandate in October 1990... Thus, we conclude that the Uruguay Round GATT negotiations did impact on CAP reform, despite the Commission's insistence at the time that these were only internally driven' (see also Garzon 2006: Chapter 6, Kjeldahl 1994: 5, Ingersent et al. 1994: 77).

Yet others try to find some middle ground between the two opposing views. For instance, Daugbjerg (1998: 115–16) concludes that 'the GATT talks and the expected budget crisis, should nothing be done, were the main driving forces behind the 1992 policy reform. Probably neither of these two factors would have been strong enough to cause major alterations in the policy by themselves. The combined effect of the two was what eventually led to reform' (see also Skogstad 1998: 472).

Cunha, the Portuguese Farm Minister who chaired the Agriculture Council at the time of the MacSharry reforms, having re-examined the events of the period, is of the view that whilst budgetary concerns were the primary initial impetus for the Commission and the Commissioner to propose the reform, these concerns progressively disappeared, to be replaced by the pressing need to accommodate the requests of its trading partners in the UR negotiations, which in turn resulted in an increase in expenditure. Nonetheless, 'budgetary pressures were emphasized in the *political speech* because it was *politically incorrect* for European politicians to recognize explicitly the GATT pressures for reform' (Cunha 2007: 167); and a Delphi survey, of senior policy makers who had taken part in the reform, that he undertook in 2006 indicated that they too believed that the GATT negotiations had been crucially important (Cunha and Swinbank 2009). Ross (1995: 278), who chronicled events in Delors's *cabinet*, has also remarked on this dual negotiation: 'One interesting detail of the entire plan was that there developed an agreed taboo to refrain from acknowledging that CAP reform was in any way connected to the Uruguay Round.'

A scrutiny of the role of budgetary concerns in the reform process does indicate that they played a less important role. Despite the alleged budgetary crises in 1991 and 1992, the Council's annual decisions on prices were not noticeably influenced by the need to remain within the Agricultural Guideline; and in any event the Commission's reform proposals could not have had an immediate effect. Nevertheless, the initial Reflections Paper does at one point say: 'In order to avoid a build up of stocks and excessive growth in spending on agriculture, a key objective of the agricultural policy has to be that of controlling production...' (Commission 1991a: 11). However, at no point is it claimed that the objective of the proposed reforms is to contain or reduce expenditure. Indeed, the document ends by debating two rhetorical objections to the Commission's proposal, one of which is: 'The guidelines outlined above may lead to higher budgetary cost insofar as part of the support now provided by the consumer (by virtue of high prices) would be henceforth charged to the budget.'

The impression given is that expenditure could increase: 'These reforms will have budgetary consequences whose significance will depend on the parameters to be chosen', but the Commission claims the money would be better spent (Commission 1991a: 17). Indeed, when MacSharry (1991: 17) addressed the European Parliament in March 1991 he acknowledged that the 'new direction' recommended 'would require additional budgetary resources'. He went on to say: 'How much...would depend on how far we should go to compensate farmers for the price reductions.'

When the Commission's formal proposals were published in July 1991 the financial annex suggested that additional annual expenditure on price and income support would amount to 2.3 billion ecu compared to the preliminary draft budget for 1992, with an additional 479 million ecu in the first year, plus 4 billion ecu over five years (1993–7) for the accompanying measures (Commission 1991b). The package as adopted by ministers in May 1992 differed in several important respects from that proposed by the Commission: for example, the proposals on milk were emasculated; but the compensation package on set-aside was more generous (Swinbank and Tanner 1996: 92). Identifying an appropriate counterfactual to benchmark the estimate of any change is difficult. However, Ackrill et al. (1997: 92) simulated the budget effects of the 1992 reform using a 1992 dataset and assuming an immediate implementation of the reform. They found 'the reform leads to a significant increase in net agricultural spending' (p. 95), with the increase in gross expenditure calculated to be 5.7 billion ecu (p. 96).

Post-UR

After the conclusion of the UR, EU agricultural policy makers explicitly and increasingly referred to the WTO when proposing, and deliberating upon, CAP reforms. Such concerns were apparent in the agricultural chapter of the Commission's Agenda 2000 proposal in which it was assumed that the forthcoming WTO negotiations would result in further trade liberalization and it was said that 'the Union has to prepare its agriculture sector for these negotiations' (Commission 1998a: 2). Furthermore, it was stated that 'the Union has to lay down the agricultural policy that it intends carrying out in the years ahead in a way that satisfies its own interests and takes a realistic view of developments in the international context. This needs to be done before the opening of the WTO negotiations so that the Union can negotiate on a solid basis and knows where it wants to go' (p. 3). The heads of state and government (the European

Council), who made the final reform decision after farm ministers had failed to reach agreement, acknowledged the Commission's view in stating that the Agenda 2000 reform had to be seen in the context of the future agricultural negotiations in the WTO, by stating that 'The European Council considers that the decision adopted regarding the reform of the CAP within the framework of Agenda 2000 will constitute essential elements in defining the Commission's negotiating mandate for the future multilateral trade negotiations at the WTO' (European Council 1999: 5). Framing the CAP in a global context demonstrated to the international community that the member states now accepted that WTO concerns were becoming institutionalized in CAP reform processes.

The 2003 CAP reform process confirmed that WTO concerns were firmly institutionalized in agricultural policy institutions. For instance, the Commission stated that the reform proposal was designed to take 'into account the need to preserve farming incomes in a less trade-distorting way' (2002: 3) and that the proposal to decouple direct payments 'will provide a major advantage in the WTO since the green box compatibility of the scheme will help secure these payments in an international context' (p. 19). In the Commission's proposal for a Council Regulation, published 21 January 2003, there was even a switch to seeing CAP reform as an offensive negotiating asset to be used to prise concessions from its trading partners. As the Commission (2003: 4) stated: 'As regards WTO aspects, the new single farm payment will be green box compatible. Decoupling will allow the European Union to maximise its negotiating capital in order to achieve its WTO objectives such as non-trade concerns. Hence, the proposals for decoupling could be crucial in getting the best deal for the European Model of Agriculture' (see also a similar statement attributed to Franz Fischler in *Agra Focus*, no. 89, July 2003). The Council declaration of 30 June 2003 re-confirmed that the WTO negotiations were a crucial concern in EU agricultural policy by stating: 'The reform is also a message to our trading partners, including in particular the developing countries. It signifies a major departure from trade-distorting agricultural support . . . ' (Council 2003: 3). The fact that the Council devoted 'half of the political declaration introducing the final compromise . . . to explaining the relationship between the newly adopted reform and the ongoing WTO negotiations' (Garzon 2006: 110) shows that WTO concerns had come to the fore in EU agricultural policy making. This 'contrasts with the concerns prevailing in 1999, where only a cursory reference was made to the WTO, or with the defensive position adopted in 1992' (p. 111). This concern to place CAP policy changes in a WTO frame has continued. For example, in

2007, in proposing reforms to the fruit and vegetables regime, the Commission said that they had been formulated 'taking into account the need for WTO compatibility' (Commission 2007*a*: 3). The changes to the EU's sugar regime, agreed in 2005–6, bringing its export subsidy practices into line with the Dispute Settlement Body's earlier ruling, as outlined in Chapter 5, signified a willingness on the part of the EU to conform with WTO provisions, even though the sugar regime was only partially liberalized in the 'reform'. Whilst the 'Health Check' (Commission 2007*b*, 2008*a*) was not explicitly legitimized by WTO concerns, it was moving in the same direction as the emerging Doha package. In promoting the Health Check to the European Association of Agricultural Economists, the Commissioner's Deputy Head of Cabinet, Klaus-Dieter Borchardt (2008) drew attention to the proposal for 'further decoupling', moving from a situation in which some arable payments were 'partially coupled' by phasing in 'full decoupling'. Borchardt (2008: 5) also noted the ambition of the Health Check to weaken the remaining elements of market price support: 'Market orientation further needs the conversion of our traditional market instruments, like intervention, private storage, export refunds and quotas, into a genuine safety net. These instruments should not be applied any more as "price setters" on the markets but as instruments that keep farmers in business in case of dramatic market disruptions.' Thus, the Health Check proposals to further decouple arable payments and to weaken market price support mechanisms could be seen as an important element in the Commission's Doha strategy (Daugbjerg and Swinbank 2008*b*).

Since the early 1980s there have been no major changes in the way the CAP's decision-making processes are organized.[2] The Commission, that is the Farm Commissioner, has retained his/her right of initiative in agricultural policy making, the Council of Agriculture Ministers has made the decision, and the European Parliament has had a limited consultative role.[3] However, the European Council, consisting of heads of state and government, has been directly involved in CAP reform on three occasions (milk quotas [adopted 1984], budgetary stabilizers [adopted 1988], and Agenda 2000 [adopted 1999]) and has made the final *de facto* reform decision in two of these—but this did not mean that the Council of Agriculture Ministers lost influence on the reform contents. When it was the prerogative of the European Council to adopt the reform decision, farm ministers were asked to negotiate the deal on CAP reform, which they failed to do. Instead they progressed the negotiations until they had pointed the European Council in the direction of a compromise, whilst falling short of a final deal. The European Council invariably followed these pointers, given that its members lacked the detailed expertise on agricultural policy, and it had other pressing issues to resolve (Daugbjerg and Swinbank 2007).

Though there has been relative stability in terms of decision-making structures, the institutional changes that have taken place can best be characterized as institutional layering. In addition to the traditional concerns in agricultural policy making, such as farm incomes and the maintenance of family farming, WTO concerns have gradually been accepted as a constraint within which the CAP evolves and which could no longer be ignored, but which instead increasingly had to be taken into consideration. From 1995 on, policy makers designing reforms would strive to ensure conformity with WTO agreements, and perhaps even attempt to anticipate future developments in the WTO.

Reforming the CAP

As a result of institutional layering—following Table 2.1—we would expect the evolving CAP to maintain its existing ideational underpinning, although this might well be rephrased. Policy measures are expected to change gradually to serve the original objectives in a new and, to critics, more acceptable, way. Thus this section analyses the nature of the policy changes since 1990 when farm ministers realized that the GATT farm trade negotiations could no longer be ignored, and compares the Mac-Sharry (adopted 1992), Agenda 2000 (adopted 1999), and Fischler (adopted 2003) reforms.

Until 1992 the key characteristic of the CAP was that it was a high-price policy in which consumers paid a significant share of the cost of subsidizing farmers. Farm incomes were supported through a system of guaranteed minimum prices set well above world market levels. These guaranteed prices were maintained by market manipulation: import levies, intervention buying, and export subsidies. To farmers this system had the advantage of hiding the real costs of agricultural support, because a large share was off budget, but abroad two of the key policy measures were particularly visible and clearly distorted world markets. These were the extensive use of export subsidies and the highly protective variable import levies, stopping EU market prices falling below politically determined price floors. The extensive use of these trade-distorting policy measures was a clear indication that the CAP took very little notice of the international trade distortions they caused, and therefore very little notice of the overall aim of the GATT to liberalize world trade. As we documented in Chapter 4, there was widespread international criticism of the CAP.

The MacSharry reform of 1992 changed the *architecture* of the CAP. There was a shift from a reliance on price support to direct payments. The main change to the CAP's price support mechanisms came in the cereals sector where intervention prices were reduced by a third, but farmers were compensated for the implied revenue loss by the introduction of a subsidy paid on each hectare of eligible land on which an eligible arable crop was grown (the arable area payments scheme). Claimants above a specified threshold had to set aside 15 per cent of their arable land, but still qualified for an arable area payment on that land; and claims were submitted, and authenticated, through an Integrated Administration and Control System (IACS) (Swinbank and Tanner 1996: Chapter 5).

In the literature on the MacSharry reform in 1992, there is some disagreement on how radical it was. Those who claim it was radical base their assessment on the fact that it put an end to open-ended support by shifting from price support to direct payments. These payments were based on area farmed and historical yields, and fixed livestock numbers. The 'radical' in this shift is that it would bring an end to ever-increasing budget costs caused by price support in a situation in which productivity was ever increasing (Ackrill 2005). Another way of seeing the shift in policy instruments as a radical reform is based on the view that the increased visibility of agricultural support would eventually mobilize strong public opposition. As Kjeldahl (1994: 7) points out: 'The switch to direct payments is making financial support to farmers more visible. Not only will it be increasingly clear to farmers how much support they each receive, but also the total payments made to farmers in each Member State can easily be seen ... Will people not forget the compensatory payment and ask why farmers should be "for ever" entitled to budgetary transfers?'

Whilst the policy instruments were changed, the whole idea of subsidizing farmers and protecting their incomes from market forces remained untouched. Thus, the CAP remained within the state-assisted paradigm. A further confirmation of this was that, during the reform process, the Commission and the member states were careful not to raise the question of whether or not the EU should subsidize agriculture, but made sure that the discussion was limited to the way it should be subsidized (Daugbjerg 1999: 420–3).

The proposals for the Agenda 2000 CAP reform were cast in the mould of the MacSharry reforms, with a further cut in intervention prices (and increase in direct payments), and an extension to milk (see Serger 2001: 125 and Ackrill 2000 for an overview). However, member states were given the option of making direct payments conditional on cross-compliance—they could be reduced if a farmer failed to comply with some environmental standard—and member states could 'modulate' (i.e. re-duce) direct payments in order to re-channel EU budget funds for other (second pillar) activities in the member state. A further innovation was the revamping of structural policy, placing the emphasis on rural develop-ment and the environment, creating the so-called second pillar of the CAP (the traditional mechanisms of price and income support comprised the first pillar). The creation of the second pillar of the CAP could, at first glance, be seen as a substantial change, but actual change was modest since the pillar would largely consist of already existing schemes and very limited additional funds would be available. The Agenda 2000 CAP reform is generally understood as 'a deepening' of the MacSharry reforms. There was an adjustment of existing policy instruments, not a shift in policy instruments, and the policy paradigm was maintained.

In its proposals for Agenda 2000 the Commission had claimed that the *European Model of Agriculture* was not the same as that 'pursued by our major competitors elsewhere', and that 'care will accordingly need to be taken to provide proper compensation for natural constraints and disad-vantages' (Commission 1998a: section 3), a view reaffirmed by the Agri-culture Council in November 1998. Very quickly the rhetoric turned to *multifunctionality*, aligning this concept with the non-trade concerns that were to be accommodated in the new round of agricultural trade negotiations envisaged in the URAA. Multifunctionality emphasized the non-marketable outputs of the farm sector—maintaining viable rural communities; contributions to the social and cultural fabric of the nation; protection of the environment, its fauna and flora, and the land-scape; water catchments; etc.—all of which could be lost if farmers were not rewarded for the provision of these public goods. Accordingly the term multifunctionality entered the lexicography of the WTO, sup-ported by many *Old World* economies. We discuss this more thoroughly in Chapter 7. However, once the Doha Round was truly underway, the EU stopped using this term in Geneva, although it remained part of the domestic policy discourse justifying the continuation of agricultural support in the Fischler reforms.

The core of the Fischler reform in 2003 involved a further change of policy instruments. Direct aid payments based on the area farmed and crops grown, and type and number of livestock kept, were further decoupled and transformed into a new Single Payment Scheme, often referred to as the single farm payment—we use the terms interchangeably (Swinbank and Daugbjerg 2006). However, the payments are not fully decoupled because to qualify for them the land had to be kept in good agricultural condition, and recipients had to be farmers. During the reform debate, it was clearly stated that there was no intention of ending agricultural support and thus there was no attempt to shift to the market-liberal paradigm. As the Farm Commissioner stated at an internal Commission seminar in April 2002: 'For us, the relevant policy question is NOT IF, but HOW to continue support for EU agriculture' (Fischler 2002a: 4, see also Fischler 2001: 4). Instead the aim was to shift support modes. As the Commission (2002: 18, 19) stated, 'One of the objectives of the process of CAP reform since 1992 has been to focus on *shifting support* for agriculture from the product to the producer', and that its proposal would 'accomplish the final step in the *shift of support...* ' (our italics).

There was no attempt to use the Single Payment Scheme to undertake a general reshuffling of the distribution of support among farmers (Haniotis 2007: 58). Indeed, the then Farm Commissioner, Franz Fischler, said at a recent conference that the financial impact of the reform for individual farmers was intended to be zero.[4] A farmer's future entitlement to payments would be based on that farm's past claims (averaged over the period 2000–2) for area and headage payments under the IACS scheme. If the average annual payment in the base period had been €A, and the number of hectares that had supported the claim was B, then the farm would be allocated B hectares of entitlements, worth €A/B per hectare. In subsequent years, in order to claim his/her subsidy in full, the farmer would have to show that B hectares remained in good agricultural condition. Set-aside conditions would be carried forward from the old regime, cross-compliance would apply across the whole farm, land had to be maintained in good agricultural and environmental condition, payments could not be claimed on land under permanent crops or growing fruit and vegetables (although this was changed later), and certain supplementary crop-specific payments would remain. Beyond that, however, farmers would no longer be obliged to grow specific crops, or keep livestock, as they had to claim area and headage payments, but would instead be free to follow whatever 'agricultural activity' they chose.

The final Council compromise, however, involved two significant derogations. First, some member states chose a partial decoupling option. The rules were complex but countries were allowed to retain—as a payment coupled to crops grown—25 per cent of the old arable area aid; and for livestock many permutations were possible. Many of the EU15, including France, opted for partial decoupling. Some others (e.g. Germany, Ireland, and the United Kingdom) followed the default variant of full decoupling. In the November 2008 Council decision on the Commission's Health Check proposals, ministers agreed to abolish the partial coupling option for the main arable crops from 2010 and of many of the livestock aids from 2012 at the latest, whilst abolishing set-aside and increasing modulation[5] (*Agra Europe*, 21 November 2008: EP/1).

Second, the 2003 Regulation allowed the Single Payment Scheme to be applied on a regionalized basis rather than in a farm-based, or historical, mode (and combinations of the two—so-called hybrids—were also possible). Under this scheme, all of the monies that would be paid in a particular region were pooled in a common pot, and then paid out at a flat rate per hectare on all eligible land in the region. This had the potential to give some farmers in the same region more subsidy (or 'income support', to adopt the language of the Council Regulation), and others less than they would have been entitled to under the farm-based model.

Garzon (2006: Chapters 12 and 13) argues that the 2003 reform notably involved a shift of policy paradigm, moving the CAP from the state-assisted to the multifunctional paradigm. In the multifunctional agriculture paradigm 'agriculture is viewed as a provider of public goods in addition to, and in many ways more important than its role as a producer of raw material for the food industry' (Moyer and Josling 2002: 35). The Commission (2002: 11, 2003: 2) clearly emphasized the multifunctional character of agriculture and the need to change policy in order to increase the provision of public goods such as environmental sustainability and services, rural development, animal welfare, and food safety. However, the argument that multifunctionalism underpinned the 2003 reform raises two questions. First, is multifunctionalism a distinct paradigm, that is, is it fundamentally different from the state-assisted paradigm; and second, assuming that it is, was the 2003 reform underpinned by it? As to the first question it can be argued that the multifunctional paradigm is no more than a newer evolved version of the state-assisted paradigm, or indeed the state-assisted paradigm in disguise. In both paradigms markets are basically regarded as unstable, creating imbalances between supply and demand. The multifunctional paradigm has broadened the notion of market imbalances, emphasizing that agricultural markets oversupply public bads and undersupply public goods (although the term 'multifunctionality' had been used to talk about public goods, and not the negative externalities of agriculture). In both paradigms public intervention is seen as essential to direct agricultural production towards the desired outcomes.

Imagining that multifunctionalism is a distinct paradigm, was the ideational underpinning of the CAP actually changed by the 2003 reform? The CAP was still based on the view that agriculture is an exceptional industry requiring special treatment. Indeed, in a seminar to fellow Commissioners, Fischler argued that agriculture remained different from other industries, and that demand and supply-side changes meant that both price and farm income volatility was higher than in the past. In addition to the 'old realities' of demand being both price and income inelastic, and supply subject to 'unexpected shocks' and weather-induced uncertainties, the 'new realities' of food safety, environmental and animal welfare concerns, and lengthening supply chains, compounded the problem (Fischler 2001: slides 4–5; see also Haniotis 2007: 60).

Furthermore, there was no intent to redistribute support to farmers according to the level of public goods produced. Neither the historical nor the regionalized mode of transforming the area and headage payments into single farm payments linked them to the production of public goods. A true shift to the multifunctional paradigm would, to a considerable extent, imply that payments would be much more directly related to the provision of public goods.

Not dissimilar to the academic debate on the origins of the MacSharry reform, a discussion on the driving forces behind the 2003 reform has emerged. Interestingly, two Commission officials, Isabelle Garzon and Tassos Haniotis, have taken opposite positions on this issue. The former (who had worked in the *cabinet* of the trade commissioner) argues that WTO concerns were the main driving force (Garzon 2006: Chapter 8), whereas the latter (who worked in Franz Fischler's *cabinet*) pinpoints internal factors as the major motivation behind reform, arguing that 'Some would add Doha, but in reality this was only the side effect, because the fundamental reason for reform of the CAP was internal' (Haniotis 2007: 57).[6]

The internal factors often mentioned as important for reform are enlargement, the budget, and a public perception that support should be switched to rural development and environmental enhancement. To what extent could these concerns be said to have exercised leverage on the EU's institutions in the early 2000s, enabling the Fischler reforms to be conceived and enacted?

There were interlinkages between the enlargement and reform debates, but CAP reform did not precede enlargement as had been widely canvassed in the 1990s. The accession package was agreed prior to the conclusion of the reform debate, but the fact that EU15 had applied a Small Farmers Scheme since 2001 (with a flat rate decoupled area payment for farmers receiving less than €1,250 in annual premiums) paved the way for the adoption of the simplified approach for direct payments in the new member states, known as the Single Area Payment Scheme, which in turn led the Commission to propose a simplified approach (the Single Payment Scheme) for EU15 (Daugbjerg 2009; Daugbjerg and Swinbank 2004). However, as things turned out, the Fischler reform was anything but simple. Had enlargement been a major driving force behind the CAP reform, reform would have preceded enlargement and would not have been undertaken subsequently. Nonetheless, the simplified approach applied in the new member states may have had some influence on the shape of the reform.

As originally tabled in 2002, the proposed Farm Income Payment would have *maintained* CAP expenditure on direct payments at prevailing levels in nominal terms. It was not designed to reduce the budget allocation; although progressively, through modulation, some expenditure would have been switched to second pillar. In October 2002, German chancellor Gerhard Schröder and French president Jacques Chirac agreed on a financing plan for the CAP through to 2013, which was then endorsed by the European Council. This placed an additional budget constraint on the CAP, and in the Fischler reform as finally adopted this translated into the new provisions for a Financial Discipline which will result in an automatic cut in direct payments if the planned expenditure on market support and direct payments threatens to exceed the annual ceiling (Swinbank and Daugbjerg 2006: 58). But, again, this does not reduce overall expenditure on the CAP. In 2003 the CAP did not face a severe budgetary crisis, as it had at the time of earlier reforms. Further, decoupling of the area and headage payments, which were linked to inputs used rather than production, did not in itself improve the ability to control the budget. In fact, the area and headage payments performed well in that respect because they set a ceiling on how much support could be paid. The introduction of the Financial Discipline reflects fears that in the future the budget ceiling might be breached as a consequence of extending the CAP to the new member states, but it could equally have been applied to area and headage payments.

The public's concern over the development of the CAP was clearly reflected in the Commission's proposal. For instance, it said: 'There are growing public concerns about both the way in which food is produced and the way in which agriculture is supported...However, policy instruments available to support food safety and quality within the common agricultural policy remain limited. Incentives and signals sent to farmers have to be in line with the objectives of safety and quality, as they have to be in line with environmental and animal health and welfare requirements' (Commission 2002: 6–7). On environmental policy objectives, the Commission stated that 'support still provided through prices and product-specific payments may discourage farmers from more environmentally friendly production methods' (p. 8). With respect to animal health and welfare, it claimed that 'many citizens rightly remain concerned that more can be done to ensure coherence with animal health and welfare objectives...The further promotion of good animal husbandry must therefore ensure that services provided by farmers beyond good farming practice are adequately remunerated' (p. 9). These statements clearly indicate that Fischler perceived a European public concern for the sustainability of European agriculture; however, these concerns were not new. Environmental issues entered the discussions in the mid 1980s, with the Commission acknowledging that intensive farming had caused environmental damage and pollution, and concerns for food safety, environmental and animal welfare were issues discussed in the Agenda 2000 reform process.

Undoubtedly, the wish to move towards more sustainable agricultural production played a role, but it was not a major driving force behind the reform. Cross-compliance, which requires farmers to comply with environmental, animal health, and welfare and food safety regulations, was introduced in the Agenda 2000 CAP reform on an optional basis for member states. Had these concerns been the major driving forces for reform, cross-compliance could have been made compulsory for the existing area and headage payments. It did not require a decoupling of support. Similarly, the risk of land abandonment in marginal areas, and its implications for rural life, could have been avoided by limiting the reform to the addition of mandatory cross-compliance to the existing area and headage payments. By linking European public concern for more sustainable farming practices with the EU's position in the WTO talks on agricultural trade, Fischler developed a forceful argument for decoupling. Greater cross-compliance alone would have achieved the EU's internal, but not its international, objectives.

Right from his inauguration as Farm Commissioner, Fischler had voiced a strong preference for moving the support system of the CAP more in the direction of rural development. In the Agenda 2000 CAP reform,

Fischler succeeded in establishing rural development as the second pillar of the CAP. However, the real change was modest. Basically, the second pillar brought together a number of earlier policy schemes, but the funds assigned to the pillar remained modest. The lion's share of the agricultural budget remained within the first pillar. Lowe et al. (2002: 4) conclude that the 'Agenda 2000 outcome was... deeply compromised... there was no "reform dividend" at the EU level (i.e. a freeing up of funds from production subsidies to be available to promote the integrated rural development agenda)'. In Fischler's 2002 reform proposal, rural development was given increased importance. However, in the final reform decision, the shift of funds from first pillar to second pillar was limited. Nonetheless, the introduction of cross-compliance and the modest switch of funds from the first to the second pillar did help to legitimize the reform to the European public. The push to develop rural development could hardly be said to be a major driving force of reform.

Since these alternative explanations of reform are not particularly forceful, we conclude that WTO concerns remain the most important motivation of the CAP reform in 2003. What the other factors did was legitimize reform within the EU and influence the shape of the reform when not in conflict with WTO concerns.

Conclusion

The ideational shift in the WTO farm trade regime, brought about by the URAA, has influenced EU agricultural policy institutions. A process of institutional layering in which the core has been preserved while new concerns have been added has taken place. In addition to the traditional concerns in EU agricultural policy making, such as farm incomes and maintenance of family farming, the WTO has increasingly been accepted as a constraint within which the CAP evolves. This institutional layering has resulted in gradual change of the CAP in which the underlying paradigm, the state-assisted paradigm, has been sustained though it has been rephrased by introducing the concept of multifunctionality. There has been a gradual change of policy instruments aimed at making the CAP more WTO compatible by applying less trade-distorting support measures.

Despite the reformist rhetoric of some member states (e.g. the United Kingdom's *Vision for the Common Agricultural Policy*: Defra and HM Treasury 2005), and the quite substantial changes in the CAP brought about by the MacSharry and Fischler reforms, the conclusion that the CAP still rests upon the state-assisted paradigm implies that it exists uneasily within a WTO framework that is far more oriented to the market-liberal paradigm. This suggests that the WTO continues to impose powerful constraints on the design and implementation of the CAP (Swinbank and Daugbjerg 2006; Daugbjerg and Swinbank 2008*a*); and that the CAP will likely remain a focus of discontent between the EU and its trade partners.

Chapter 7

Setting the Limits: CAP Reform and WTO Farm Trade Rules

In Chapter 6 we showed that the Common Agricultural Policy (CAP) is changing as a result of the WTO agenda; but it still remains an important constraint to the global liberalization of farm trade. In this chapter we show how the CAP sets limits for WTO agreements, whilst re-emphasizing that the CAP is not a static policy complex. Instead it is dynamic, and thus it continuously moves the boundaries for a feasible set of WTO agreements on farm trade.

In particular two conditions influence the EU's bargaining position. As pointed out in Chapter 1, the EU's agricultural sector has comparatively limited competitiveness, meaning that European famers have been dependent on import protection and agricultural subsidies. Conventional economic analysis suggests that, despite considerable agricultural adjustment costs, there would be valuable economic welfare benefits for the EU from CAP reform. European consumers and taxpayers would reap the benefits of trade liberalization whilst Europe's farmers and landowners, agriculture's ancillary industries, and possibly the environment, would bear the brunt of the adjustment costs.

During the trade talks the EU was under strong pressure from important trading partners to change its farm policies. In the Uruguay Round (UR) the agriculture negotiations were organized around three sets of disciplines, or 'pillars'—market access, domestic support, and export competition—and this continued into the Doha Round. As a high-cost exporter to world markets, the EU made extensive use of all three.

An important reason why EU farmers were able to maintain high levels of protection and support is the EU's institutionally constrained ability to agree to liberalize agricultural trade. At any particular moment the existing CAP, to a very large extent, defined the mandate that the EU's Member States were willing to give its negotiators (the European Commission); but with each successive reform of the CAP the EU's room for manoeuvre was enlarged. Although the Treaty empowered the Council of Ministers to reach decisions on the CAP by qualified majority vote, the norm of consensual decision making is very strong. This is not to say that decisions are always reached by unanimity, but simply that considerable effort is made to get all Member States 'on board' before a decision is made, and thereby avoid a formal vote.

As noted in Chapter 2, the consensual norm means that the preferences of the least reform-minded Member States tend to dominate when formulating the EU's negotiating position: it tends to give them veto powers. To ensure that the Commission, which negotiates on behalf of the Member States, does not concede more concessions than is acceptable to the *status quo*-minded states, the Commission will be granted restricted competence in trade negotiations, causing the EU to adopt a conservative position. There is not much leeway for the Commission negotiators to exceed the mandate given. They have occasionally done so, but this is a risky strategy because it can provoke fierce criticism within the EU, in particular from France, and could weaken the authority of the College of Commissioners. In other words, the EU has a small win-set which it is able to convert into bargaining power in international negotiations, making the EU a tough bargainer. An EU negotiator can forcefully claim that concessions demanded by other WTO Members stand a limited chance of being ratified by the Council of Ministers. Thus, we suggest as a hypothesis, that the EU's internal voting rules and decision-making norms enable the EU to obtain considerable bargaining power, setting limits for GATT/WTO farm trade agreements. This hypothesis would be supported if it could be demonstrated that the lack of CAP reform stalemates GATT/WTO negotiations on agriculture, and that reform of the CAP facilitates progress.

Accordingly in this chapter we account for developments in the agriculture negotiations in the UR, the failure to launch a Millennium Round, and the stalled Doha Round; and we show how lack of CAP reform led to stalemate. We also discuss the extent to which, and how, CAP reforms facilitated progress. The CAP *has* changed, allowing the EU's conservative stance to be relaxed; and the position of the least reform-minded Member States in the late 2000s is quite different from that of the late 1980s and early 1990s.

From Punta del Este to Heysel

The state-assisted agriculture paradigm institutionalized in GATT 1947 was clearly challenged at an early stage in the UR when the United States submitted its *Proposal for Negotiations on Agriculture* in July 1987 (GATT 1987*a*). Dubbed by some 'zero-2000', the proposal was radical. The zero-2000 proposal asked for a complete change in the rules governing trade in agricultural products. The main elements of the proposal were: 'A complete phase-out over 10 years of all agricultural subsidies which directly or indirectly affect trade . . . Freeze and phase-out over 10 years of the quantities exported with the aid of export subsidies . . . A phase-out of import barriers over 10 years' (GATT 1987*a*). The zero-2000 proposal did allow for the use of subsidies, but only those that would not distort trade (later to be known as green box subsidies). Nevertheless, the zero-2000 proposal was a clear expression of agricultural normalism and with it a desire to move domestic agricultural policies from the state-assisted paradigm to the market-liberal paradigm. The adoption of zero-2000 would imply that world market shares would be determined by comparative advantage rather than agricultural subsidies.

This was clearly emphasized when US Trade Representative (USTR) Yeutter diagnosed the problems of farm support. As he argued: 'We are on a subsidy treadmill . . . The false price signals which result encourage surplus, prices fall, and we have to subsidize more to make up for low prices. It's a vicious cycle. There is a growing recognition that the problem is excessive government support of agriculture' (Yeutter 1988: 267). The US solution to these problems was to liberalize agricultural trade. As Yeutter (1988: 266) stated: 'We . . . expect all countries, not just the United States, to benefit from this approach. All will benefit from restoration of order. Some producers in each country adjust to employment that offers greater rewards than their present production. Others will profit from a more competitive environment in which prices are no longer driven down by government programs. Consumers will benefit. Taxpayers will benefit.' Thus, the United States viewed government support, and not the market, as the root cause of the imbalance in farm trade.

While the United States chose an offensive strategy right from the launch of the negotiations, the EU adopted a reactive strategy of damage control: 'The Community chose to react to proposals for reform tabled by others, most notably the United States and the Cairns Group of agricultural exporting countries' (Ingersent et al. 1994: 61). A major priority of the EU in the Round was to defend the CAP and its support mechanisms.

145

During the first phase of the Round, the EU considered the US zero-2000 proposal to be unrealistic and therefore did not take it seriously. Clearly, the EU hoped that due to major disagreements among the parties, agricultural trade would eventually be taken out of the round or play a minor role. However, this was a misjudgement. The United States and the Cairns Group were committed to major reform in international agricultural trade rules.

According to Paemen, who was lead EU negotiator in the UR, the EU's October 1987 offer had 'no substance at all' (Paemen and Bensch 1995: 107). But this is perhaps a harsh judgement. Josling et al. (1996: 143) note that it was 'initially welcomed in Washington for the extent to which it broke ground with previous EC positions'. It was a guarded document that talked about the need for 'a significant, concerted reduction in support coupled with a readjustment of . . . external protection in order to achieve a reduction of the distortions which are the source of, or contribute to, the present world market disequilibria' (GATT 1987*b*: 19). It certainly did not advocate the removal of support. Indeed, in presenting the paper the EU's spokesperson somewhat more frankly said 'we believe a system in which agricultural activity would be left entirely to the play of world market forces, without any kind of support or aid, does not seem viable' (GATT 1987*c*: 2); and the press release from the General Affairs Council that had approved the Commission's mandate read in part: 'The Council noted that the Commission will ensure that throughout the negotiations . . . the basic principles and mechanisms of the CAP will be preserved' (Council 1987*a*: 7).[1] These statements of the United States and the EU demonstrated that the two major agricultural trading powers did not share the same basic ideas on the causes of the problems of farm trade and the solutions to them. The US position was based upon the idea of agricultural normalism, whereas the EU still adhered to agricultural exceptionalism. These opposing basic perceptions prevailed until the final stages of the Round and explain the difficulties of finding common ground between the United States and the EU on farm trade. What was proposed by the EU for the first stage of the negotiations was a managed-market approach, with for example the EU extolling those GATT members who had not signed up to the International Dairy Agreement, negotiated during the Tokyo Round, to now respect its export price disciplines (GATT 1987*b*: 3). Furthermore, in presenting the proposal the EU's spokesperson emphasized the importance of the need for a 'rebalancing of protection' (GATT 1987*c*: 2)—an oblique reference to the fact that the EU's border protection for cereals was significant, whilst that for 'cereal substitutes' (protein-rich oilseed cake, carbohydrates such as cassava, etc., which when blended together produced an animal feed that replaced highly-priced cereals in EU farmers' feed rations) was slight, and the EU wished to remedy this.

A mid-term ministerial meeting was held in Montreal in December 1988. Negotiators had made good progress in many of the other trade issues, but the basic impasse over agriculture remained as meaningful negotiations had not really begun. The United States was still insisting on its zero-2000 proposal, which called for 'an elimination' of all trade-distorting subsidies and import barriers. To underline its commitment to the proposal, 'the US demanded a prior commitment by all parties to the eventual elimination of support, before negotiations could begin on merely reducing it in the short term' (Ingersent et al. 1994: 64). Since such a commitment would go far beyond its win-set, the EU was strongly opposed. As Ingersent et al. (1994: 65) point out: 'the EC remained implacably opposed to the zero option on any timescale'.

From January 1989 there were new teams in place in both Brussels and Washington. President Reagan gave way to President Bush (senior), and Clayton K. Yeutter replaced Richard E. Lyng as Secretary of State for Agriculture. Yeutter's previous role—of USTR—was filled by Carla Hills (Paemen and Bensch 1995: 135). Jacques Delors was reappointed president of the European Commission, and a newcomer to the college of commissioners, Ray MacSharry, took over as farm commissioner. The previous incumbent in this post, Frans Andriessen, became trade commissioner. MacSharry and Yeutter led the agriculture negotiations.

One immediate task for MacSharry was to revive the agriculture negotiations following the failure in Montreal. Under the guidance of Arthur Dunkel, GATT's Director-General, and with a good deal of flexibility on the part of the United States, the mid-term review (which had been the business for Montreal) was signed off in Geneva in April 1989, and the UR was back on track (Paemen and Bensch 1995: 141, 145). The text on agriculture in the Geneva Accord talked of a long-term objective of establishing 'a fair and market-oriented agricultural trading system' and of 'substantial progressive reductions in agricultural support and protection' (GATT 1989a: 3). This wording allowed both parties to claim victory (Josling et al. 1996: 148).

However, fundamental disagreement between the United States and the EU remained and became evident when they submitted their 'comprehensive proposals' later in the year. Though the United States had agreed on 'substantial reduction' rather than 'elimination' in Geneva in April 1989, its comprehensive proposal, submitted in October 1989, reverted to the zero-2000 option (GATT 1989*b*). As Hillman (1994: 40) put it: 'The US zero-option remained intact . . . Ideological positions, once taken by great powers, die reluctantly.' On domestic support, the proposal distinguished between three categories. The most trade-distorting subsidies were those linked directly with production (e.g. price support and deficiency payment) and should be phased out over a 10-year period. The least trade-distorting subsidies were agricultural budgetary outlays not linked to production (e.g. government support for research, environmental subsidies, 'income support policies not linked to production or marketing', etc.). These would not be subject to reduction commitments. Agricultural support schemes falling between these two extreme categories, such as investment subsidies, would be subject to reduction and GATT disciplines (GATT 1989*b*: 8). Export subsidies should be phased out completely over five years, meaning that the agricultural provisions of Article XVI of GATT 1947, one of the cornerstones of agricultural exceptionalism in international agricultural trade, would have to go. It was only on import barriers that the comprehensive proposal approached the Geneva Accord, in conceding that import taxes would be eliminated or reduced to low levels over 10 years. However, the agricultural provisions of Article XI of the GATT 1947 were to be eliminated, meaning that this other safeguard of agricultural exceptionalism would be abolished (GATT 1989*b*: 2–3).

Meanwhile, in Brussels, events were not proceeding smoothly under MacSharry's watch. In February 1988 the European Council had agreed on a CAP 'reform' that would restrict the growth in budget expenditure on the CAP, and trigger automatic price cuts on some products if the increase in output exceeded specified limits. But in the course of the 1989/90 farm price review it became all too evident that farm ministers did not have the stomach to inflict the price cuts that they had been mandated to do by the over-hyped CAP 'reforms' of 1988 (Swinbank and Tanner 1996: 86–8). As Manegold (1989: 45) remarked: 'Thus, the much-touted CAP reform has perhaps ended before it really got to the core.' Nevertheless, the EU had to come up with a GATT offer; but its inability, or unwillingness, to change the CAP severely troubled the process of agreeing on an offer.

The EU submitted its 'Global Proposal' to the GATT Negotiating Group on Agriculture a few days before Christmas 1989. As the world market had improved since the launching of its initial proposal of 1987, it no longer demanded short-term market management. However, the proposal was firmly based upon the idea of agricultural exceptionalism:

Agricultural production has its own characteristics which explain the special characteristics of current agricultural policies and the specific rules which currently apply to this sector in the framework of GATT.

The demand for agricultural products has a weak price elasticity, which explains the very large price variations and which leads to the imbalances which appear between supply and demand.

Production does not develop steadily, because it is influenced by climatic variations and because it responds excessively to price variations.

Without public intervention on prices, agricultural production adjusts abruptly in a succession of cyclical crises. This is why existing agricultural policies in most industrialized countries pursue, with very different mechanisms, the same objectives: to guarantee and stabilize the prices received by producers and to ensure security of supply at reasonable prices for consumers. These policies respond to the diversity of agricultural situations and also take into account social concerns.

(GATT 1989c: 1–2)

It explicitly rejected agricultural normalism in stating: 'Basing protection exclusively on customs tariffs and envisaging, after a transition period, the reduction of these tariffs to zero or very low levels would lead to trade in agricultural products on a totally free and chaotic basis. The Community remains convinced that such arrangements are not viable' (GATT, 1989c: 6). Perhaps reflecting the budgetary burden of the CAP, the proposal did concede that the 'the aim of the negotiation' was 'to progressively reduce support to the extent necessary to re-establish balanced markets and a more market-oriented agricultural trading system' (GATT 1989c: 2), but it did not quantify the reductions. Furthermore, the EU was only prepared to commit itself to making reductions in *domestic* support, arguing that when domestic support was reduced, border protection and export subsidization would automatically be reduced as well. In terms of border protection, the EU was 'prepared to consider including elements of tariffication ... given that the problem of rebalancing can be solved in the context of tariffication' (GATT 1989c: 6). For the EU 'it was essential to maintain a mechanism which would permit markets and prices to be regulated, in order to avoid cyclic crises ... Therefore no proposal which envisaged the elimination of the Community's system would be accepted; total tariffication or total decoupling were thus excluded' (GATT 1990a: paragraph 13). This position constrained the EU's negotiators, ensuring they were unable to offer concessions to the United States and thus reach a compromise. Substantial CAP reform was needed to allow EU negotiators more flexibility. The GATT

Secretariat's report of the meeting went on to say: 'Several participants expressed agreement with the EEC's approach, endorsing for example its acknowledgement of the specific characteristics of agriculture. One stated that reconciling these with GATT rules was a fundamental question for the negotiation. The Community's attention to non-commercial concerns in agricultural policy was also welcomed, though some participants would have put more specific emphasis on these' (GATT 1990*a*: paragraph 15). Clearly agricultural exceptionalism still appealed to some of GATT's Contracting Parties.

As late as July 1990, less than five months before the UR was scheduled to be concluded, EU Farm Commissioner MacSharry showed little (public) faith in trade liberalization in a spirited defence of the CAP, saying: 'there can be no question of setting aside the achievements of the CAP or to put them at risk in the pursuit of dubious textbook economic theories of comparative advantage and international specialisation...The CAP exists because of the importance given to agriculture and to the rural society of Europe' (*Agra Europe*, 20 July 1990: P/3); but, as we shall see below, MacSharry and his colleagues were already planning for a CAP reform. Furthermore, only a couple of weeks later, at Dromoland Castle in Ireland, whilst hosting an informal meeting of farm ministers from Australia, Canada, Japan, and the United States, MacSharry surprised his guests, EU farm ministers ('who had received no prior notice of MacSharry's plans') and his fellow commissioners ('No such plan had been discussed by the Commission executive') by proposing to reduce 'global subsidies to agriculture by 30% over a ten-year period between 1986 and 1996' (*Agra Europe*, 3 August 1990: E/1).

Another crucial event of 1989/90 was the report of the oilseeds panel. Prompted by the American Soybean Association, in 1988 the United States had challenged the EU's oilseeds regime, and a panel had been established (Paarlberg 1997: 438). First the United States claimed that, in granting a subsidy to oilseed crushers when they processed EU-grown, but not imported, oilseeds, the EU had infringed the national treatment provisions of GATT Article III (GATT 1989*d*: paragraph 36). Second, by encouraging the production of oilseeds in the EU, the measure had the effect of nullifying or impairing the tariff bindings entered into in the Dillon Round (paragraph 53). The panel, which reported on 30 November 1989, concluded that the national treatment provisions of Article III had been violated, and the EU was requested to change its policies. The panel also found 'that benefits accruing to the United States...in respect of the zero tariff bindings for oilseeds...were impaired as a result of the introduction of production subsidy schemes which operate to protect Community producers of oilseeds completely from the movement of prices of imports and thereby prevent the tariff concessions from having any impact on the competitive relationship between domestic and imported oilseed' (paragraph 156). It suggested the EU 'consider ways and means to eliminate the impairment of its tariff concessions for oilseeds', but noted that a modification of the EU's support regime, to make it compatible with Article III, 'could also eliminate the impairment of the tariff concessions' (paragraphs 156 and 157). The panel's report was adopted by GATT's Contracting Parties on 25 January 1990 (GATT 1991*a*: paragraph 7).

The Commission records that the EU 'declared its intention to conform with the recommendations and to make appropriate changes to its legislation when implementing the results of the Uruguay Round' (Commission of the European Communities 1992*b*: 122). This is an oblique reference to its position on 'rebalancing': *increasing* its tariffs on oilseeds in exchange for a reduction of border protection on cereals, which was bitterly opposed by the United States and others (Swinbank and Tanner 1996: 131–2). However, the UR was not concluded in December 1990 in Brussels, and the EU recognizing 'that it could not postpone indefinitely its obligation to modify its oilseeds system' changed the system of support so that an area payment was paid, replacing the processing subsidy on EU-grown oilseeds that had flouted the principle of national treatment (Commission 1992*b*: 122, 60). This was a similar area payment scheme to the one then under consideration for cereals, and later adopted in May 1992, as the key component of the MacSharry reforms (Swinbank and Tanner 1996: 90).

The Heysel breakdown

The UR was scheduled for conclusion at a Ministerial meeting to be held at the Heysel conference centre in Brussels, in December 1990. In what Josling et al. (1996: 153) call 'a milestone in the Round, and indeed in agricultural trade relations in general', Aart de Zeeuw, the Chairman of the Agricultural Negotiating Group, had tabled a draft *Framework Agreement* in July (GATT 1990*b*). Although it lacked numbers, it was a clear precursor of the eventual Uruguay Round Agreement on Agriculture (URAA) in that it set out disciplines on internal support, border protection and export competition. It was time to get serious. The text requested that, by 1 October 1990, detailed tables setting out existing levels of internal support, border protection, and export subsidies, should be made available, and declared that 'Participants will negotiate the amount and duration of the substantial and progressive reductions in support and protection as soon as the country lists are tabled...' (GATT 1990b: 7).

On October 15, the United States submitted its 'final' proposal, which indicated that the United States had now moved from the zero-2000 option, but only to a limited extent. It demanded that budget outlays for export subsidies and the quantities of subsidized exports be reduced by 90 per cent over 10 years (six years for processed products). On market access, the proposal stated that non-tariff barriers should be converted into bound tariffs and reduced by 75 per cent over 10 years. Further, it demanded minimum access commitments of 3 per cent of domestic consumption. On domestic support directly linked to production, the United States demanded a 75 per cent reduction over 10 years (as published in *International Trade Reporter*, 17 October 1990: 1595–9.[2] See also Josling et al. 1996: 154).

The EU's text was much delayed. It was only after a series of stormy meetings in first the Commission, and then the Council, that on 7 November 1990, the EU was able to table its offer (Swinbank and Tanner 1996: 76–8; Daugbjerg 1998: 117–20). It comprised: (a) a 30 per cent reduction in an Aggregate Measure of Support, as first suggested by Mac-Sharry before the summer recess, for certain products, from a 1986 base (the reader will recall that the United States was asking for 75 per cent)[3], (b) a limited form of tariffication *with* rebalancing (the United States wanted to cut tariffs by 75 per cent, and was opposed to rebalancing), and (c) 'a concomitant adjustment of export restitutions' (the United States wanted a 90 per cent reduction) (Commission 1990).

Despite these limited offers to reduce support, it is noteworthy that in this document the EU had given up its ideational struggle with the United States and the Cairns Group. This is evident when the document is compared to its 'Global Proposal' of December 1989 (GATT 1989c). In that the EU had made very clear ideational statements on the special characteristics of agricultural production, as we showed earlier in this chapter. The GATT offer of November 1990 contained no such ideational statements, but was entirely devoted to operational aspects. The main purpose of the offer seemed to be one of damage limitation in maintaining the incomes of European farmers even if this required a shift in support mechanisms.

Negotiators had not been able to agree on a framework agreement before their ministers met at the Brussels Ministerial. This made the exercise extremely difficult. After little progress over the first few days, the Swedish Minister of Agriculture Mats Hellström, who chaired the agricultural negotiating group at ministerial level, asked all delegations to respond to six questions. The Commission indicated that it was willing to give new concessions. On the basis of these responses, Hellström prepared a compromise non-paper and circulated it in the afternoon of 6 December. It suggested a 30 per cent reduction of internal support, border protection, and export subsidies. At first glance this seemed to coincide with the EU's offer. However, the non-paper suggested that reductions would be based on 1990 support levels. The EU had suggested 1986 as base year, a year when support levels were high as a result of low world market prices. In 1990, prices in the world market had improved and consequently support was lower. Thus, had 1990 been decided as the base year, a 30 per cent cut would have resulted in deeper cuts than suggested in the EU proposal.[4] The United States, as well as the Cairns Group and other delegations, supported the Hellström non-paper as the basis for the negotiations. In doing so, the United States was making a major concession because the compromise in the non-paper was quite distant from its original zero-2000 option, and its October 1990 almost-zero-2000 proposal. EU Farm Commissioner MacSharry 'submitted a somewhat cautious but broadly positive response' to the compromise proposal, and 'for a few hours it appeared there was a breakthrough' (Josling et al. 1996: 155). However, he had to retreat when Ireland and France claimed that he had exceeded his negotiating mandate. Once it became apparent that the ministerial group on agriculture could make no further progress 'all the Latin American negotiators stood up as one man and walked out of the night sessions in which they had been working . . . the Brussels Conference was over' (Paemen and Bensch 1995: 186; see also Croome 1999: 240). The breakdown starkly demonstrated that the EU's unwillingness to undertake substantial reform of the CAP had blocked the Round; and farm ministers in the EU eventually realized that they had to embark on reform to restart the negotiations.

From Heysel, through Blair House, to Marrakesh

A small group of Commission officials had been preparing for a CAP reform for some time. Kay (1998: 99) dates this from early 1989 when Commission president Jacques Delors, concerned that the 1988 reforms 'would be only a medium-term measure to control the rate of increase of the CAP's budget costs', became convinced of the need for further CAP reform, and that MacSharry would be 'a suitable proponent of such reforms'. Ross (1995: 110–11) suggests the process began 'in early 1990' and gives Delors a more central role in the deliberations than does Kay (who emphasizes more MacSharry's role) and suggests that the ongoing trade tensions of the UR and the oilseeds dispute were important motivating factors. To him, the failure of the Heysel meeting was 'a disguised blessing' for it gave 'Delors and his team...precious time to get CAP reform through the Commission and then win Council approval' (p. 112). The plans went public in February 1991, and the internal debate on the reform proposal began.

Following the aborted Heysel Ministerial, the Secretary General of GATT, Arthur Dunkel, called an emergency meeting in Geneva at which the Contracting Parties agreed to continue negotiations (Ingersent et al. 1994: 78). However, progress was limited until late 1991, when the United States at an EU–United States summit on November 9 relaxed its demands on subsidy and protection reductions. In December 1991, Dunkel presented a draft for an Agreement on Agriculture with the aim of concluding the Round. It was based on the de Zeeuw July 1990 draft, but was more concrete, and it went beyond Hellström's non-paper. It suggested tariffication of non-tariff barriers and a 36 per cent reduction on the basis of the 1986–8 average, a 36 per cent cut in export subsidy outlays, and a 24 per cent reduction in the volume of subsidized export on the basis of the 1986–90 average. Domestic support was to be reduced by 20 per cent on the basis of the 1986–8 average (GATT 1991*b*). While the United States, the Cairns Group, and most of the other GATT members accepted the Dunkel draft, the EU had severe reservations. The Dunkel draft did not include 'rebalancing' as the EU wished, it suggested larger cuts than the EU was willing to accept, it did not give full credit for supply management in reduction commitments, it put limits on subsidized export volumes, and it implicitly questioned whether the area and headage payment under discussion in the MacSharry reform process could be considered 'green' (i.e. minimally trade distorting) and thus exempt from reduction commitments (Ingersent et al. 1994: 80–1; Josling et al. 1996: 158).

In the meanwhile, CAP reform was being negotiated in Brussels. The Dunkel draft had stated that by 1 March 1992, countries should submit their detailed offers. The EU, in the midst of tough negotiations on CAP reform, failed to do so.

With the MacSharry reform negotiations continuing, Cunha (2007: 158) writes:

One of the main concerns of some ministers, with Ignaz Kiechle *[the German Farm Minister]* in the lead, was the need to guarantee that the new compensatory payments should be included in the *green box*, in order to ensure that the agricultural direct aids would not be reduced under the GATT rules. At this time, in response to the Dunkel Working Document of December 1991, the EC had raised in the Uruguay Round negotiations the claim that a *blue box* should be aimed at covering adjustment subsidies during a certain transition period. During March and April, intense trade negotiations took place between EU and USA officials. By that time it was reported that a deal had been closed between both parties on establishing a *blue box* to accommodate the EU compensatory payments... The positive evolution of the *blue box* issue was a determinant moving some ministers into the final negotiation phase. The French minister had finally accepted that a GATT agreement was inevitable and the best way to reduce its impact on farm incomes and preserve the CAP in the future was negotiating its reform.

Having agreed upon the MacSharry reform in May 1992 and having agreed with the United States to shelter the livestock premiums and the newly introduced area payments in the blue box, the EU was better prepared for the bilateral negotiations between the EU and the United States that resulted in the Blair House accord, agreed between the US Secretary of Agriculture and the EU Farm Commissioner in November 1992. This clarified the Dunkel draft, and most importantly it added new elements to it. It introduced the blue box as a separate category for domestic support. The Peace Clause[5] was inserted to preclude dispute settlement actions against agricultural support schemes that complied with the agreement (see the Commission text of the Blair House accord in *Agra Europe*, 27 November 1992, no.1519, E/1–4).

The oilseed dispute between the EU and the United States also played its role in the Blair House accord. The view of the United States was that, with the new support system agreed in October 1991, the EU had still not met its GATT obligations (GATT 1991*a*: paragraphs 11 and 16). Thus the original panel was reconvened, and it reported in March 1992 (GATT 1992). The panel concluded that the 'benefits accruing to the United States... in respect of the zero tariff bindings for oilseeds... continue to be impaired by the production subsidy scheme' (GATT 1992: paragraph 90), although the scheme was no longer GATT-illegal in flouting the national treatment provisions. Paemen and Bensch (1995: 209) comment that it would have been 'suicidal to ignore its recommendations', although the EU did question the legal basis of the panel ruling. Accordingly, on 30 April 1992, whilst formally opposing adoption of the report, the EU offered to renegotiate its oilseeds tariff bindings. This was accepted by the GATT Council in June (GATT 1992: footnote 1). But the United States was not willing to countenance rebalancing, and in the absence of a negotiated agreement the EU faced trade sanctions. This is what brought the EU to the Blair House meeting in November 1992, and the beginning of the long-drawn-out final phase of the UR negotiations on agriculture.

France opposed the Blair House accord and forced the EU and the United States to enter a new round of bilateral negotiations. In early December 1993 the two parties reached a final agreement (sometimes known as Blair House II), which allowed both to subsidize exports of larger quantities than originally provided for in the Dunkel text (see Swinbank and Tanner 1996: Chapters 6–7 for an account of the EU domestic and international negotiation process). Further, the final agreement convinced reluctant EU farm ministers (particularly the French) that the GATT deal posed no immediate threat to EU farm policy (Swinbank and Tanner 1996: 104–11). Thus Blair House II paved the way for agreement of the URAA later in December 1993, when the other GATT signatories accepted the EU–United States deal as a *fait accompli* as part of the Single Undertaking. It was signed in Marrakesh, Morocco, in April 1994.

The agricultural negotiations of the UR clearly demonstrated that there could be no breakthrough until the EU had decided to embark on CAP reform and that a deal between the EU and the United States could not be reached until after the MacSharry reform was decided in May 1992.

From Marrakesh to Doha: defending the special status of EU agriculture

With the implementation of the Uruguay Round Accords from January 1995, the EU settled into the life of the new organization. The Commission claimed that it participated 'actively' in the work of the new Agriculture and SPS (Sanitary and Phytosanitary) Committees, where 'it was closely monitoring the implementation by its GATT partners of their Uruguay Round commitments' (European Commission 1996: 153). Unfortunately it soon found itself embroiled in the banana and beef hormone disputes, as we saw in Chapter 5, which tarnished its reputation. Nonetheless, the Commission said that the EU had 'played a decisive role in the successful conclusion of the Uruguay Round and the establishment of the World Trade Organization (WTO)'; and that the 'EU, the biggest trader on the world stage, has a strong interest in consolidating the new WTO structures and in *promoting further international trade liberalisation* beyond that which is already programmed' (Commission 1997: 4, 43, emphasis in original).

However, it was not evident that this professed interest in further trade liberalization extended to agriculture. When, in 1998 for example, it toyed with the idea of a *New Transatlantic Marketplace*, linking the EU and the United States, it made abundantly clear that this would exclude agriculture (Hindley 1999: 52). Although the EU emerged as an early advocate of a new multilateral round of trade negotiations (that it promoted as the Millennium Round), this was because it was reluctant to agree to an *agricultural* round, or to an early start to new reductions in agricultural protection. It will be recalled that Article 20 of the URAA committed the WTO Membership to begin a new round of negotiations for trade liberalization in agriculture before the end of 1999. The American president, Bill Clinton, told the WTO Ministerial meeting in Geneva in 1998 that 'Starting next year, we should aggressively begin negotiations to reduce tariffs, subsidies, and other distortions that restrict productivity in agriculture. . . . And I propose that even before negotiations near conclusion, WTO Members should pledge to continue making annual tariff and subsidy reductions—ensuring that there is no pause in reform' (Clinton 1998). As expected, Europe's response was negative. As Sir Leon Brittan, the EU Commissioner in charge of trade negotiations, was later to explain to the United Kingdom's premier farming audience, 'negotiations have a much better chance of success if there are possibilities to achieve trade-offs between differing sectors. It is not in our interest for the focus to be exclusively on agriculture' (Brittan 1999). In the end the Americans too came to the view that a comprehensive round, rather than one with a narrow focus, should be launched; and plans were hatched to do so at the WTO Ministerial convened for November 1999 in Seattle.

Internationally the pressure for further CAP reform had been growing. *Agra Europe*'s report on the 1998 Ministerial in Geneva quoted various spokespersons criticizing aspects of the CAP, including a specific demand from Uruguay's Trade Minister for abolition of the blue box (*Agra Europe*, 22 May 1998: EP/5). The EU was defensive, but even so it was said that the CAP reform proposed in Agenda 2000 was motivated in part by the need to 'improve the competitiveness' of EU agriculture, and to 'help prepare the [EU] for the next WTO Round' (Commission 1997: 31), as we noted in Chapter 6. However, as we shall see, the reform provided little leeway for giving the concessions necessary to reach agreement in the forthcoming WTO negotiations on agricultural trade.

The URAA's reference to *non-trade concerns* potentially left the EU, and others, some leeway to protect their agricultural sectors in future trade rounds, despite the prevalence of agricultural normalism in the WTO agreements, and thus they set about articulating their non-trade concerns. The WTO Ministerial meeting in Singapore, in November 1996, on the invitation of the Committee on Agriculture, had established a process of analysis and information exchange (AIE) that became an informal part of the Committee's work (WTO 1999*a*: Annex III). At the eighth AIE meeting, in September 1998, substantive discussions took place on non-trade concerns, including debate on a paper from Norway on 'Non-Trade Concerns in a Multifunctional Agriculture'; and the EU tabled a paper on 'The Multifunctional Character of Agriculture' for later discussion (WTO 1999*a*: 43).[6] The same meeting also discussed domestic support, with the EU defending the blue box on the grounds that it 'was a policy instrument necessary to facilitate the adjustment towards less trade-distorting support' (WTO 1999*a*: 45).

The EU's institutions had been late in adopting the word 'multifunctional', and even later in including 'multifunctionality' into their rhetoric; but in November 1997, during the Agenda 2000 discussions, the EU's Council of Agriculture Ministers had declared:

> In order to keep alive the fabric of the countryside throughout Europe, multifunctional agriculture has to be spread throughout Europe, including regions facing particular difficulties. Care will have to be taken in particular to provide proper compensation for natural constraints and disadvantages and fairly reflect the contribution made by farmers in land care, maintenance of the countryside and conservation of natural resources. (Council of the European Union 1997: 6)

In March 1998 in its formal Agenda 2000 proposals for CAP reform, as noted in Chapter 6, the European Commission took up more or less the same words in commenting that 'care will . . . need to be taken to provide proper compensation for natural constraints and disadvantages' (Commission 1998*a*: Section 3). Given that comparative cost structures, determined in part by geographic and climatic differences, are major determinants of trade, the EU's wording was problematic: it did look as if the EU wished to isolate and protect its farm sector from competitive producers elsewhere. This view was reinforced by the claim that there was a *European Model of Agriculture* that differentiated Europe from other parts of the world:

> The fundamental difference between the European model and that of our major competitors lies in the multifunctional nature of Europe's agriculture and the part it plays in the economy and the environment, in society and in preserving the landscape, whence the need to maintain farming throughout Europe and to safeguard farmers' incomes (Commission 1998*b*: 8).

This language was still prevalent in the preparations for the Seattle Ministerial. The opening paragraph of the Agriculture Council's Press Release following its meeting in September 1999, which defined the Commission's mandate for the forthcoming negotiations, read:

> The Agriculture Council stresses that safeguarding the future of the European model of agriculture, as an economic sector and as a basis for sustainable development, is of fundamental importance because of the multifunctional nature of Europe's agriculture and the part agriculture plays in the economy, the environment and landscape as well as for society. Thus the contribution of agriculture remains vital to the European economy and society (Council of the European Union 1999).

The idea that farming activities impact on the environment, and society, in a number of ways, with both positive and negative effects that are not reflected in market transactions, is long-standing. After all, the landscape in many parts of the *Old World* has been shaped by many generations of farm families. Thus the notion of multifunctionality was not new, but the word was; and the EU's trading partners in the *New World* were suspicious that, if used in an abstract or blanket fashion, talk of multifunctionality could serve as a smokescreen to deflect attention from the EU's real intent, which was, they believed, protectionist (Swinbank 2002). Anderson (2000: 491), together with other critics, suggests that conventional instruments to address market failures would be more efficient, and less trade distorting, than blanket support for agriculture. He asserts that 'A key question at stake is: do they require exceptional treatment or are the WTO provisions sufficient to cater for them, for example via the URAA's "green box"? The short answer...appears to be that the WTO provisions are adequate...'

After Seattle

The Seattle Ministerial failed to launch a new trade round, and consequently in March 2000, in Geneva, negotiations on agriculture, as mandated by Article 20 of the URAA, began (Swinbank 2005a: 89–90). Although some WTO members, particularly from the Cairns Group, argued that this was a 'stand-alone' negotiation that could be undertaken and concluded as such, others (including the EU) still wanted to see it wrapped into a wider round (WTO 2000c).

Although it had been claimed that the purpose of the Agenda 2000 CAP reform, agreed in March 1999, had been to pave the way for EU enlargement, and to meet the challenges of the next WTO trade round, it fulfilled neither of these original purposes. As Swinbank (1999b: 404) had concluded: 'Agenda 2000 . . . was motivated more by the need to tackle the current problems faced by the CAP (beef "mountains", the expiry of the legislation providing for milk quotas in 2000, and the prospects of massive set-aside if the GATT export constraints on wheat were to be met) than by challenges of enlargement or the Millennium Round' (see also Ackrill 2000). As a 'deepening' of the MacSharry reform, with further reductions in support prices for cereals and beef, the reform did not provide much leeway for the EU on domestic support, because the enhanced area and headage payments continued to be categorized in the contested blue box. Therefore, the EU would have to defend the blue box in the forthcoming negotiations. There had been no reform of the sugar regime, and the dairy reforms had been postponed so that they would only apply from 2005. The failure to tackle these key sectors meant the EU had little scope to offer significant liberalization of border protection, or to accept further constraints on export subsidies, in the agriculture negotiations.

In that initial *pre-negotiation* in Geneva, which in effect continued the AIE programme that had been launched in Singapore in 1996, and prior to the launch of the Doha Round in November 2001, the EU tabled five papers outlining its negotiating stance: in June 2000 on: the blue box and other domestic support policies; food quality and the improvement of market access; and animal welfare, a long-standing EU concern (Swinbank 2006a); and in September 2000 on export subsidies.[7] These were followed, in December 2000, with its 'Comprehensive Negotiating Proposal' (WTO 2000b). In its Comprehensive Proposal, on market access the EU suggested: a continuation of the UR process of tariff reductions and tariff rate quotas (TRQ) expansions, but without specifying the magnitude of the change; the need to protect Geographical Indications of Origin; and a prolongation of the Special Safeguard provisions on agriculture (WTO 2000*b*: paragraphs 1–4). On export subsidies it stressed the need to discipline export credits and the abuse of food aid, and then said: 'On the condition that all forms of export subsidisation are treated on an equal footing, the EC stand ready to negotiate further reductions in export subsidies' (paragraph 9). On domestic support it said it was willing to negotiate further reductions, provided the concept of the blue and green boxes was retained (paragraph 10). However, in a move that would impact specifically on the United States, the EU also proposed a reduction in the *de minimis* allowance, and 'specific disciplines' on 'variable' amber box supports, which acted to 'boost export performance' (paragraphs 11 and 14).

Under the heading 'Non-trade concerns' it stressed the need to recognize the 'multifunctional role of agriculture', the need to protect the environment and 'sustain the viability of rural areas', food safety, and the need to clarify WTO rules over the precautionary principle, the need to examine WTO rules on labelling to allow consumer concerns to be addressed, and the need for an examination of various means to protect animal welfare (paragraphs 15–19). In addition it made various suggestions about Special and Differential Treatment for Developing Countries; and it closed (paragraph 25) with a suggestion that the Peace Clause needed to be renewed.

A group of countries (often dubbed 'The Friends of Multifunctionality') met in Norway in July 2000 to discuss non-trade concerns, and again in Mauritius in May 2001 (WTO 2000*a*; European Commission 2001). However, following the initial hostile reaction in the WTO, the EU's enthusiasm for defending the concept in Geneva had waned, and at neither meeting did it promote the word 'multifunctionality'. At the first, in a paper entitled 'Agriculture's contribution to environmentally and culturally related non-trade concerns', which was in effect a defence of multifunctionality, it did not use the word (or even 'multifunctional'), and in its 2001 paper the word 'multifunctional' appeared only once, in a paragraph about Japan. Otherwise 'multifunctionality' was absent. Even the Norwegian paper made only one reference to multifunctional agriculture (Norway 2001: 1). Nonetheless, multifunctionality had led to a work programme in the OECD (e.g. OECD 2003), academics continued to discuss the concept at conferences and in journal articles (e.g. Harvey 2003) and, as noted in Chapter 6, it did form part of the discourse that justified the Fischler reforms to a domestic audience. Indeed, for some

Member States it remained a key concept, as evidenced by a book published by the Spanish Ministry of Agriculture 'to commemorate the tenth anniversary of the introduction of the multifunctional concept into the European Council' (according to *Agra Europe*, 8 February 2008: N/6. See Gómez-Limón and Hurlé 2007).

Everything but Arms (EBA)

The pending trade negotiations on agriculture were not the only WTO-inspired pressure on EU farm policy. Its Lomé Convention, dating back to the 1970s, had long been viewed by its non-ACP (African, Caribbean, and Pacific States) trading partners as an infringement of GATT rules. In their eyes it could not qualify as a free-trade area under GATT Article XXIV because it was non-reciprocal: although the EU gave (almost) free access to its markets for ACP goods, there was no corresponding obligation on the ACP states to reciprocate on EU-sourced products. Nor could this infringement of the most-favoured-nation clause of GATT be justified under the Enabling Clause, agreed in the Tokyo Round (see Box 3.2 in Chapter 3), because the Lomé Convention discriminated between developing countries: only ACP states, and not GATT Signatories in Asia and Latin America, benefited. For Latin American producers of bananas this was a particular grievance.

One consequence of the second Banana Panel, which reported (but was not adopted) in 1994 under the old GATT Dispute Settlement procedure, was that the EU and the ACP States decided to seek a waiver from the most-favoured-nation clause to allow the tariff preferences of the Lomé Convention to continue (WTO 1997: 304. For a discussion see McQueen 1998: 429). On the switch in regime to the WTO in 1995 this waiver was carried forward, so that 'the provisions of paragraph 1 of Article I of the General Agreement shall be waived, until 29 February 2000, to the extent necessary to permit the European Communities to provide preferential treatment for products originating in the ACP States as required by the relevant provisions of the Fourth Lomé Convention, without being required to extend the same preferential treatment to like products of any other contracting party' (WTO 1997: 304).

For a variety of reasons that cannot be discussed in depth here, but related in part to the hostility of the Latin American banana producers, the EU decided that the Lomé waiver could not be extended beyond 2000. Alternative trade arrangements would have to be negotiated. So the EU with its ACP partners concluded an interim deal, the Cotonou Agreement, which would prolong the Lomé preferences on a temporary basis until GATT Article XXIV-compatible free-trade areas could be negotiated with the ACP States. Six Economic Partnership Agreements (EPAs) were to be negotiated with four groupings in sub-Saharan Africa, one with the Caribbean, and one with the Pacific ACP states, and these would apply from January 2008.

However, this plan also required a waiver. The EU hoped to secure this at the Seattle Ministerial, but that proved unattainable. As part of its diplomatic offensive in the WTO, however, the EU had been promising it would grant duty- and quota-free access to its markets for 'essentially all' goods from the (now 50) Least-Developed Countries (LDCs) on the UNCTAD list, on a non-discriminatory basis under the Enabling Clause. In September 2000 the phrase 'essentially all' was expanded to cover *all* products (except arms and ammunition), including agricultural goods to the chagrin of the EU's farm lobby, and the policy was implemented from 2001 (Page and Hewitt 2002).[8] For bananas, rice, and sugar, however, there was to be a phased introduction, with totally free access delayed until 2009. A waiver covering the Cotonou Agreement, through to 31 December 2007, was secured at the Doha Ministerial; but with special conditions attached for bananas (WTO 2001*a*).

It lies beyond the scope of this book to explore the politics of the initiative: was it an innocent move on the part of Directorate-General (DG) for Trade that DG Agriculture failed to spot before it was too late; was DG Agriculture outmanoeuvred by other interests in the Commission who saw this as an opportunity to force further changes on the CAP; was DG Agriculture (or at least its Commissioner) itself a covert Machiavellian supporter of the initiative, seeing this as an excuse to secure reform of the sugar regime in the face of powerful vested interests? And what role did the Member States, the European Parliament, the farm and sugar processing lobbies, and the development NGOs play? (See various chapters in Faber and Orbie 2007; and Pilegaard 2006, for a discussion of these factors).

If the LDCs were to be granted unlimited access to the EU's coveted sugar market, an unreformed sugar regime looked unsustainable (Swinbank, 2008*a*). In presenting his 2002 reform plan to the European Parliament, which included a halving of the support price for rice (with compensation through the Single Payment Scheme), Commissioner Fischler made a clear connection, pointing out that: 'The progressive reduction in import tariffs for rice under the Everything but Arms initiative will lead to a dramatic deterioration in conditions on the EU rice market' (Fischler 2002*b*).

Doha, and the Doha Round

The Doha Round (or, to give it its official title, the Doha Development Agenda) was launched at the fourth WTO Ministerial Meeting, which was held in Qatar in November 2001. As with the UR, and aside from some possible clarifications and improvements to the Dispute Settlement Understanding, it was agreed that 'the conduct, conclusion and entry into force of the outcome of the negotiations shall be treated as parts of a single undertaking.' (WTO 2001*b*: paragraph 47). Quite how the round was to be *concluded* as a Single Undertaking was a little unclear: an issue to which we return in Chapter 8.

Agriculture was a key concern addressed in the Ministerial Declaration (effectively the mandate for the negotiations), but not the only one. The existing Committee on Agriculture, meeting in Special Session, was given responsibility to progress the agriculture negotiations, overseen by the Trade Negotiations Committee (essentially the WTO's General Council meeting in a different format) chaired *ex-officio* by the WTO's Director-General.

Establishing the Doha mandate on agriculture was not without its drama. The text as it finally appeared is reproduced in Box 7.1. According to Cunha (2004: 161), 'the reference to the *phasing out* of export subsidies as a possible goal of the negotiations, was imposed by the WTO Director-General with the support of the United States and the Cairns Group. The ... qualification that all the goals referred to in the declaration are stated *without prejudging the outcome of the negotiation*, was imposed by the EU and its *friends of multifunctionality'*. The text restated the URAA objective 'to establish a fair and market-oriented trading system'. WTO Members reconfirmed their commitments to this objective and thus to agricultural normalism as the ideational underpinning of the WTO farm trade regime. Deadlines were set: draft modalities for agriculture were to be agreed by 31 March 2003, with details of the new tariff and domestic support and export subsidy commitments tabled before the next WTO Ministerial (in Cancún, Mexico, in September 2003). Quite how the agriculture negotiations were to be settled by then, if this was to be a Single Undertaking with nothing agreed until everything was agreed, was never quite clear.

Box 7.1 EXTRACT FROM THE DOHA MINISTERIAL DECLARATION: AGRICULTURE

---

13. We recognize the work already undertaken in the negotiations initiated in early 2000 under Article 20 of the Agreement on Agriculture, including the large number of negotiating proposals submitted on behalf of a total of 121 Members. We recall the long-term objective referred to in the Agreement to establish a fair and market-oriented trading system through a programme of fundamental reform encompassing strengthened rules and specific commitments on support and protection in order to correct and prevent restrictions and distortions in world agricultural markets. We reconfirm our commitment to this programme. Building on the work carried out to date and without prejudging the outcome of the negotiations we commit ourselves to comprehensive negotiations aimed at: substantial improvements in market access; reductions of, with a view to phasing out, all forms of export subsidies; and substantial reductions in trade-distorting domestic support. We agree that special and differential treatment for developing countries shall be an integral part of all elements of the negotiations and shall be embodied in the Schedules of concessions and commitments and as appropriate in the rules and disciplines to be negotiated, so as to be operationally effective and to enable developing countries to effectively take account of their development needs, including food security and rural development. We take note of the non-trade concerns reflected in the negotiating proposals submitted by Members and confirm that non-trade concerns will be taken into account in the negotiations as provided for in the Agreement on Agriculture.
Source: WTO (2001*b*).

The whole round was to be concluded by 31 December 2004. But these deadlines were not met.

The United States, in June 2002, demanded that export subsidies be eliminated over a five-year period, supported by the Cairns Group, but this received a hostile response from the EU (*Agra Europe*, 7 June 2002: EP/1). The French, *Agra Europe* suggested, would be particularly opposed. Another headline from the *US Proposal for Global Agricultural Trade Reform* elaborated in 2002 was that all trade-distorting domestic support (both amber *and* blue) should be limited to 5 per cent of the value of farm production, with reductions implemented over a five-year period, which would hit the CAP hard. At the time the United States did not use, or intend to use, the blue box to shelter its domestic support payments. Finally, tariffs should be sharply reduced using the 'Swiss formula'.[9] Under this, the new tariff T_1 would be a function of the old tariff T_0 and a coefficient a, according to the expression

$$T_1 = (T_0 \; x \; a)/(T_0 + a).$$

The effect is to reduce larger tariffs (tariff peaks) by a proportionally greater amount than smaller tariffs, and the maximum tariff will never exceed a. Under the US proposal, with $a = 25$, the EU's maximum tariff would have been reduced to 25 per cent over five years. Again this was highly problematic for the EU: Agenda 2000 had not prepared the CAP for this.

The Agenda 2000 CAP reform had given the Commission a window of opportunity for further reform, for it provided for mid-term reviews of its provisions in 2002/03. The Commission launched its *Mid-term Review* in July 2002. If adopted, the reform plan would give the EU much more scope to accept tighter WTO constraints in a new Agreement on Agriculture. The decoupling of direct payments, with the proposed Farm Income Payment replacing the area and headage payments of the MacSharry reforms, would shift blue box expenditure into the green box and enable the EU to be proactive on domestic support in the negotiations (although, as outlined in Chapter 5, there are reasons to believe that these might not be legitimate green box payments). The acceleration, and deepening, of the milk reform (already agreed in Agenda 2000) would make cuts in import tariffs and export subsidies easier to bear. But as yet these were only proposals from the Commission; they did not represent the agreed policy of the Member States, and so they could not easily be reflected in any mandate the Council could grant the Commission for the Doha talks.

Somewhat to everyone's surprise, the European Commission tabled proposals for an EU offer on agriculture on 16 December 2002 (European Commission 2002). The Council unanimously adopted a (very) slightly modified text on 27 January 2003 (European Commission 2003). The language of the EU's proposal was buoyant, with its talk of slashing import tariffs and export subsidies, and its emphasis on a 'radically better deal for developing countries'. But, aside from the rhetoric, it was rather light on content.

On market access the EU rejected the use of the Swiss formula, and offered a repeat of the UR: 'an overall average reduction of 36 per cent and a minimum reduction per tariff line of 15 per cent' (European Commission 2003: 2). Simple arithmetic suggests that the same percentage cut (36 per cent), when applied to a lower base (post URAA) would result in a smaller cut in absolute terms than that achieved in the UR. But, more aggressively, for products originating within the LDCs, developed countries and 'all advanced developing countries' should provide duty- and quota-free access, reflecting the EU's own *EBA* initiative. On domestic support, the EU proposed a 55 per cent reduction in the Aggregate Measurement of Support (AMS) limit, but insisted that the blue box should be retained. However, in a move that would hit the United States quite hard, it suggested that the *de minimis* provisions that had 'been used by some Members as an important loophole in disciplining trade-distorting support' should be eliminated (European Commission 2003: 4). On export competition, the EU proposed that the aggregate expenditure limit on export subsidies be reduced by 45 per cent, with an 'average substantial cut' in the volume of subsidized exports: however, given the low budget spend on export subsidies at the time, this implied no cutback for the EU at all (Swinbank 2005*b*: 553). The lack of ambition shown in the EU's text reflects the state of the post-Agenda 2000 CAP, but it was hardly likely to convince the United States, the Cairns Group, and others, of the EU's commitment to the talks.

The late delivery of the EU's paper was probably a contributory factor delaying preparation of the modalities of the new Agriculture Agreement, which according to the Doha timetable were to be agreed by 31 March 2003. The Chairman of the agriculture negotiations, Stuart Harbinson, tabled his revised *Draft of Modalities for the Further Commitments* on 18 March 2003 (Ruffer and Swinbank 2003: 7; WTO 2003*b*). The *Harbinson Draft* never commanded the support of WTO Members, being seen as too ambitious by some, and lacking in ambition by others, and the Doha deadline of 31 March 2003 was missed, but the text was nonetheless important in the development of thinking in the round, and for that reason, in Table 7.1, we compare its provisions with those contained in the EU's opening bid of January 2003, and in the Falconer text of July 2008 (WTO 2008*a*, 2008*b*).

One precedent that the Harbinson draft clearly set was that the structure of the URAA was to be retained in any new agreement, with its three pillars (import access, domestic support, and export competition), but expanded and modified as appropriate.

Meanwhile, in the EU, the Commission and Commissioner were determined to press ahead with CAP reform, despite opposition from some Member States; and the reform package that emerged in June 2003 clearly gave the EU scope to enlarge its offer in the WTO.

Perhaps misinterpreting what was expected of them, the EU and the United States then met in August 2003, the outcome of which was a 'joint initiative ... presented ... to trade partners ... with a view to advancing the negotiations in the Doha Round towards a successful conclusion in Cancún *as requested by our other trading partners*' (EU/USA 2003, emphasis added). This text, on agriculture, was replete with square brackets, but short on numbers, although it did propose an expansion of the blue box to accommodate the countercyclical payments of US farm policy that the

Table 7.1 Contrasting key features of the EU's January 2003 'offer', the Harbinson text of March 2003, and the Falconer package of July 2008, for developed countries

EU offer January 2003	Harbinson text March 2003	Falconer package July 2008
On *import access* the EU proposed a repeat of the UR formula: an average tariff cut of 36%, with a minimum of 15% on any tariff line.	Harbinson proposed three tariff bands (with *ad valorem* tariff rates of ≤ 15, 15–90, >90%), and a tariff reduction in the top band of [45–60] %, implemented over a five-year period.	Four tariff bands. For the top band (>75%) a cut of 70% over five years. However, countries could designate 4% of tariff lines as *sensitive products*, with smaller tariff cuts but with an expansion of TRQs (6% if 30% or more of tariff lines were in the top band). However, the minimum average cut would be 54%.
The Special Safeguard Clause (SSG) would be retained.	SSG might be abolished.	The SSG would either expire at the outset of the new Agreement, or be limited to 1.5% of tariff lines.
On *domestic support* the AMS limit would be reduced by 55%, the *de minimis* exemption for developed countries would be eliminated; but the blue box would be retained.	A 60% reduction in the bound AMS over five years; a halving of the *de minimis* exemption; and either a 50% reduction in the actual level of blue box expenditure, or inclusion of blue box expenditure into the AMS limit.	Three disciplines would apply to the AMS. The EU's AMS would be reduced by 70% over five years, its OTDS (Overall Trade-Distorting Domestic Support, which includes the blue box and *de minimis*) by 80%; and product-specific AMSs would be capped. The *de minimis* exemption would be reduced by 50%, and blue box expenditure would be capped at 2.5% of the value of farm production in 1995–2000. Eliminate by 2013.
On *export competition*, the overall expenditure limit would be reduced by 45%, and there would be an 'average substantial cut' in the volume of subsidized exports. Export credits would be disciplined	Eliminate export subsidies over a 10-year period, and impose equivalent disciplines on export credits	

Note: Square brackets [] are a common drafting device indicating a range of possibilities.

Source: Compiled by the authors from Ruffer and Swinbank (2003), European Commission (2003), WTO (2003b), and WTO (2008a, and 2008b) together with the Secretariat's 'unofficial notes on the web version of this text'). Be advised, however, that these are terse summaries of complex documents. A fourth revision of the draft modalities was circulated in December 2008, but it is the July text (WTO 2008a) that has acquired iconic significance.

United States now feared would not fit in the green box. It was widely seen as a dilution of the already weak Harbinson draft, a considerable back-tracking by the United States from its 2002 'Global Proposal', and an affront to the wider WTO membership. The UR had been dominated by the United States and the EU, but after Seattle the Doha Round was supposed to be different, involving *all* WTO members.

The initiative was also believed to influence too strongly the pre-Cancún draft modalities on agriculture circulated by the conference chairman, Luis Ernesto Debrez; and on 20 August 2003 a group known as the G20 tabled a more ambitious proposal (WTO 2003*a*).[10] Although this con-tained no numbers, and to that extent its level of ambition was unclear, it did advocate the elimination of export subsidies and the blue box, and suggest that direct payments in the green box should 'as appropriate' be 'capped and/or reduced for developed countries'.

The Cancún Ministerial (10–14 September 2003) was unable to reconcile these differences over the agriculture text, mediate effectively between a group of African States (Benin, Burkina Faso, Chad, and Mali) and the United States over the latter's subsidy programme for cotton, or deal with other issues, and it ended in failure (Bhagwati 2004). Amid the recrimin-ations it was hard to see how the talks could be revived, particularly in a US Presidential election year.

Despite these fears, the EU reconfirmed its commitment to multilateral-ism in November 2003, and said that it was willing to disentangle the 'Singapore' Issues from the Single Undertaking (*Agra Europe*, 28 November 2003: EP/1). In January 2004 the USTR, Robert Zoellick, signalled the United States's intent to progress the round in 2004 (*Agra Europe*, 16 January 2004: EP/2). And in May 2004, with the second tranche of the Fischler reforms for cotton, olive oil, and tobacco agreed (*Agra Europe*, 23 April 2004: EP/1), Commissioners Lamy and Fischler wrote to WTO trade ministers saying, *inter alia*:

On *agriculture*, we believe that we have a historic opportunity for a breakthro-ugh... We are prepared to play our role... as two major reforms of the Common Agriculture Policy in the span of less than a year demonstrate', and noting 'it is clear that the objective of eliminating all forms of export support is one which is shared by the great majority of participants... [B]efore Cancún, the EU offered to eliminate export subsidies on a list of products of interest to developing countries, and we subsequently made clear that there would be no *a priori* exclusions, so all our export subsidies are effectively on the table. However, the list approach has not worked, and we need to take this into account. If an acceptable outcome emerges on market access and domestic support, we would be ready to move on export subsidies (Lamy and Fischler 2004).

The EU's willingness to abandon export subsidies was widely seen as an historic step in the evolution of the CAP, and of the EU's stance in the WTO. This was a different negotiating position from that adopted by the EU in Doha in November 2001. Although other factors were undoubtedly at work, key events in the intervening period had been the Fischler reform, the emergence of the G20 as a strong negotiating group, and the failure of the Cancún Ministerial. Quite quickly a *Framework for Establishing Modalities in Agriculture* was agreed (in July 2004), allowing the Doha Round to progress through 2005 (WTO 2004c: Annex A). The *Framework* was just that: a framework. It lacked the quantification that Harbinson's draft modalities had tried to determine. The next 'deadline' was December 2005, when WTO Ministers were to meet in Hong Kong. But once again, progress was stymied, and the hoped-for 'first approximation' of the modalities, planned for late July 2005, failed to materialize (Anania and Bureau 2005: 542).

At this juncture the United States raised the stakes. Until 2005 the Harbinson numbers had been much in people's minds. In October 2005 the United States tabled an ambitious proposal—that the highest tariffs be reduced by up to 90 per cent for example, and that the EU's AMS be reduced by 83 per cent—prompting a somewhat less ambitious counter-proposal from the EU two weeks later (European Union 2005; Office of the United States Trade Representative 2005). The Hong Kong Ministerial (13–18 December 2005) achieved little—but there again very few observers had believed it would—apart from a confirmation that export subsidies would be abolished in the new agreement. Nonetheless the shape, and ambition, of a new Agreement on Agriculture was talking shape, as the number of square brackets decreased, and the numbers crystallized, in successive texts, and these were not challenged by the membership.

However, the 2006 deadlines set in Hong Kong could not be met and, in July 2006, Pascal Lamy, by now Director-General of the WTO, dramatically 'suspended' the negotiations, with no clear indication of how or when they might be resuscitated. With the election of Democrat majorities to both the Senate and the House of Representatives in the United States mid-term elections in November 2006, and with the fast-track procedure[11] expired by 30 June 2007, the possibility of a Bush presidency successfully concluding the round seemed slim.

Once again talks were revived. Multilateral negotiations in Geneva were resumed in February 2007; but a meeting of the G4 (Brazil, India, the EU, and the United States) in Potsdam, Germany, in June 2007, however, failed to progress the negotiations. Then, in July 2007, the Chairman of the agriculture negotiations, Crawford Falconer, published another *Draft Possible Modalities on Agriculture*, with somewhat fewer square brackets, and a smaller range in the square-bracketed numbers tabled. This document was revised a number of times, slowly narrowing the range of possible outcomes and expanding its scope, but progress remained glacially slow. The third revision (WTO 2008*a*) was the focus of discussion in July 2008 when, as we saw on page 1 of this book, talks were again suspended. There was some hope that even at this late stage in the Bush presidency a deal could be concluded before the end of 2008, and trade ministers were on standby to attend a ministerial meeting in Geneva, but on 18 December Pascal Lamy (2008*b*) was forced to concede to the General Council that 'we had to recognize the reality that calling Ministers to try to finalise modalities by the end of the year would be running too much of a risk of failure which could damage not only the Round but also the WTO system as a whole'. Thus, the Doha Developmental Agenda (DDA) is not dead, but as this text is prepared for publication it remains in deep freeze with little sign of a thaw.

The ostensible cause of the July 2008 deadlock on agriculture was a dispute between the United States and India over the proposed *Special Safeguard Mechanism* for developing countries under which, for a limited number of products, developing countries could impose an additional import tax if faced with an import surge or depressed import price (Hanson 2008: 11; WTO 2008*a*: 21). The United States wanted to limit the total import charge to the pre-Doha bound rate; India did not. Crawford Falconer warned: 'It is perhaps worth underlining that such differences were not some purely "technical" matter . . . the impasse was not technical. It was political' (WTO 2008*b*: 3). However, this was only the proximate cause of the breakdown. Cotton was 'not addressed in a substantive way', and 'other very significant issues were not even dealt with' (WTO 2008*b*: 4, 1).

Conclusion

In the introduction to this chapter, we set out to analyse the impact of the EU's bargaining power in the GATT and WTO farm trade negotiations, suggesting that limited competiveness of the EU agricultural sector and the EU's internal voting rules and decision-making norms would give the EU's negotiators substantial bargaining power, enabling them to set limits for GATT/WTO farm trade agreements. This hypothesis was supported by our analysis which demonstrated that the lack of CAP reform stalemated GATT/WTO negotiations on agriculture, and that reform of the CAP led to progress in the negotiations. The breakdown of the UR in Brussels in December 1990 was caused by the EU's unwillingness to reform the CAP, and it was not until the CAP was reformed in 1992 that agreement with the United States could be achieved and the UR closed. In parallel with bilateral negotiations with the United States, in which the blue box support category was agreed, the EU undertook a reform of CAP in which price support was transformed into direct payments designed for the blue box. This enabled the EU to give concessions on amber box domestic support, tariffs, and export subsidies.

In the Doha Round, little progress was achieved until after the CAP reform in July 2003. The EU's negotiating position was locked in by the 1992 and 1999 reforms of the CAP, which gave little leeway for concessions on domestic support. The EU's trading partners wanted blue box support eliminated, or subjected to substantial reductions, which the then version of the CAP did not allow. Progress in the Doha Round would not have been possible without the Fischler reforms of 2003, although the EU's ability to accept the domestic subsidy constraints rests heavily on its Single Payment Scheme expenditure falling within the green box; and high world market prices in 2007 and 2008 had made the removal of export subsidies and significant cuts in border protection easier to contemplate.

Although the Doha talks are currently in deep freeze, and it is by no means certain that Crawford Falconer's July 2008 package could be thawed out if the talks were to resume, Table 7.1 does indicate how far the EU was willing and able to go on each of the three pillars, and how far it had moved from January 2003. It was willing to countenance the elimination of export subsidies; and accept major reductions in the allowable levels of domestic support. On import access, where it had originally suggested an average tariff cut of 36 per cent and retention of the Special Safeguard Clause, it was now willing to consider a cut of 70 per cent in the highest tariff band, and a significant reduction in coverage of special safeguards; but it was still vulnerable to *further* demands for increased market access.

It had long since abandoned (in Geneva) the rhetoric of multifunctionality, and indeed had never tabled any drafting amendments to enlarge the scope of the green box to embrace multifunctionality. Its other non-trade concern, animal welfare, not discussed in this volume, had been quietly abandoned. As the Commissioner conceded: 'We've tried extremely hard in the Doha Round to make "non-trade concerns" a part of any new agricultural trade agreement, but the resistance has been fierce. So for the time being, we have no legal powers to insist that agricultural imports were produced according to our environmental and animal welfare standards' (Fischer Boel 2008: 3). The EU was, nonetheless, still hoping for concessions on Geographical Indications of Origin (again not discussed in this volume).

Significantly, it had not been blamed for the suspension of the talks: that role was now assigned to the United States, because of its negotiating stance and its 2008 Farm Bill (the *Food, Conservation, and Energy Act*) that seemed to pay scant regard to any likely Doha Round disciplines on farm support (Murphy and Suppan 2008).

Chapter 8

Beyond Doha: Conclusions and Prospects

The Uruguay Round (UR) was a turning point in the international trade regime. Not only did it transform GATT into the WTO, but the trade regime's decision-making rules were radically changed. The Single Undertaking meant that any new rules that were negotiated had to be applied by *all* WTO members, unlike the *GATT a la carte* that had characterized the Tokyo Round accords, and moreover it involved a switch from a request–offer model, that had characterized tariff negotiations in preceding GATT rounds, to a formula approach. This changed the game in the agricultural negotiations, and implied that farm trade became a more integral part of the WTO, albeit with its own sectorial agreement (the Uruguay Round Agreement on Agriculture, URAA). Furthermore, dispute settlement changed radically and has proved a powerful tool for countries seeking trade liberalization since it allows them to pursue this objective through the judicial arm of the WTO in parallel with political efforts to negotiate liberalization.

The fuller integration of farm trade into the international trade regime and the reformed dispute settlement system moved farm trade up the agenda. The UR's Single Undertaking meant that agricultural trade had to be part of the package if the Round was to be successfully concluded. It was particularly evident that the Common Agricultural Policy (CAP) was vulnerable. It was also apparent that the EU put far more political weight into a defence of the CAP than the farm sector's economic importance would suggest. EU negotiators vigorously defended the CAP against the United States's Zero-2000 proposal aimed at abolishing all trade-distorting farm subsidies and tariffs by the year 2000. This was a clash between giants with very different understandings of the nature of agricultural production and markets, and of the appropriate role for agricultural policies.

Eventually, the EU and the United States resolved the conflict in the so-called Blair House Accords which, as anticipated, paved the way not only for a WTO agreement on farm trade, but also for the conclusion of the UR. In the Doha Round the CAP was again a contested issue and, as in the UR, under pressure, but the EU's decision to decouple direct payments to farmers in the 2003 reform shifted (it hoped) the bulk of them into the green box for which there would be no reduction commitments. This enabled the EU to adopt a more offensive negotiating strategy in the Doha Development Agenda (DDA). As a result, the DDA's focus on trade-distorting domestic support shifted from EU to US agricultural policy. The EU was no longer the sole scapegoat when negotiations deadlocked. Nonetheless, since the EU still operates market price policies in a number of commodity sectors (e.g. beef, dairy, and sugar), the EU was still defensive over market access, which itself was in danger of bringing the Round to a halt on several occasions. Thus, as we have demonstrated, it is difficult to understand the WTO process of agricultural trade liberalization without an appreciation of how this interacts with CAP reform and EU decision making.

The theoretical challenges of the book

The way the conflict between the EU and the United States, supported by the Cairns Group, played itself out in the UR points towards ideational theory as a useful analytical tool providing a deeper understanding of the difficulties in reaching agreement on farm trade in the GATT and WTO. Ideational theory is still in its infancy, but it is a growing and challenging literature within political science. Nevertheless, it proved a useful analytical framework for studying the underlying factors making agricultural trade an issue of high politics during both the Uruguay and the Doha rounds. However, as ideational theory has mostly been applied in domestic settings, we had to develop the theory further to make it applicable for an analysis of international trade policy. Since most of the accounts in the literature on the GATT/WTO farm trade negotiations have been essentially descriptive, they had limited ability to provide new insights into the nature of the farm trade conflict and fully to uncover the causal mechanisms driving the design of farm trade agreements. Our ideational approach provided a novel theoretical perspective on international farm trade negotiations, providing an analytical framework that potentially may be applied to other trade issues as well.

We have argued that particular emphasis should be put upon the EU's pivotal position in agricultural trade negotiations. Due to the comparatively limited competitiveness of the EU's agricultural sector, and the EU's institutionally constrained ability to undertake CAP reform, the CAP has set limits for agricultural trade liberalization. Whilst lack of international competitiveness is a direct cause of the EU's stubbornness over farm trade, the decision-making rules within the Council of Ministers further constrain its ability to grant concessions. Formally a qualified majority is required to adopt changes to the CAP, but this decision rule is often emasculated by a strong norm to reach consensus, or to ensure that key member states are not outvoted, particularly with respect to French sensitivities.

Though this perspective is not particularly novel, it is nevertheless a key factor which cannot be neglected in a study of the evolution of the WTO farm trade regime. But we have gone beyond this, and emphasized the role of *ideas*. This perspective enabled a better appreciation of the deeper layers of conflict reflected in disagreements over farm trade negotiations, and of the way the CAP evolves in response to WTO developments. This also allowed us to understand how developments in the CAP feed back into the trade negotiations, setting the scene for those negotiations, facilitating some compromises but at the same time placing constraints on what can be achieved.

We have argued that the URAA involved an ideational shift from agricultural exceptionalism to agricultural normalism. However, this did not immediately lead to a recognizably more liberal international farm trade regime. Rather it set the stage for a *future* scaling down of agricultural support and protection. Farm protection and support remained substantial more than a decade after the WTO farm trade regime was established. To explain this paradoxical outcome we distinguished between the *operational* and the *ideational* levels of farm trade agreements. The former referred to the specific commitments to reduce agricultural support and protection, which in the URAA were limited, while the latter refers to the elite assumptions on the nature of agricultural production and markets, which in the URAA were more profound. An ideational shift was clearly expressed in the URAA, which called for the establishment of 'a fair and market-oriented trading system'. This was a long-term objective. The URAA allowed countries to maintain high levels of support and protection, through to the end of the 1990s, but these countries were warned that they should then anticipate 'substantial progressive reductions in support' as part of an 'ongoing process', and that they should be prepared to provide farm support in less trade-distorting ways. The URAA made clear that farm trade was an integral part of the WTO legal system, with sector-specific disciplines.

This peculiar outcome is a challenge to ideational theory. First, as noted above, it forced us to distinguish between the operational and the ideational levels of international trade agreements. Second, in ideational theory there is a strong tendency to assume that ideational change leads to radical institutional and policy paradigm change. However, there is a growing realization among analysts that policy reform induced by ideational change may take a variety of forms (see Skogstad 2008). As demonstrated by Coleman et al. (1997) there can be a gradual and cumulative trajectory to shifts in policy paradigms induced by the introduction of new ideas. Thus, the immediate impact of new ideas in public policy may not be dramatic; instead they may lead to gradual adjustments of policy over a long period of time, perhaps cumulating in a genuine change of policy paradigm. Thus we suggested that policy makers may react in four different ways. They can: (*a*) undertake rapid and fundamental policy reform; (*b*) change policy through gradual shifts of policy instruments to bring policy into conformity with the new idea; (*c*) maintain the existing ideational underpinning by disguising it through rephrasing whilst gradually changing policy instruments to serve the original objective in new ways; or (*d*) defend the existing policy and the idea upon which it is based, but undertake some symbolic acts to deflect attacks on policy.

In this book we analysed negotiations taking place simultaneously at two levels. The rules of the WTO farm trade regime, and reduction commitments, are decided in negotiations that take place both internally and internationally. Thus the EU's trade negotiators have to come up with a package that satisfies both its WTO partners across a whole range of trade issues (the Single Undertaking), whilst commanding the support of the EU's member states through the Council of Ministers (but also in the European Parliament). Developments in domestic agricultural policies influence negotiations on farm trade rules, as suggested by Putnam's two-level game model (Putnam 1988). However, it is also important to emphasize that trade negotiations in the GATT/WTO are historically embedded since they take place over relatively long periods and they are affected by previous trade rounds and agreements. Therefore trade negotiation analysis also has to include an assessment of the impact of previous trade rounds and agreements on not only the agenda of new negotiations but also how they affect the negotiating positions of the parties. We demonstrated that the ideational underpinning of the URAA had an important impact on the evolution of the CAP, and showed how this influenced the EU's negotiating position. These changes to the CAP took place over more than a decade in three broad CAP reforms (1992, 1999, and 2003/4) in which WTO concerns increasingly shaped the institutional setting in which the reforms were hammered out. However, although substantial, these reforms could not readily be termed *radical*; they remained based upon the existing policy paradigm. Thus, the gradualist model of ideationally induced policy change, and our distinction between the ideational and operational levels of an international trade regime, proved especially useful in analysing a two-level game in which an international trade regime underwent change in its ideational underpinning, and member governments adapted to this.

Major findings

In the introductory chapter we asked a sequence of related questions focused on the interrelationship between GATT/WTO and the CAP: an interrelationship that we considered central to our understanding of the process of farm trade liberalization, and of CAP reform. The first question related to ideational change in the GATT/WTO farm trade regime. At the ideational level of the URAA we identified a shift from agricultural exceptionalism to agricultural normalism. So we asked: *Why and how was agricultural exceptionalism eventually eroded in the UR?* An important catalyst for ideational change arose within the academic community in the development of analytical tools to measure the magnitude of agricultural support and its economic consequences. In particular work carried out within FAO, OECD, and the Australian agricultural research institute ABARE, was key in this process. Further, the phasing out of agricultural support in Australia and New Zealand attracted attention. In the United States, President Reagan's attempt to bypass the farm lobby in Congress by using the GATT to force through domestic agricultural policy reform, put further pressure on the supporters of agricultural exceptionalism. But most importantly, a change of decision rules within the GATT had a decisive impact. By agreeing not only to *open* the UR as a *Single Undertaking*, but also to *close* it as such, the EU and the United States were forced to compromise on agriculture. While this compromise allowed the EU (and also the United States) to maintain high levels of agricultural support, a substantial part of the EU's market-price support was transformed into direct payments with production-limiting obligations.

Since domestic farm policies were only to be marginally affected by the specific reduction commitments of the URAA, and some of the text was open to alternative readings, it was inevitable that disputes would arise and that the new Dispute Settlement Understanding (DSU) would be invoked, and so it was. Therefore, the second research question asked: *Have proceedings in the Dispute Settlement Body (DSB) resulted in further farm trade liberalization?* Several rulings have challenged the commitments of countries that had believed their agricultural policies were in conformity with WTO rules, but were then told the contrary. Nevertheless, even when cases go against a member, rulings are in general considered legitimate, and even the major trading powers, including the United States and the EU, usually seek to comply, at least to some extent. The DSU has thus eroded the exceptional treatment of agriculture in the WTO and advanced the liberalization of farm trade further than was envisaged when the URAA was negotiated and agreed. This has forced the losing defendants to move their agricultural policies in the direction of the liberal market paradigm. Under the new dispute settlement system, the EU seems to be more willing to comply with judicial rulings on agricultural trade than it was under the old system. However, its response varies, depending upon which set of EU institutional decision-making rules apply. Although cases are too few for any firm conclusions to be drawn, we suggest that the EU is able to conform when the dispute relates to decisions on *farm* policy, whereas those involving *food safety* (e.g. beef hormones, GMOs) are less amenable to WTO-imposed policy changes. In contrast to agricultural policy, in which the Council of Agriculture Ministers has the sole decision-making authority, food safety legislation is in part determined by the European Parliament, an institution which seems to emphasize EU public concerns about food safety rather than WTO trade rules.

Although the CAP occupies a pivotal position in WTO negotiations, potentially leading the EU to block negotiations, it is not a static policy, but one that evolves in response to both internal and external developments, for instance the ideational shift from agricultural exceptionalism to agricultural normalism in the GATT/WTO farm trade regime. Therefore our third research question asked: *In what way has the ideational underpinning of the URAA influenced EU agricultural policy institutions and CAP reform?* We demonstrated that EU agricultural policy makers gradually adopted WTO concerns when proposing, and deliberating upon, CAP reforms. In particular, the 1992 and 2003 reforms were shaped to accommodate GATT/WTO pressure. There was a shift from market price to partially decoupled support in 1992, and in 2003 these direct payments were largely decoupled from production. Despite the increased influence of WTO farm trade negotiations, the CAP is still based on the view that agriculture is an exceptional industry requiring special treatment, but newer versions of agricultural exceptionalism have emerged emphasizing the public goods provided by the agricultural sector (to which the EU applies the term *multifunctionality*).

The interrelationship between CAP reform and WTO negotiations is dynamic. Our fourth research question, therefore, asked: *How do CAP reforms feed back into the WTO negotiations setting limits for what can be achieved?* We demonstrated how the 1992 reform allowed the United States and the EU to reach a compromise on farm trade and thus pave the way not only for the URAA but also for the whole UR package of agreements. At the same time, the 1992 CAP reform set limits for the Agreement on Agriculture, with the result that the URAA was much less ambitious than originally envisaged by the Americans. However, the United States had a decisive say on the ideational foundation of the URAA, defining a built-in agenda for future negotiations. The CAP is a dynamic policy complex, and as it changes it continuously moves the boundaries for a feasible set of WTO agreements on farm trade. When viewed in a longer time perspective the interrelationship between CAP reform and the WTO negotiations is clearly dynamic. We showed how the 1992 and 1999 reforms influenced the EU's stance before the launch of the Doha Round, and how lack of progress in the Doha negotiations then put pressure on EU agricultural policy makers to complete the 2003 CAP reform in an attempt to avert a breakdown at the Ministerial in Cancún in September 2003. Although this meeting ended in failure, the 2003 CAP reform did facilitate further progress on domestic support leading to the 2004 *Framework Agreement*, but it also placed constraints on the level of ambition for the Doha Round. Despite decoupling in several commodity sectors, the EU still made heavy use of market price support, limiting the tariff reductions it could readily concede. This played a role in the suspension of the Round in July 2006, but the EU's 2003 reform had isolated the United States on the question of domestic support, and US unwillingness to move on this issue was another important factor in creating deadlock, both in July 2006 and again in July 2008.

The book has demonstrated that ideas are important in trade policy. Not only do they influence domestic trade policies; they also play an important role in international trade negotiations. The establishment or reform of trade regimes involves a struggle over ideas and, once the ideational struggle is settled, ideas affect the functioning of trade regimes, and how they evolve, by setting the direction for future negotiations on trade rules. The ideational underpinning of an international trade regime may also affect domestic policy evolution by influencing the domestic policy debate. Policy makers will attempt to anticipate developments in the trade regime so as to adapt and safeguard domestic policies against external pressure, and perhaps even facilitate further evolution of the trade regime.

Post-Doha scenarios

When they met in Seattle in 1999, WTO Ministers failed to launch a Millennium Round of multilateral trade negotiations. In part this was because the meeting had been inadequately prepared; in part the ambiance of the meeting was shattered by street riots; but the developing world's antipathy towards the continuation of an EU/US hegemony also played a role. Thus the new negotiations on agriculture, mandated by Article 20 of the URAA, began in 2000 without any clear framework within which to proceed. The launch of the DDA in 2001 was possibly facilitated by a lessening of *trade* tensions as a result of heightened security concerns following terrorist attacks on New York and Washington in September 2001. The Doha Round, as with its predecessor the UR, was to be a Single Undertaking, with the agriculture dossier an integral and important part. According to the rather ambitious schedule included in the Doha Ministerial statement, the Round was to be concluded by 1 January 2005. Initially, the failure to meet this deadline could be dismissed as inconsequential: after all, the UR was eventually concluded despite a number of setbacks, and some years after its advertised completion in December 1990.

In Chapter 7 we chronicled, briefly, the ups and downs of the agriculture negotiations. By July 2008 a substantial, and detailed, Chairman's draft (WTO 2008*a*) was under discussion; but, detailed as it was, there was still some crucial detail missing. EU Trade Commissioner Peter Mandelson's decision to take a cabinet post in the British government in October 2008 did not signal strong EU commitment to conclude the talks; and indeed there was to be no outcome by the end of the year. The change in the US presidency, with the election of Barack Obama in November 2008, inevitably means it will be some time before the new US administration will be ready to resume negotiations, and possibly even longer before the new president can turn to Congress to seek a renewed fast-track negotiating mandate. In India, a key player in the July 2008 impasse, a general election is to be held before May 2009.

Complicating the negotiations was the turmoil in commodity and financial markets in 2008. Oil prices that had peaked at over $140 a barrel in the summer, with knock-on effects for transport costs, fertilizer prices, etc., dipped below $70 in October (*Financial Times*, 17 October 2008: 41), and continued to fall. Soft commodities began their price rise in 2006, peaking in the summer of 2008 when all the talk was of a world food crisis (more on this below), and then fell away again. All of this tested the international community's commitment to a more open trading system. In part prices began to tumble because of growing fears of a looming world recession, triggered by a financial crisis that had been developing since 2007. South East Asia, Latin America, and Russia had had financial crises in recent years; but the realization that banks and other financial institutions at the heart of the US and EU economies might fail spread fear around the world. One paragraph from the front page of the *Financial Times* on 13 October 2008 (chosen almost at random) conveys the sombre mood: 'World leaders were last night scrambling to finalize rescue plans for their banking systems before stock markets open today, amid fears the global financial system is on the brink of collapse.' Whether these pressures will result in a return to trade protection, as in the interwar years, or result in a revival of the Bretton Woods spirit of 1944 that helped in the revival of the global economy in the aftermath of the Second World War, only time will tell.

But the foregoing discussion raises a number of important questions. For example, can the Doha Round be revived in the near term, or a new round launched at some time in the future? If so, can the agricultural dossier be 'dusted off', and talks resumed where the negotiations left off in 2008, or will they start with a clean (or cleanish) sheet of paper? As the book goes to press, no clear answers to these questions are in sight.

The single undertaking: still fit for purpose?

The Single Undertaking served the EU and the United States well in the UR, but is this decision-making mode still fit for purpose? If not, what alternative strategies might countries pursue? If there is no Doha agreement, and no immediate prospect of an agreement, how will the existing UR package of agreements cope with the challenges of the world trading system: can trade liberalization and reform proceed through dispute settlement, for example? In this book we have stressed the importance of the Single Undertaking in the UR: as a negotiating procedure, a decision-making rule, and in implementation.[1] The decision-making rule that 'nothing was agreed until everything was agreed' bound all economic sectors into a complex web of deals and side-deals; and consequently industrial and other commercial interests were willing to exert leverage on the agriculture negotiators. The Doha Round was also billed as a Single Undertaking, and the negotiations proceeded on that basis; but can it, or any successor round, be concluded as a Single Undertaking?

Amongst policy makers and trade policy analysts there is a growing suspicion that the Single Undertaking decision-making procedure is no longer workable. Compared with the UR, the DDA is a narrow trade round, focusing mainly on trade in services, agriculture, and non-agricultural market access (NAMA). Nevertheless, the round ran late, and then stalled, *despite* a very detailed set of draft modalities on the table in July 2008. At first sight this may seem somewhat of a paradox; why could the Single Undertaking decision-making rule be applied in the broad UR and not in the narrow DDA? One possible obvious answer is that the 'ball game' has changed. As in the UR, agriculture is a key component in the package of draft agreements that also embrace trade in services and NAMA. In the UR, the EU and the United States were the major 'players' and their Blair House Accord was the magic formula for reaching agreement on the whole package. The Cairns Group, which represented large agricultural exporters such as Australia and Brazil, played a modest role, occasionally mediating between the EU and the United States.

The Doha Round has had different dynamics. The power relations in the WTO are no longer bipolar with the United States and the EU as *the* major and dominating trading powers. New states, or rather groups of states, in particular the G20, have emerged as key players. In Seattle developing countries blocked the launch of a new trade round. Consequently, Doha was billed as the *development* round to assuage the concerns of developing countries.[2] During the Ministerial conference in Cancún in September 2003 it became even more evident that the rules of the game had changed. A joint text of the EU and the United States on the modalities of an agricultural agreement did not produce progress; rather it proved counterproductive by angering a number of developing countries, triggering the formation of the G20.

Although the EU and the United States can no longer dominate the farm trade negotiations, a change in power relations is not a full explanation for the difficulties of applying the Single Undertaking decision-making rule in the Doha Round. Even though the Single Undertaking closed the UR, it never worked as intended. It did not enable *all* contracting parties to reach agreement on *all* parts of the UR package of agreements by consensus. Instead it was an exercise of power. As the Round progressed it had become apparent to the United States and the EU that a large number of developing countries were reluctant to agree to all parts of the UR package. Therefore they agreed to apply an 'exit tactic' to close the Round, as we outlined in Chapter 4. The Marrakesh Agreement establishing the WTO created a package of agreements and legal instruments that would be binding on all WTO members. With the WTO in place, both the United States and EU withdrew from the GATT 1947. The consequence of this exercise of power was that to regain access to EU and US markets on an MFN basis, countries had to become members of the WTO. This procedure was not a Single Undertaking in the sense that 'nothing is agreed until everything is agreed': that was true only for those countries that actively supported the establishment of the WTO and its *entire* package of agreements. Others were reluctant parties, and it was only a Single Undertaking for them in the sense that they chose to subscribe to the whole package of WTO agreements rather than abandon the international trade regime. Thus, there is no record of the Single Undertaking being applied as a successful consensually based decision-making rule; or to suggest that the United States and the EU would want, or be able, to repeat the exit 'trick' again. Presumably, it would require a grouping such as the G7 (EU, the United States, Brazil, India, Japan, Australia, and China) to agree a deal between themselves, collectively resign their membership of WTO 1995, and then re-enact the existing WTO agreements, supplemented by Doha, as WTO mark 2. But is there any guarantee that the rest of the existing WTO membership would follow, re-imposing upon themselves the disciplines of TRIMS, TRIPS, etc.? Consequently, there is every reason to consider alternative decision-making procedures.

This was one of the challenges addressed by the Warwick Commission. The Single Undertaking was a procedural innovation introduced in the UR, in part to eliminate the flexibility that applied in the Tokyo Round. This had allowed the Contracting Parties to opt into, or out of, the agreements; whilst all GATT members benefited as a consequence of the Most-Favoured-Nation (MFN) principle. The Warwick Commission recommended the re-introduction of this flexibility, by using *critical-mass decision making*. The Single Undertaking would still proceed on the basis that 'nothing is agreed until everything is agreed', but crucially some elements of the negotiated package would only apply to those WTO members that had signed up to the new element. In short, the critical-mass decision-making method allows a group of WTO members to negotiate an agreement between themselves, embedded in the Single Undertaking, extending all the rights of the agreement to the whole WTO membership, whilst the obligations would fall only on the signatories to the agreement.

Emphasizing the non-radical nature of their recommendation, the Warwick Commission stressed that this decision rule was successfully applied in negotiating market access for telecommunications, financial services, and information technology (Warwick Commission 2007: 30–1). They did not, however, discuss the possible use of critical-mass decision making to facilitate agreement in farm trade negotiations. Thus, since trade liberalization is the essence of the farm trade negotiations, we need to reflect on the extent to which critical-mass decision making would enable agreement on farm trade liberalization.

To some extent the critical-mass decision-making method has already been applied in the Doha and UR farm trade negotiations. First, the bilateral negotiations between the EU and the United States in the UR, culminating in the Blair House Accords, could be conceived of as a critical-mass constellation. In the Doha Round, the constellation of the critical mass has been extended. Various constellations have formed the core negotiating group reflecting the intensity of interests in the issues negotiated. At various times these have been the G4 (EU, the United States, Brazil, and India), G5 (EU, the United States, Brazil, India, and Australia), G6 (the United States, EU, Brazil, India, Australia, and Japan), and G7 (EU, the United States, Brazil, India, Japan, Australia, and China). However, although each of these constellations has consisted of a limited number of WTO member states they have not succeeded despite intensive efforts. It is not that these meetings have reached an agreement, and then failed to sell it to the wider WTO membership as part of the Single Undertaking: they have not reached agreement between themselves. Thus there is little evidence to suggest that a workable critical mass for a Doha farm trade agreement could be found. Furthermore, a precondition for the EU to commit itself to farm trade liberalization in the WTO is that a farm trade agreement is an integral part of a broader package of agreements. It is absolutely essential for the EU to link the farm trade talks with NAMA and trade in services since there are very few 'gains' (from a trade negotiator's perspective) for the EU in farm trade liberalization. The 'concessions' given on farm trade have to be legitimized domestically by 'gains' elsewhere. In short, liberalization in farm trade depended upon the Single Undertaking in the UR, and the same seems to hold for the

DDA. As D. Gale Johnson (1973: 265) in *World Agriculture in Disarray* envisaged more than three decades ago, a WTO framework is necessary because 'one trade concession demands another in return... [S]eparate agricultural negotiations are doomed before they start'.

Rather than blaming decision-making rules in the WTO for being unable to facilitate a conclusion to the Doha Round, attention should perhaps be shifted to the domestic level, in particular in the EU and the United States. As a result of the increased international orientation of the EU's industrial firms, and reflecting the fact that the EU is the leading exporter and importer of services, the EU pressed strongly for market opening in these two important economic sectors (Young 2007). Representatives of *BusinessEurope*,[3] giving evidence to the United Kingdom's House of Lords Select Committee on the European Communities, refuted the suggestion that European business interests had been insufficiently vocal in supporting trade liberalization, but commented that because the Round had gone on for so long, interest had waned, and it was consequently difficult to attract press coverage for its 'positive messages on trade liberalisation' (House of Lords 2008: Q 262). Moreover, the business community had become sceptical about a Doha success: 'As scepticism grows, it becomes more difficult to mobilize people, even when they believe fundamentally in trade liberalisation' (Q 261). But another problem was that 'The EU has privileged its defensive interests in agriculture over its offensive interests in industry' (Q 267).

Since progress in both the UR and DDA was heavily dependent on progress in the farm trade talks, domestic institutional reform is a more likely key to facilitate future agreement. In the United States and the EU, farm interests are privileged by favourable institutional arrangements. Special political and administrative institutions in the agricultural sector—such as ministries or departments of agriculture, agricultural committees of legislatures, and administrative agencies assigned responsibility for administering farm support schemes—provide farm interests with venues which are responsive to their advocated needs and which are well placed to pursue those interests in the broader trade policy process. The core institutions of the EU providing easy access to the trade policy process for farm interests are the Council of Agriculture Ministers, a commissioner specifically responsible for agriculture and rural development and the Directorate-General for Agriculture and Rural Development.

Furthermore, the EU's decision-making rules are favourable to protectionist interests. Apart from some isolated examples, such as the milk quota regulations, CAP legislation typically has no expiry date built in: it continues indefinitely unless changed. A policy can only be modified if the Commission takes the initiative and tables a proposal that then gets qualified majority support in the Council of Agriculture Ministers. Qualified majority voting and the still strong consensus norm favour the *status quo* and enable a minority group of member states with protectionist interests to block concessions on agriculture in WTO negotiations. Since the established agro-political institutions have provided farm interest with a disproportionately strong voice in the broader trade policy process, it could be argued that these institutions should be reformed to reflect better the economic and electoral realities of the farming sector. In some EU member states, most notably in the United Kingdom, agricultural ministries have been reformed and renamed to balance farm with consumer, environmental, and broader rural development interests. This attempt to shift the balance is not yet reflected at EU level, but the *Treaty of Lisbon*, if ratified, would enhance the European Parliament's co-decision rights over the CAP, sharing decision making with the Council, and this may weaken farm interests in the EU.[4]

A second element of the critical mass, flexibility, can already be found in URAA and in a likely Doha agreement. Though WTO members cannot, on a voluntary basis, choose whether or not to opt-in in relation to the agreements of the Single Undertaking, the URAA and a likely Doha agreement *do* differentiate between countries, both in terms of reduction commitments and the specificity of rules. Thus the URAA differentiated between developed and developing countries, and LDCs, with more stringent provisions applying for developed countries, and *Special and Differential Treatment* applying to developing countries. These distinctions were carried forward into the negotiations for a new Doha agriculture agreement (again we stress it was the Doha *Development* Agenda), but with even more differentiation than in the URAA. For example, although not mentioned in the draft agreement by name, the EU was to accept larger reductions (in percentage terms) in its Aggregate Measurement of Support (AMS) and Overall Trade-Distorting Domestic Support (OTDS) bindings; and the proximate cause of the July 2008 breakdown in the negotiations was disagreement over the proposed Special Safeguard Mechanism for *developing* countries. In reality the July 2008 package (WTO 2008*a*) could be interpreted as a collection of country-specific provisions grouped together under a common umbrella.

The frustrations caused by recurrent halts and delays in the negotiations have also refocused attention on bilateral trade agreements in Brussels, both as an alternative and as a supplement to the Doha Round. The Warwick Commission (2007: 45–53) discusses the motives that lead to the formation of regional trade agreements (RTAs) and their impact on the multilateral trading system. A rich political science and economics literature has discussed the advantages and disadvantages of RTAs, asking for example whether they are building blocks or stumbling blocks to multilateral trade liberalization. We shall not repeat this discussion here, but simply focus on such agreements' possible impact on the post-Doha trade conflict over agriculture. RTAs often focus on the 'easy' sectors, exempting 'sensitive' products from the agreement and leaving them to be dealt with in the multilateral trade negotiations (Warwick Commission 2007: 50). However, it is unlikely that the EU, and the United States, can negotiate bilateral RTAs which safeguard their agricultural policies. There are major gains for countries like Brazil (and other Latin American countries) and Australia in opening markets in North America and Europe. These WTO member states have demonstrated their willingness to challenge agricultural support in the EU and the United States as illustrated by the EU sugar case and the US–Upland cotton case. So why should these countries agree to bilateral RTAs which safeguard EU or US agricultural policies? Indeed, the bilateral strategy could prove counterproductive for the EU and the United States, because other WTO members could still mount legal challenges in the dispute settlement system, forcing the EU and United States to undertake substantial reform of their agricultural policies. Reaching a new WTO agreement on agriculture, with a renewed Peace Clause, may be a better way of safeguarding their agricultural policies, allowing the farm sector time to adjust to new economic realities.

However, a new Doha agreement, with a Peace Clause, does not necessarily exclude the possibility of further disputes being raised against the farm policies of the EU and the United States. For instance, the 2003 CAP reform that enabled the EU to accept major cuts in its bound levels of amber and blue box domestic support, since it shifted direct payments from the blue to the green box, might be vulnerable. The area and headage payments that had characterized the CAP from the 1992 MacSharry reforms through to the 2003 reform were blue box payments, whereas the more decoupled Single Farm Payment introduced by the 2003 reforms was assumed to be in the green box. However, as argued in Box 3.5 in Chapter 3, this assumption can be questioned on the grounds of the annual nature of the support claim, and the link with *farm*land.

The 2008 world food 'crisis' and the CAP

We have argued in this book that CAP reform has mainly been driven by developments in the GATT/WTO. Therefore an important concern is whether the momentum of CAP reform can be maintained—indeed whether the existing reforms can be sustained—if fears of world food shortages recur. A price spike similar to that of 2008 occurred in the early 1970s. How did EU agricultural policy makers respond then, and again in 2008?

In the early 1970s many commodity prices soared, giving rise to global concerns about world food security, fuelled by neo-Malthusian pundits who had warned about *Limits to Growth* (Meadows et al. 1972). A variety of causal factors might be suggested, including: excess international liquidity as a result of a major US trade deficit (which led to the suspension of the convertibility of dollars into gold in August 1971); the *Yom Kippur* War of October 1973, which led the Arab states to impose an oil embargo; the Great Grain Robbery of 1975, in which Soviet buyers secured a large part of the US stocks of wheat and other cereals before the grain trade had realized the extent of their purchases (Morgan 1979: 17–22); and the 1972 *El Niño* which led to a collapse of the Peruvian anchovy fishery, and inflated prices for proteins for animal feed. Countries around the world, including the EU, attempted to protect their consumers from a sharp increase in food prices by restricting, or banning, the export of important food crops, such as cereals, thus exacerbating the impact of the shortages on world market prices. For less than a week in early summer 1973 the United States placed an embargo on the export of soybeans (an important source of protein—soybean meal—used in animal feeds), and other products, with further export controls lasting through the summer (Cooper 1987: 31).

The price spikes soon abated, but the EU's domestic response to the world food crisis was alarming. Despite the 1973 enlargement of the EU to include two states with rather more liberal attitudes to farm trade (Denmark and the United Kingdom), the CAP in the 1970s became more protectionist, not less. The reaction to the US soybean embargo was the development of its own oilseeds policy, to make the EU less dependent on imported protein feeds (Cooper 1987). This led to the oilseeds dispute with the United States outlined in Chapter 7. UK accession to the EU and the abrogation of the *Commonwealth Sugar Agreement* expelling Australian sugar from the UK market, and a 35 per cent increase in the quantities of sugar entitled to market price support in the 1975 quota review, caused the then EU of nine member states to flip from a net importer to a net exporter of sugar: By 1980 its net exports accounted for over 10 per cent of world exports (Swinbank 2008a). Growing production of milk, cereals, and other products was reflected in increased levels of self-sufficiency across the board.

The price spikes of 2008 were equally abrupt and (at the time of writing) short-lived, as illustrated in Figure 8.1, although allowing for inflation

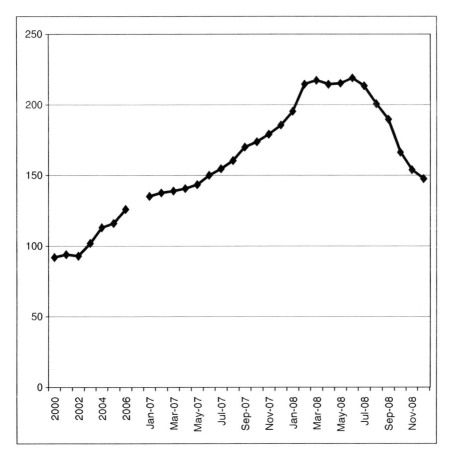

Figure 8.1 FAO food price index, 2000–8

Note: (1998–2000 = 100) Annual indices 2000–6; monthly 2007–8.

The FAO food price index is an index of indices covering cereals (including rice), vegetable oils, and animal fats, sugar, dairy products, and meats, with weighted export trade shares 1998–2000. For details see the FAO website. Because of its extensive coverage, and the differing behaviour of the commodities covered, the index does not show the more dramatic price spikes evident when the prices of individual products are graphed.

Source: http://www.fao.org/worldfoodsituation/FoodPricesIndex/en/ and personal communication from the World Food Situation division within the FAO.

they were not as severe as those of the 1970s (OECD/FAO 2008: 42). Many countries waived import duties; others imposed export taxes, and some export bans. The impact on the international rice market was particularly severe. As in the 1970s, a number of alternative explanatory factors compete for attention: excessive world liquidity, with investors looking for new investment vehicles, prior to the financial collapse later in 2008; a weak US dollar; high oil prices feeding through into higher production (particularly fertilizers) and transport costs, and linking with maize and vegetable oil prices because of government policies promoting (even mandating) the use of biofuels; rapid economic growth and urbanization in China and India; a succession of poor harvests in various parts of the globe; and global warming (Piesse and Thirtle 2009).

The EU's response, however, has been quite different to that of the 1970s (even the mid 1990s) when it imposed taxes on the export of cereals. On this occasion it did not tax exports, and the Commission (2008b: 5) gently criticized other countries that had 'responded to rising prices with restrictive export policies' by pointing out that these measures 'further tighten international agricultural markets to the detriment especially of food importing developing countries. In a medium-term perspective, such restrictions send the wrong market signal, reducing incentives for farmers to invest and increase production and contributing to imbalances on regional markets'. It is, however, perhaps important to note that the Commission has the responsibility to decide whether or not export taxes should be charged: had the initiative lain with the member states, rather different priorities might have come to the fore.[5] And it argued that part of an appropriate response to the world food 'crisis' was 'continuing to promote an open trade policy and working towards an early conclusion of the DDA' (Commission 2008b: 12). This rejection of export taxes reflects the fact that the agricultural normalist underpinning of the post-UR global farm trade regime *has* influenced the agricultural debate in the EU. For the Commission at least, trade-distorting interventions in agricultural markets are no longer on the agenda.

Some member states went further, the United Kingdom for example proposing, *inter alia*, 'a fundamental reform of Europe's agricultural sector' including 'phasing out of all elements of the CAP that are designed to keep EU agricultural prices above world market levels' and 'an end to direct payments to EU farmers'; and 'a close examination of the direct and indirect effects of EU biofuels policy, including a full assessment of its effect on food prices . . . ' (Darling 2008). A quite different perspective came from France, with President Nicolas Sarkozy reportedly saying: 'In a world where there are 800 million poor people who cannot satisfy their hunger and where a kid dies every 30 seconds from hunger, I will never accept a reduction in agricultural production on the altar of global liberalism' (as quoted in *Agra Europe*, 4 July 2008: A/1). Thus the CAP remains a contested policy arena, with some member states much more clearly wedded to the market-liberal paradigm, and others—their suspicions buttressed by the recent gyrations of world market prices—unconvinced. How this will play out in the forthcoming review of EU policies in preparation for the budget period post 2013 (the *Financial Perspective*) will only be revealed after this book has gone to press. Without a successful conclusion to the Doha discussions, we are far from convinced that internal EU concerns will drive further CAP reform (Daugbjerg and Swinbank 2008*b*). Therefore the most important role of a Doha Round farm trade agreement is perhaps not that of promoting further reductions in trade-distorting support and import protection, but instead to lock in the 2003 and subsequent CAP reforms, including the further decoupling from 2010 agreed in the Health Check reform adopted in November 2008. With a Doha farm trade agreement in place, the EU would not be able to roll back the reforms and re-couple direct payments to production requirements such as the area of land farmed with specific crops or number of livestock kept.

Nor is it easy to decide whether the 2008 world food 'crisis' makes a Doha outcome more or less likely. In the WTO it has focused attention on export taxes and restraints, in addition to its fundamental concerns about import taxes and export subsidies (Meilke 2008), but whether broadening the agenda makes an outcome more or less plausible is difficult to call. Tim Josling has suggested another variant of a critical-mass agreement if the Doha outcome is delayed.[6] This would be an 'exporter code', a new WTO agreement or binding, among exporters representing say 80 per cent of the exports of a particular commodity, to discipline the use of export subsidies *and* export taxes and restraints. One might imagine that the EU and Argentina could be moderately interested in such a pact: the EU agreeing to forego the use of export subsidies if Argentina similarly abandoned its use of export restraints. But how Japan, a main 'demander' of WTO constraints on export taxes and bans, would exercise any leverage in this critical mass is difficult to imagine, as Japan has nothing to offer on export subsidies. The deal Argentina would presumably wish to strike with Japan relates to market access and domestic support.

When world market prices were high it was possible to argue that tariff reductions were fairly 'harmless', and therefore more politically acceptable, because competitively priced imports were not available. But farm groups were nonetheless worried about any potential collapse in world market prices, arguing they needed to retain the 'safety net' of high tariffs, and these concerns were reinforced by the subsequent downturn in commodity prices. As noted earlier in this chapter, one of the sticking points in July 2008 was the proposed Special Safeguard Mechanisms for developing countries to protect against *low* world market prices. Thus we cannot see that the 2008 world food 'crisis' has improved the chances of a Doha settlement in the immediate future.

With or without a Doha settlement, disagreements over farm trade, and the underlying rationale for intervention in agricultural markets, will continue to be a source of trade conflict in the WTO. Some of these disagreements will be contested in the DSB. These disputes will be more heated and contentious without a Doha settlement, straining the whole UR construct; and European (and US) farm policy will feature prominently.

Notes

Chapter 1

1. These three topics, together with a fourth (trade facilitation) were dubbed the Singapore Issues because they referred to four working groups established by the WTO Ministerial meeting in Singapore in 1996. For a brief introduction to the Singapore Issues see, for example, Woolcock (2005: 394) or Young (2007: 803).
2. There are, nonetheless, others who contest the prevailing view. Ray and Schaffer (2007: 225) for instance, in asking: 'What if conventional wisdom is dead wrong in the case of domestic price and income programs for agriculture?', imply that it is. They go on: 'What if the worldwide elimination of all the trade-distorting price and income programs that have been identified by the WTO will not or cannot achieve the expected results?'
3. Not only in a multilateral context, which is the main focus of this book, but also within the framework of Regional Trade Agreements (RTAs) established under GATT Article XXIV. As Fiorentino et al. (2007: 26) note: 'RTAs rarely address comprehensively sensitive sectors such as agriculture'; partly 'because domestic lobbies resistant to the multilateral liberalization of such sectors will do so also at the bilateral level'. The EU has spun a web of preferential trade agreements around itself (in the Mediterranean, with the ACP states and MERCOSUR, etc.), and it is in the process of allowing duty- and quota-free access for products from the world's 50 Least Developed Countries (LDCs) under its *Everything but Arms* initiative, so a large part of its agricultural imports enter at less than the MFN (Most Favoured Nation) tariff.
4. For a critical overview see Gardner (1992). See also Coleman et al. (2004: 100) and Kay (1998: 12–13).
5. Nonetheless, the world's population continues to grow; increasing incomes in countries like China and India result in a switch to livestock products which require more land than a vegetarian diet; more land cannot readily be brought into agricultural use without adverse environmental consequences; the world's oceans are depleted of fish stocks; soil erosion, pollution, water shortages, and maybe global warming, place further potential constraints on agriculture and aquaculture; and there are pressures to devote more land to bioenergy production in an attempt to reduce greenhouse gas emissions, and dependence on

fossil fuels. Sharp increases in world commodity prices in 2007 and 2008 led to renewed European interest in food security. We will discuss this in Chapter 8.

6. A variable import levy is an import tax which is altered periodically to reflect the varying difference between a policy-determined minimum import price and a moving (and lower) world market price. For cereals the EU used to determine this gap on a daily basis (Harris et al. 1983: 47–8).

7. Moyer and Josling (2002) refer to a *competitive agriculture paradigm*, but essentially the meaning of the two terms is similar.

8. It must be said that the URAA allows for *non-trade concerns* such as food security and environmental protection, and there are provisions in the Agreement for states to promote such concerns through state intervention. However, such intervention has to be minimally trade distorting.

9. The *Producer Support Estimate* (PSE) expresses the share of farmers' gross farm receipts which can be attributed to direct or indirect support (OECD 2002: 236; Legg 2003).

10. In the next sentence of this text, published before the conclusion of the UR, she went on to say: 'As evidenced by the Uruguay Round, Americans have had only limited success.' But as we shall demonstrate in Chapter 7, whilst the United States was not successful in influencing the specific reduction commitments of the URAA, it had a decisive say on the Agreement's ideational underpinning.

11. *Official Journal of the European Union* (2007).

12. There are currently nine different configurations: *http://www.consilium.europa. eu/cms3_fo/showPage.asp?id=427&lang=EN&mode=g*, last accessed on 10 December 2008.

13. Cunha (2007: 160), the Portuguese Farm Minister, who was chairing the Council when the MacSharry reforms were adopted (at the end of a long negotiation) in May 1992, suggests that he was able to deflect an Italian attempt to invoke the Luxembourg compromise (prompted by concerns about the size of Italy's milk quota) by leaving the Italian delegation to last. By the time Italy was given the floor there was a qualified majority in favour of the package, which accordingly was passed with Italy dissenting.

14. For a flavour of the scene, see, for example, the daily 'blog' written in Geneva by Peter Mandelson during the failed meeting on 21–29 July 2008 (Mandelson 2008).

Chapter 2

1. Davis (2003) argues that the more trade institutions link multiple sectors in a negotiation, the more likely that trade liberalization can be expected. She applies a quantitative approach to analyse EU–US and Japan–US agriculture negotiations and trade disputes over the period 1970–99. While we do not

challenge her argument, we do believe that Davis overlooks key ideational and institutional reforms that changed the game. In particular, she fails to differentiate between the period up to 1995 (with the 'old' GATT rules) and post-1995 (with the new WTO), and so fails to acknowledge that the URAA marked a seminal change in international agricultural trade relations.

2. Patterson (1997) expands the model to three levels when analysing the negotiating position of the EU.

3. During the debate on the MacSharry reforms there was a brief discussion of the bond scheme proposed by the Danish Minister of Agriculture in November 1991. This involved an explicit discussion of the problems of switching from price support to decoupled, time-limited, direct payments (see Daugbjerg 2003: 426–31 for an analysis of the bond scheme debate, and Swinbank and Tangermann 2004 for an exposition of the bond scheme). As one of several steps in moving from price support to decoupled bonds, the proposal would have involved a transformation of price support to direct decoupled compensatory payments. Farm Commissioner Ray MacSharry highlighted the problems of this exercise. He was particularly concerned that, under the bond scheme, future payments would be fixed and consequently adjustments could not be made.

Chapter 3

1. The family of agreements administered by the WTO includes the GATT dating back to 1947, but now known as GATT 1994, various additional agreements on trade in goods expanding on, and sometimes derogating from, GATT, a General Agreement on Trade in Services (GATS), and an Agreement on Trade-Related Aspects of Intellectual Property Rights (the TRIPS agreement). All can be downloaded from the WTO website: *www.wto.org*.

2. Wilcox (1949), who led the US delegation in the negotiations (Diebold 1952: 4), provides a detailed overview of the history and content of the draft ITO Charter. Diebold (1952), in a lively paper, outlines US apathy and opposition to the charter, and details its demise. Without US support the charter had no chance of success.

3. The draft charter is reproduced in Wilcox 1949.

4. Under the Protocol of Provisional Application, Parts I and III of GATT were applied unconditionally, whilst Part II (Articles III to XXIII) was to be applied 'to the fullest extent not inconsistent with existing [national] legislation' (Jackson 1997: 40). Thus GATT members secured so-called *grandfather rights*, in that domestic legislation on 'customs procedures, quotas, subsidies, anti-dumping duties, and national treatment', in place in 1947, was unchallenged by more restrictive GATT provisions.

5. Reference is frequently made to RTAs in discussions of free-trade areas and customs unions, even when formed from geographically disparate states.

6. When members negotiate tariff levels either on accession to GATT/WTO, or in the periodic *Rounds* of multilateral trade negotiations, those tariffs are said to be bound. Once a tariff is bound it forms an integral part of that member's GATT/WTO obligations, and a *higher* tariff rate cannot be applied. Members can be released from GATT/WTO bindings only as a result of GATT Article XXVIII negotiations (Hoekman and Kostecki 2001: 148–9).

7. A primary product is defined in the text as 'any product of farm, forest or fishery, or any mineral, in its natural form or which has undergone such processing as is customarily required to prepare it for marketing in substantial volume in international trade'. The Tokyo Round's subsidies code, discussed below, removed minerals from this list.

8. The DSU, and the role of panels, will be outlined in Chapter 5.

9. This text is available on the WTO website. GATT Article VI deals with countervailing measures, and Article XXIII with the 'nullification and impairment' of members' rights.

10. Although not forced to assume the obligations of the Subsidies Code, non-signatories did assume all the rights granted by those GATT contracting parties that did sign (Steinberg 2002: 357).

11. The URAA applies to agricultural raw materials and processed food and drink products, as set out in Annex 1 to the URAA, *but not to fish, fish products, wood or cork*.

12. Although in practice most countries had worked this out long before.

13. Determining tariff equivalents through tariffication, as specified in the modalities document, was a complex—but supposedly exact—process (which nonetheless, as we have seen, led to accusations of dirty tariffication). Recognizing that tariffication could be problematic for developing countries, particularly if they had simply banned imports in the past, developing countries were allowed to set *ceiling bindings*. Many chose to fix high ceiling bindings (say at 100%) as their *bound* rate, whilst actually charging a lower *applied* rate on imports. When the import tariffs that countries apply are lower than their bound rates, trade policy analysts refer to a tariff *overhang*. It gives countries scope, in tariff negotiations, to agree on reductions in bound rates that translate into much smaller, or even no, reductions in applied rates.

14. See also Josling and Swinbank (2008) for shadow estimates of EU domestic support through to 2013/14.

Chapter 4

1. In the latter instance the country had imported from a low-cost supplier before the formation of the customs union, despite having trade restrictions in place.

When trade restrictions were removed on a selective basis, imports from the customs union partner appeared cheaper to consumers than imports from third countries that still faced import restrictions.

2. The EEC wanted a formula approach covering all farm support, rather than GATT's traditional 'offer and request' tariff negotiations. The margin of support would be 'equal to the difference between the price of the product on the international market and the remuneration actually obtained by the . . . producer' (GATT 1964: paragraph 18). Thus the proposal was to bind the overall level of support, rather than to negotiate on particular policy mechanisms. The EEC suggested that, if adopted, 'by binding its own amount of support it would limit considerably . . . the existing scope of its levy mechanism' (paragraph 25). Internal support prices could not readily be increased. However, the external reference price would be *fixed*: derived from world market prices in some historical period (paragraph 41).

3. Clayton Yeutter returned to serve as USTR under President Reagan, and then as Secretary for Agriculture under the first President Bush, in the UR, with an ambition to achieve what had proved unattainable in the Tokyo Round. Indeed Oxley (1990: 62), writing before its completion, suggested somewhat prematurely that 'The Uruguay Round is Yeutter's Round.'

4. On the Swiss formula, see Winham (1986: 163) and Chapter 7 of this volume.

5. Like many before, and since, Gundelach was no novice when it came to debating agricultural policy and GATT rules. He served as Commissioner for the Internal Market and Customs Union in the Commission headed by François-Xavier Ortoli (1973–7) and then as Vice-President and Commissioner for Agriculture (1977–80) under the Presidency of Roy Jenkins. He was just beginning his second term as Commissioner for Agriculture when he died in January 1981. He had headed the Danish mission in Brussels during the accession negotiations. As a career diplomat he was well versed in the GATT, having served as a Deputy-Director-General of GATT before moving to Brussels, and was said to have had 'a major hand in the outcome of the Kennedy Round' (Ruggiero 1998). Back in 1958, as Denmark's representative at the meeting establishing Committee II, the minutes record his contribution as follows: 'Discussion of agricultural protectionism was of special concern to Denmark. . . . He hoped that the new approach would give good results' (GATT 1958b: 168).

6. And yet earlier in the same volume Hudec (1993: 131) had written that by late 1978 'the United States had already signed off on a rather weak Subsidies Code', and moreover that the United States had agreed to provide 'a secret letter assuring the Community that the Subsidies Code would not be used to attack the fundamental character of the Common Agricultural Policy'. If this secret assurance was given, it does not appear to have protected the CAP from attack.

7. *Citrus* focused on the EU's tariff preferences for its Mediterranean Associates, and the compatibility with GATT Article XXIV dealing with customs unions and

free-trade areas, rather than with the CAP *per se*; but the preferences were valuable (and hence contested) because of agricultural protectionism.

8. In the 1980s the then Australian government-funded Bureau of Agricultural Economics (later the Australian Bureau of Agricultural and Resource Economics) published a series of reports that attempted to expand the policy discourse: for example, in 1985 they toured Europe promoting a substantial text which appeared to be designed to explain the CAP to European policy analysts and policy makers! (Bureau of Agricultural Economics 1985).

9. The Cairns Group originally comprised Argentina, Australia, Brazil, Canada, Chile, Colombia, Fiji, Hungary, Indonesia, Malaysia, New Zealand, the Philippines, Thailand, and Uruguay. Hungary subsequently withdrew; but as of December 2008 the Group's website listed 19 members: *http://www.cairnsgroup.org/index.html*, accessed 12 December 2008.

10. The loan rate provided *market* price support. In addition, farmers who participated in the programme by setting aside part of their acreage received deficiency payments if the market price fell below the target price.

11. The Punta del Este declaration is reprinted in Croome's semi-official 'history' of the UR (Croome 1999) and in Paemen and Bensch (1995). See Chapters 1 and 2 of Croome for his account of the preparations for, and launch of, the UR.

12. Alternatively, see Barton et al. (2006: 65–6).

13. According to Hudec (1993: 193) this 'all-or-nothing approach' was 'a product of political needs of the Uruguay Round', an attack on 'free riders', and 'not really necessary to a stronger legal design'. His verdict: 'developing country "free riders" would be told to pay in full or leave'.

Chapter 5

1. Thompson (2007: 26) suggests that the US position also has to be viewed in terms of domestic politics: 'By more thoroughly embedding US trade policy—especially regarding the settlement of disputes and the imposition of retaliation—within the GATT/WTO framework, the Uruguay Round minimized the discretion available to US trade officials and transferred power (in a relative sense) from Congress to the executive branch.'

2. The following paragraphs, and Figure 5.1, draw heavily on the WTO's own description at: *http://www.wto.org/english/thewto_e/whatis_e/tif_e/disp1_e.htm*, accessed 19 February 2007.

3. Furthermore, as we saw in Chapter 3, the Subsidies Agreement and the UR *Agreement on Safeguards* allow Members to implement various Trade Defence Mechanisms without recourse to the DSU (anti-dumping duties, countervailing levies to offset subsidies, and emergency action on imports to counter unforeseen developments). Similarly the URAA has its own special

safeguard provisions. However, a Member's use of any of these mechanisms could be challenged and thus become subject to a DSU proceeding.

4. However, in *European Communities—Export Subsidies on Sugar* the panel found that the EU's export subsidy regime contravened various provisions of the URAA, but declined on grounds of judicial economy to rule whether these elements amounted to prohibited subsidies under Article 3 of the SCM Agreement (WTO 2005*a*: paragraph 321). Had the DSB found the export subsidies to be prohibited subsidies, then under Article 4.7 of the SCM Agreement the panel could have recommended removal of the offending subsidies 'without delay', whereas a longer phase-out was eventually determined.

5. This might imply that the rule is only operative against large countries, depending on a panel's interpretation of the provisions: a small country could, for example, apply a contested green box policy that encouraged domestic production but which nonetheless had no discernable impact on *world* production or internationally traded quantities.

6. http://www.wto.org/english/thewto_e/whatis_e/tif_e/disp1_e.htm, accessed 19 February 2007.

7. See for example, Stovall and Hathaway's discussion (2003) of how Chiquita was instrumental in persuading the US government to prosecute the banana case against the EU.

8. Busch and Reinhardt (2002) discuss the difficulties inherent in a study of this sort.

9. Davis (2006) discusses two cases in which Peru challenged the European labelling of scallops and sardines.

10. The EU negotiated TRQs with Thailand and Brazil to limit the quantities of salted and cooked chicken that could be imported at the lower tariff rates (*Agra Europe*, 1 December 2006).

11. There is an extensive literature outlining, and analysing, the lengthy banana saga. See for example, Read (2005), although with subsequent developments this is now a dated source.

12. WTO's summary of Dispute DS320 at *http://www.wto.org/english/tratop_e/dispu_e/cases_e/ds320_e.htm*, accessed 15 December 2008.

13. In a rather badly drafted footnote to its schedule of commitments, the EU said: 'Does not include exports of sugar of ACP and Indian origin on which the Community is not making any reduction commitments. The average of export in the period 1986–90 amounted to 1.6 million tonnes.'

14. Somewhat controversially, it continued to issue export licences until 22 May 2006 (*Agra Europe*, 26 May 2006).

15. Following the political decision in the Council in November 2005 to accept the package, there was a delay in formal adoption as the Council had to wait for the Parliament to proffer its advice. Although there was no obligation to heed Parliament's views, some minor amendments were accepted (Noble 2006).

16. Chile did change its policy, but was subject to a further complaint from Argentina. In May 2007 the Appellate Body ruled that Chile was still 'acting inconsistently with its obligations under Article 4.2 of the Agreement on Agriculture and has not implemented the recommendations and rulings of the DSB' (WTO 2007b: paragraph 254).

17. In other publications we have used the acronym SPS to designate the Single Payment Scheme. However, in this text we use 'SPS' for 'sanitary and phytosanitary measures', as in the UR's SPS Agreement.

18. However, soaring world market prices led the EU to remove all export subsidies on dairy products in June 2007 (*Agra Europe*, 15 June 2007: EP/8).

19. Although the sugar quota buyout failed initially, a revamped scheme meant that by 2008 the Commission was not expecting to export in 2009. Consequently, a draft budget for 2009 (covering the period from mid October 2008 to the same time in 2009) was presented that did not provide for export subsidies on sugar (*Agra Europe*, 6 June 2008: EP/7). With the export subsidy on sugar set at zero then, under the URAA rules, no subsidy can be paid on the sugar incorporated into processed products.

20. *http://www.wto.org/english/tratop_e/dispu_e/dispu_by_country_e.htm*, accessed 15 December 2008.

Chapter 6

1. However, in a subsequent edition of this essay, Rieger (2005: 180) wrote: 'The new politics of international trade relations have probably had more impact on CAP reform than intra-EU budgetary pressures and internal factors.'

2. The 1982 farm price package was adopted by qualified majority vote. See Butler 1986 (158–63), a former British Permanent Representative to the EU, on this and more generally on qualified majority voting. We think Swinnen (2008: 138) misleads in implying that the Single European Act of 1987 introduced qualified majority voting into the CAP; and wrong in writing: 'the 1999 CAP reforms... were a watershed: for the first time a major country (France) was outvoted in relation to a major CAP reform'. Although France was in the minority in the Agriculture Council, the 1999 reforms were settled unanimously by the European Council after French concerns were addressed (Ackrill 2000: 346–7).

3. This will change if and when the *Treaty of Lisbon* is ratified and comes into force, as this will enhance the powers of the European Parliament.

4. Personal notes, the 109th EAAE seminar, 'The CAP after the Fischler reform', Viterbo, Italy, 20–21 November 2008.

5. As agreed in 2003, the first €5,000 in single farm payments receivable by the farm were to be paid in full, whereas payments above €5,000 were 'modulated' (i.e. taxed) with the proceeds channelled into second pillar expenditure.

6. Interestingly, in a personal conversation with one of the authors at the 109th EAAE seminar, 'The CAP after the Fischler reform', Viterbo, Italy, 20–21 November 2008, former Farm Commissioner Franz Fischler disagreed with his former aid on this. He said that the core measure of the reform, the decoupling of direct payments, was aimed at enabling the EU to offer something on domestic support in the WTO.

Chapter 7

1. It is interesting to note that the Agriculture Council was also in session, and in the same location, but its press release carries no mention of the GATT negotiations (Council of the European Communities 1987b).
2. We have been unable to locate both this document from the United States, and the EU's document referred to in the next paragraph, in the *List & Index of Uruguay Round Documents issued between 1986 and 1994* produced by the GATT Secretariat in December 1994.
3. But, in an attempt to appease Germany, facing elections in December, EU farm ministers had been promised that farmers would receive compensation 'in the form of direct income supports that do not stimulate production' ('EC deal on farm aid could save Uruguay Round', *Financial Times*, 24 October 1990: 3): a precursor of the CAP reform proposals to be tabled early in 1991. The Council Press Release, following the unanimous approval of the EU's GATT 'offer', notes that 'the Commission undertook to submit in the very near future measures designed to soften the effect on Community agriculture of the reductions in support which will ensue from the Community offer' (Council of the European Communities 1990).
4. For example, the EU's text recorded the level of support to cereals and rice in 1986 as 15.6 billion ecus, but only 13.4 billion in 1990. The EU's offer was to reduce support to 10.9 billion in 1995: a 30 per cent reduction on the 1986 level, but only 19 per cent on 1990 (Commission 1990: Annex 1A).
5. See Chapter 3, Box 3.3 for a description of the Peace Clause.
6. These papers do not appear to be publicly available from the WTO. However, this particular document was published a year later (European Commission 1999). The AIE was concluded prior to the Seattle Ministerial.
7. Documents 17, 18, 19, and 24 in the series G/AG/NG/W/...
8. But rules of origin apply. For a discussion of the impact of rules of origin see McQueen (1982).
9. The *US Proposal for Global Agricultural Trade Reform (2002)* was made available on the USDA's Foreign Agricultural Service website at *http://www.fas.usda.gov/ itp/wto/proposal.htm* (accessed 21 February 2008).
10. The original group (of 20) was Argentina, Bolivia, Brazil, Chile, China, Colombia, Costa Rica, Cuba, Ecuador, El Salvador, Guatemala, India, Mexico,

Pakistan, Paraguay, Peru, Philippines, South Africa, Thailand, and Venezuela. Brazil was seen as its leader.

11. Fast track, or trade promotion authority as it is formally named, treats an international trade agreement as a congressional–executive agreement and not as a treaty. Congressional–executive agreements can be adopted by simple majority vote of each chamber of Congress. Treaties require a two-thirds majority (Grimmett 2001). To ratify a trade agreement under the fast-track procedure, the president submits an implementing bill to both houses which decide on ratification in up-or-down-vote on the whole agreement without the option to amend it. The ratification process is deadline driven and is only allowed limited debate (Shapiro and Brainard 2003: 14–16).

Chapter 8

1. The Warwick Commission (2007: 30) expressed this slightly differently, suggesting that there are 'two different but not necessarily mutually exclusive meanings that attach to the concept of a single undertaking'. The first relates to the negotiation: 'nothing is agreed until everything is agreed'. The second 'relates to obligations rather than procedure': 'all Members are obliged to subscribe to all the constituent parts of a negotiated package'. The Warwick Commission was not set up by a government or international agency, but instead it was established by the University of Warwick to address issues of global importance. Composed of selected international scholars from Warwick and elsewhere, its aim was 'to make thought-provoking contributions to the debate thereby assisting policymakers to find solutions to sometimes seemingly intractable problems' (Warwick Commission 2007: iv).

2. Arguably it also raised their expectations to unattainable levels. For trade diplomats, a *negotiation* implies that all parties trade requests and offers, and these trade-offs are the cement of the Single Undertaking. However, in some quarters, the expectation of the DDA was that it would be more one-sided, with developed countries granting more concessions to developing countries than vice-versa.

3. Until January 2007 this was the Union of Industrial and Employers' Confederations of Europe (UNICE).

4. Set against this thought, however, is our earlier observations that the EU's greater apparent willingness to abide by the DSB's rulings on *farm* policy issues, compared to its lesser capacity to comply with rulings related to *food safety* concerns, might be related to the European Parliament's enhanced role in the latter. This institutional difference would disappear with ratification of the Lisbon Treaty.

5. The current regulation (No. 1234/2007, 'establishing a common organisation of agricultural markets and on specific provisions for certain agricultural

products (Single CMO Regulation)', *Official Journal of the European Union*, L299, 16 November 2007) makes no specific provision for export taxes, although export licences can be withheld, in particular to allow the EU to remain within WTO export subsidy constraints. However, Article 187, under the heading 'Disturbances caused by quotations or prices on the world market', does read: 'Where, with regard to the products of the cereals, rice, sugar and milk and milk products sectors, the quotations or prices on the world market of one or more products reach a level that disrupts or threatens to disrupt the availability of supply on the Community market and where that situation is likely to continue or to deteriorate, the Commission may take the necessary measures for the sector concerned. It may in particular suspend import duties in whole or in part for certain quantities.' Import taxes on cereals were suspended, but then reintroduced in October 2008 (*Agra Europe*, 17 October 2008: EP/1).

6. For example, at a seminar in Wye, the United Kingdom, on 28 October 2008 (*Agra Europe*, 31 October 2008: EP/10).

Bibliography

Ackrill, R. W. (2000), 'CAP Reform 1999: A Crisis in the Making?', *Journal of Common Market Studies*, 38/2: 343–53.

—— (2005), 'The Common Agricultural Policy' in van der Hoek (ed.), *Handbook on Public Administration and Policy in the European Union* (Boca Raton: Taylor & Francis), pp. 435–87.

—— Hine, R. C., Rayner, A. J. and Suardi, M. (1997), 'Member States and the Preferential Trade and Budget Effects of the 1992 CAP Reform: A Note', *Journal of Agricultural Economics*, 48/1: 93–100.

Agra Europe, various issues.

Agra Focus, no. 89, July 2003.

Alter, K. J. and Meunier, S. (2006), 'Nested and Overlapping Regimes in the Trans-atlantic Banana Trade Dispute', *Journal of European Public Policy*, 13/3: 362–82.

Ames, G. C. W. (2001), 'Bananas, Beef, and Biotechnology: Three Contentious US–EU Trade Disputes', *Review of Agricultural Economics*, 23/1: 214–22.

Anania, G. and Bureau, J.-C. (2005), 'The Negotiations on Agriculture in the Doha Development Agenda Round: Current Status and Future Prospects', *European Review of Agricultural Economics*, 32/4: 539–74.

Anderson, K. (2000), 'Agriculture's "Multifunctionality" and the WTO', *Australian Journal of Agricultural and Resource Economics*, 44/3: 475–94.

—— and Martin, W. (2006), 'Agriculture, Trade Reform, and the Doha Agenda', in Anderson and Martin (eds.), *Agricultural Trade Reform and the Doha Development Agenda* (Basingstoke: Palgrave Macmillan and the World Bank), pp. 3–35.

Anton, J. and Cahill, C. (2005), 'Towards Evaluating "More Decoupled" Payments: An Empirical Approach', paper presented at the symposium *Pressures for Agricultural Policy Reform: WTO Panels and the Doha Round Negotiations*, organized by the International Agricultural Trade Research Consortium and the European Commission Joint Research Centre, Seville, Spain, 19–21 June.

Bagwell, K. and Sykes, A. O. (2004), 'Chile—Price Band System and Safeguard Measures Relating to Certain Agricultural Products', *World Trade Review*, 3/3: 507–28.

Barton, J. H., Goldstein, J. L., Josling, T. E. and Steinberg, R. H. (2006), *The Evolution of the Trade Regime: Politics, Law and Economics of the GATT and WTO* (Princeton: Princeton University Press).

Bibliography

Baumgartner, F. R. and Jones, B. D. (1993), *Agendas and Instability in American Politics* (Chicago: The University of Chicago Press).

Benitah, M. (2005), 'U.S. Agricultural Export Credits after the WTO Cotton Ruling: The Law of Unintended Consequences', *The Estey Centre Journal of International Law and Trade Policy*, 6/2: 107–14.

Benvenuti, A. (1999), 'Australia's Battle against the Common Agricultural Policy: The Fraser Government's Trade Diplomacy and the European Community', *Australian Journal of Politics and History*, 45/2: 181–96.

Bergsten, C. F. and Cline, W. R. (1983), 'Conclusion and Policy Implications', in Cline (ed.), *Trade Policy in the 1980s* (Washington, DC: Institute for International Economics), pp. 747–78.

Bhagwati, J. (2004), 'Don't Cry for Cancún', *Foreign Affairs*, 83/1: 52–63.

Blonigen, B. A. (2004), 'Food Fight: Antidumping Activity in Agricultural Goods', in Anania, Bohman, Carter and McCalla (eds.), *Agricultural Policy Reform and the WTO: Where Are We Heading?* (Cheltenham: Edward Elgar), pp. 568–92.

Blustein, P. (2004), 'Cotton Crisis Betrayal', *Washington Post*, 12 May: E01.

Blyth, M. M. (1997), ' "Any More Bright Ideas?" The Ideational Turn of Comparative Political Economy', *Comparative Politics*, 29/2: 229–49.

—— (2002), *Great Transformations: Economic Ideas and Institutional Change in the Twentieth Century* (Cambridge: Cambridge University Press).

Borchardt, K. -D. (2008), 'Health Check', text of a speech prepared for the Brussels Session of the EAAE Congress, 28 August.

Botterill, L. C. (2003), 'Uncertain Climate: The Recent History of Drought Policy in Australia', *Australian Journal of Politics and History*, 49/1: 61–74.

Brink, L. (2007), *Classifying, Measuring and Analyzing WTO Domestic Support in Agriculture: Some Conceptual Distinctions*, Working Paper 07–02, International Agricultural Trade Research Consortium: Minnesota (http://iatrcweb.org/).

Brittan, L. (1999), 'The Next WTO Negotiations on Agriculture—a European View', paper for the 53rd Oxford Farming Conference.

Brooks, J. (1996), 'Agricultural Policies in OECD Countries: What Can We Learn from Political Economy Models?', *Journal of Agricultural Economics*, 47/3: 366–89.

Bureau of Agricultural Economics (1985), *Agricultural Policies in the European Community: Their Origins, Nature and Effects on Production and Trade*, Policy Monograph no. 2 (Canberra: Australian Government Publishing Service).

Burnett, J. (1979), *Plenty and Want. A Social History of Diet in England and Wales from 1815 To the Present Day*, revised edn., republished 1983 (London: Methuen).

Busch, M. L. and Reinhardt, E. (2002), 'Testing International Trade Law: Empirical Studies of GATT/WTO Dispute Settlement', in Kennedy and Southwick (eds.), *The Political Economy of International Trade Law. Essays in Honor of Robert E. Hudec* (Cambridge: Cambridge University Press).

Butler, M. (1986), *Europe: More than a Continent* (London: Heinemann).

Clinton, B. (1998), 'Statement by H.E. Mr. William J. Clinton, President', Geneva WTO Ministerial 1998, http://www.wto.org/english/thewto_e/minist_e/min98_e/anniv_e/clinton_e.htm, accessed 3 October 2008.

Cloke, P. (1989), 'State Deregulation and New Zealand's Agricultural Sector', *Sociologia Ruralis*, 29/1: 34–47.

Cohn, T. H. (1993), 'The Changing Role of the United States in the Global Agricultural Trade Regime', in Avery (ed.), *World Agriculture and the GATT* (Boulder and London: Lynne Rienner), pp. 17–38.

Coleman, W. D., Grant, W. and Josling, T. (2004), *Agriculture in the New Global Economy* (Cheltenham: Edward Elgar).

——Skogstad, G. D. and Atkinson, M. M. (1997), 'Paradigm Shifts and Policy Networks: Cumulative Change in Agriculture', *Journal of Public Policy*, 16/3: 273–301.

——and Tangermann, S. (1999), 'The 1992 CAP Reform, the Uruguay Round and the Commission', *Journal of Common Market Studies*, 37/3: 385–405.

Commission of the European Communities (1981), *Mandate of 30 May 1980: Guidelines for European Agriculture. Memorandum to Complement the Commission's Report on the Mandate of 30 May 1981*, COM(81)608 (Brussels: CEC).

—— (1985), *Perspectives for the Common Agricultural Policy. The Green Paper of the Commission*, COM(85)333 (Brussels: CEC).

—— (1990), *Uruguay Round. Agriculture. European Communities Offer Submitted Pursuant to MTN.TNC/15*, 7 November, unpublished.

—— (1991*a*), *Communication to the Council: The Development and Future of the CAP. Reflections Paper of the Commission*, COM(91)100 (Brussels: CEC).

—— (1991*b*), *Communication of the Commission to the Council and the European Parliament. The Development and Future of the Common Agricultural Policy. Follow-up to the Reflections Paper (COM(91)100 of 1 February 1991—Proposals of the Commission*, COM(91)258/3 Revised Version (Brussels: CEC).

—— (1992*a*), *Agriculture in the GATT Negotiations and the Reform of the CAP*, SEC(92) 2267 (Brussels: CEC).

—— (1992*b*), *The Agricultural Situation in the Community 1991 Report* (Luxembourg: Office for Official Publications of the European Communities).

—— (1997), *Agenda 2000—Volume I—Communication: For a Stronger and Wider Union* (Brussels: CEC).

—— (1998*a*), *Agenda 2000. The Future for European Agriculture. Explanatory Memorandum* (Brussels: CEC).

—— (1998*b*), *Proposals for Council Regulations (EC) Concerning Reform of the Common Agricultural Policy*, COM(1998)158 (Brussels: CEC).

—— (2002), *Communication from the Commission to the Council and the European Parliament. Mid-Term Review of the Common Agricultural Policy*. COM (2002)394 (Brussels: CEC).

Commission of the European Communities (2003), *Proposal for Establishing Common Rules for Direct Support under the Common Agricultural Policy and Support Schemes for Producers of Certain Crops*, COM(2003)23 final (Brussels: CEC).

——(2006), 'Notice of initiation of an antidumping proceeding concerning imports of frozen strawberries originating in the People's Republic of China', *Official Journal of the European Union*, C14, 19 January.

——(2007a), *Proposal for a Council Regulation Laying Down Specific Rules as Regards the Fruit and Vegetable Sector and Amending Certain Regulations*, COM(2007) 17 (Brussels: CEC).

——(2007b), *Communication from the Commission to the Council and the European Parliament: Preparing for the "Health Check" of the CAP reform*, COM(2007)722 (Brussels: CEC).

——(2008a), *Proposal for a Council Regulation Establishing Common Rules for Direct Support Schemes for Farmers under the Common Aricultural Policy and Establishing Certain Support Schemes for Farmers . . .* , COM(2008)306/4 (Brussels: CEC).

——(2008b), *Tackling the Challenge of Rising Food Prices. Directions for EU Action*, COM(2008)321 (Brussels: CEC).

Cooper, A. F. (1987), 'The Protein Link: Complexity in the US–EC Agricultural Trading Relationship', *Journal of European Integration*, XI/1: 29–45.

Council of the European Communities (1987a), *1195th Council meeting—General Affairs—Luxembourg*, 19 and 20 October, Press Release 8725/87 (Presse 166).

——(1987b), *1196th Council meeting—Agriculture—Luxembourg*, 19 and 20 October, Press Release 9018/87 (Presse 167).

——(1990), *Special Council Meeting Agriculture—with the participation of the Ministers for Foreign Trade—Brussels*, 5 and 6 November. Press Release 9721/90 (Presse 73).

Council of the European Union (1997), *2045th Council Meeting—Agriculture—Brussels*, 17, 18 and 19th November, Press Release 12241/97 (Presse 343).

——(1999), *2202nd Council Meeting—Agriculture—Brussels*, 27 September, Press Release 11277/99 (Presse 284).

——(2003), *CAP Reform—Presidency Compromise (in agreement with the Commission)*, Note from Presidency to Delegations, 30 June, 10961/03 (Brussels).

Croome, J. (1999), *Reshaping the World Trading System. A History of the Uruguay Round*, 2nd edn. (The Hague: Kluwer Law International).

Cunha, A. (2004), 'A Role for Direct Payments? The Doha Round, EU Enlargement and Prospects for CAP Reform', in Swinbank and Tranter (eds.), *A Bond Scheme for Common Agricultural Policy Reform* (Wallingford: CABI Publishing).

Cunha, A. M. (2007), *A Political Economy Analysis of the 1992, 1999 and 2003 CAP Reforms*, unpublished PhD dissertation, University of Reading.

Cunha, A. and Swinbank, A. (2009), 'Exploring the Determinants of CAP Reform: A Delphi Survey of Key Decision Makers', *Journal of Common Market Studies*, 47/2: 235–61.

Curzon, G. and Curzon, V. (1976), 'The Management of Trade Relations in the GATT', in Shonfield (ed.), *International Economic Relations of the Western World 1959–1971. Volume 1 Politics and Trade* (Oxford: Oxford University Press).

Dam, K. W. (1967), 'The European Common Market in Agriculture', *Columbia Law Review*, 67/2: 209–65.

Darling, A. (2008), letter to Dr Andrej Bajuk, Minister of Finance, Slovenia, 13 May: http://www.hm-treasury.gov.uk/media/4/1/chx_letter130508.pdf, accessed 10 September 2008.

Daugbjerg, C. (1998), *Policy Networks under Pressure: Pollution Control, Policy Reform, and the Power of Farmers* (Aldershot: Ashgate).

——(1999), 'Reforming the CAP: Policy Networks and Broader Institutional Structures', *Journal of Common Market Studies*, 37/3: 407–28.

——(2003), 'Policy Feedback and Paradigm Shift in EU Agricultural Policy: the Effects of the MacSharry Reform on Future Reform', *Journal of European Public Policy*, 10/3: 421–37.

——(2008), 'Ideas in Two-level Games: The EC–United States Dispute over Agriculture in the GATT Uruguay Round', *Comparative Political Studies*, 41/9: 1266–89.

——(2009), 'Sequencing in Public Policy: The Evolution of the CAP over a Decade', *Journal of European Public Policy*, 16/3: 395–411.

—— and Swinbank, A. (2004), 'The CAP and EU Enlargement: Prospects for an Alternative Strategy to Avoid the Lock-in of CAP Support', *Journal of Common Market Studies*, 42/1: 99–119.

—— ——(2007), 'The Politics of CAP Reform: Trade Negotiations, Institutional Settings and Blame Avoidance', *Journal of Common Market Studies*, 45/1: 1–22.

—— ——(2008a), 'Curbing Agricultural Exceptionalism: The EU's Response to External Challenge', *The World Economy*, 30/5: 631–52.

—— ——(2008b), 'Explaining the Health Check: The Budget, WTO, and Multi-functional Policy Paradigm Revisited', paper prepared for the 109th EAAE Seminar The CAP after The Fischler Reform: National Implementations, Impact Assessment and the Agenda for Future Reforms, Viterbo, Italy, November 20–1.

—— ——(2009), 'Ideational Change in the WTO and Its Impacts on EU Agricultural Policy Institutions and the CAP', *Journal of European Integration*, 31/4: 311–27.

Davis, C. L. (2003), *Food Fights over Free Trade. How International Institutions Promote Trade Liberalization* (Princeton: Princeton University Press).

——(2006), 'Do WTO Rules Create a Level Playing Field? Lessons from the Experience of Peru and Vietnam', in Odell (ed.), *Negotiating Trade: Developing Countries in the WTO and NAFTA* (Cambridge: Cambridge University Press).

——(2007), 'A Conflict of Institutions? The WTO and EU Agricultural Policy', unpublished manuscript: http://www.princeton.edu/cldavis/research/index.html (accessed 9 May 2007).

de Gorter, H. (2004), 'Market Access, Export Subsidies, and Domestic Support: Developing New Rules', in Ingco and Winters (eds.), *Agriculture and the New*

Trade Agenda: Creating a Global Trading Environment for Development (Cambridge: Cambridge University Press), pp. 151–75.

—— and Swinnen, J. (2002), 'Political Economy of Agricultural Policy', in Gardner and Rausser (eds.), *Handbook of Agricultural Economics. Volume 2B: Agricultural and Food Policy* (Amsterdam: Elsevier), pp. 1893–1943.

Defra and HM Treasury (2005), *A Vision for the Common Agricultural Policy* (London: Stationery Office).

Desta, M. G. (2002), *The Law of International Trade in Agricultural Products. From GATT 1947 to the WTO Agreement on Agriculture* (The Hague: Kluwer Law International).

Diebold Jr., W. (1952), *The End of the ITO*, Essays in International Finance No. 16 (Princeton, NJ: Princeton University).

Downs, A. (1957), *An Economic Theory of Democracy* (New York: Harper & Row).

EU/USA (2003), 'Joint Initiative by EU and USA presented today (13/8/2003) to trade partners in Geneva (WTO) with a view to advancing the negotiations in the Doha round towards a successful conclusion in Cancun as requested by our other trading partners', pdf document downloaded from http://ec.europa.eu/agriculture/external/wto/archive/index_en.htm (last accessed October 3 2008).

European Commission (1996), *The Agricultural Situation in the European Union 1995 Report* (Luxembourg: Office for Official Publications of the European Communities).

—— (1999), *Contribution of the European Community on the Multifunctional Character of Agriculture*, Info-paper (Brussels: CEC).

—— (2001), *Environment as a Non-Trade Concern*, Discussion Paper Two, International Conference on Non-Trade Concerns in Agriculture, Mauritius, 28–31 May.

—— (2002), *WTO and Agriculture: European Commission Proposes More Market Opening, Less Trade Distorting Support and a Radically Better Deal for Developing Countries*, Press Release IP/02/1892, 16 December 2002 (Brussels).

—— (2003), *WTO and Agriculture: The European Union Takes Steps to Move the Negotiations Forward*, Press Release IP/03/126, 27 January 2003 (Brussels).

—— (2006), 'Does the "trade talk" match the "trade walk"? Exploding the Myths Surrounding World Trade', *Monitoring Agri-Trade Policies (MAPs)* No. 03–06 (Brussels: CEC).

—— (2007), 'CAP Reform: Fruit and Vegetable Reform Will Raise Competitiveness, Promote Consumption, Ease Market Crises and Improve Environmental Protection', Press Release IP/07/810 (*http://europa.eu/rapid/pressReleasesAction.do?reference*=IP/07/810&format=HTML&aged=0&language=EN&guiLanguage=en).

European Council (1999), 'Presidency Conclusions: Berlin European Council 24 and 25 March 1999', Press Release: Brussels, Nr. SN 100.

European Union (2003), 'A Proposal for Modalities in the WTO Agriculture Negotiations. Specific Drafting Input: EC', paper for the Committee on Agriculture, Special Session. JOB(03)/12 (Geneva: WTO).

—— (2005), *Making Hong Kong a Success: Europe's Contribution*, 28 October: http://trade.ec.europa.eu/doclib/docs/2005/october/tradoc_125641.pdf (retrieved 30 April 2009).

Evans, L. (1987), 'Farming in a Changing Economic Environment', in Bollard and Buckle (eds.), *Economic Liberalisation in New Zealand* (Wellington: Allen & Unwin in association with Port Nicholson Press), pp. 102–20.

—— Grimes, A., Wilkinson, B. and Teece, D. (1996), 'Economic Reform in New Zealand 1984–95: The Pursuit of Efficiency', *Journal of Economic Literature*, XXXIV/4: 1856–1902.

Faber, G. and Orbie, J. (eds.) (2007), *European Union Trade Politics and Development: 'Everything but Arms' unravelled* (London: Routledge).

FAO (1973), *Agricultural Protection: Domestic Policy and International Trade*, C73/LIM9 (Rome: FAO).

Feindt, P. H. and Müller, F. (2007), 'Reagieren oder Gestalten? GAP-Reform und WTO-Verhandlungen by', in Feindt and Lange (eds.), *Agrarpolitik im 21. Jahrhundert: Wahrnehmungen, Konflkite, Verständigungsbedarf*, Loccumer Protokolle 30/07 (Rehburg-Loccum: Evangelische Akademie Loccum), pp. 91–104.

Financial Times, various issues.

Fiorentino, R. V., Verdeja, L. and Toqueboeuf, C. (2007), *The Changing Landscape of Regional Trade Agreements: 2006 Update*, Discussion Paper No. 12 (Geneva: WTO).

Fischer Boel, M. (2008), 'Observations on a CAP for the Future', Congress of European Farmers 2008 organised by COPA/COGECA Brussels, 30 September, SPEECH/08/472 http://europa.eu/rapid/pressReleasesAction.do?reference=SPEECH/08/472&format=HTML&aged=0&language=EN&guiLanguage=en, accessed 7 October 2008.

Fischler, F. (2001), 'CAP—State of Play', presentation by Commissioner Franz Fischler, April, http://ec.europa.eu/agriculture/capreform/comsem1.pdf (retrieved 31 July 2007).

—— (2002a), 'The Mid term Review of the CAP', presentation at the Commission Seminar on the MTR, April, http://ec.europa.eu/agriculture/capreform/comsem2.pdf (retrieved 31 July 2007).

—— (2002b), 'Towards Sustainable Farming—Presentation of the CAP Mid-term Review', Speech/02/330 (Brussels: CEC).

Fukuda, H., Dyck, J. and Stout, J. (2003), *Rice Sector Policies in Japan*, Electronic Outlook Report from the Economic Research Service RCS-0303–01, USDA: www.ers.usda.gov.

Gardner, B. L. (1992), 'Changing Economic Perspectives on the Farm Problem', *Journal of Economic Literature*, XXX/1: 62–101.

Garzon, I. (2006), *Reforming the Common Agricultural Policy: History of a Paradigm Change* (Basingstoke: Palgrave).

GATT (1958a), *Trends in International Trade. A Report by a Panel of Experts* (Geneva: GATT) (The Haberler Report).

—— (1958b), Thirteenth Session, *Summary Record of the Seventeenth Meeting Held at the Palais des Nations, Geneva, on Monday, 17 November 1958, at 2.30 p.m.*, SR.13/ 17 (Geneva: GATT).

—— (1960), Sixteenth Session, *Second Report of Committee II. Note by the Chairman of Committee II*, L/1192 (Geneva: GATT).

—— (1961), Eighteenth Session, *Third Report of Committee II. Note by the Chairman*, L/1461 (Geneva: GATT).

—— (1962), Twentieth Session, *Report of Committee II on the Consultation with the European Economic Community*, L/1910 (Geneva: GATT).

—— (1964), *Statement by the Representative of the European Economic Community Before the GATT Committee on Agriculture Regarding the Negotiating Plan of the EEC for the Agriculture Part of the Kennedy Round*, TN.64/AGR/1 (Geneva: GATT).

—— (1982a), Contracting Parties Thirty-Eighth Session, *Ministerial Declaration Adopted on 29 November 1982*, L/5424 (Geneva: GATT).

—— (1982b), *Working Party—Sugar. Report to the Council*, L/5294 (Geneva: GATT).

—— (1987a), *United States Proposal for Negotiations on Agriculture*, MTN. GNG/NG5/ W/14 (Geneva: GATT).

—— (1987b), *European Communities Proposal for Multilateral Trade Negotiations on Agriculture*, MTN.GNG/NG5 /W/20 (Geneva: GATT).

—— (1987c), *Negotiating Group on Agriculture 26–27 October 1987 Statement by European Communities*, MTN.GNG/NG5/W/24 (Geneva: GATT).

—— (1989a), *Trade Negotiations Committee Meeting at Level of High Officials*, Geneva, 5–8 April 1989, MTN.TNC/9 (Geneva: GATT).

—— (1989b), *Submission of the United States on Comprehensive Long-Term Agricultural Reform*, MTN.GNG/NG5/W/14 (Geneva: GATT).

—— (1989c), *Global Proposal of the European Community on the Long-Term Objectives for the Multilateral Negotiation on Agricultural Questions*, MTN.GNG/NG5/W/145 (Geneva: GATT).

—— (1989d), *European Economic Community—Payments and Subsidies Paid To Processors and Producers of Oilseeds and Related Animal-feed Proteins. Report of the Panel.* L/6627 (Geneva: GATT).

—— (1990a), *Summary of the Main Points Raised at the Eighteenth Meeting of the Negotiating Group on Agriculture (19–20 December 1989) Note by the Secretariat*, MTN.GNG/NG5/W/149 (Geneva: GATT).

—— (1990b), *Framework Agreement on Agriculture Reform Programme. Draft Text by the Chairman*, MTN.GNG/NG5/W/170 (Geneva: GATT).

—— (1991a), *European Economic Community—Payments and Subsidies Paid to Processors and Producers of Oilseeds and Related Animal-feed Proteins. Follow-up to the Panel Report. Communication from the United States.* L/6933 (Geneva: GATT).

—— (1991b), *Draft Final Act Embodying the Results of the Uruguay Round of Multilateral Trade Negotiations.* MTN.TNC/W/FA (Geneva: GATT).

—— (1992), *Follow-up on the Panel Report 'European Economic Community—Payments and Subsidies Paid to Processors and Producers of Oilseeds and Related Animal-feed Proteins'. Report of the Members of the Original Oilseeds Panel.* DS28/R (Geneva: GATT) (Published as BISD 396/91).

—— (1993), *Modalities for the Establishment of Specific Binding Commitments under the Reform Programme, Note by the Chairman of the Market Access Group*, MTN.GNG/MA/W/24 (Geneva: GATT).

Goldstein, J. (1993), *Ideas, Interests, and American Trade Policy* (Ithaca: Cornell University Press).

—— and Keohane, R. H. (1993), 'Ideas and Foreign Policy: An Analytical Framework', in Goldstein and Keohane (eds.), *Ideas and Foreign Policy: Beliefs, Institutions, and Political Change* (Ithaca: Cornell University Press), pp. 3–30.

Gómez-Limón, J. A. and Hurlé, J. B. (2007), *La Multifuncionalidad de la agricultura en Espana: Concepto, aspectos horizontals, cuantificatión y casos pácticos* (Madrid: Ministerio de Agricultura, Pesca y Alimentacion).

Gourevitch, P. A. (1989), 'Keynesian Politics: The Political Sources of Economic Policy Choices', in Hall (ed.), *The Political Power of Economic Ideas: Keynesianism across Countries* (Princeton: Prince University Press), pp. 87–106.

Grant, W. (1995), 'Is Agricultural Policy Still Exceptional?', *The Political Quarterly*, 66: 156–69.

—— (1997), *The Common Agricultural Policy* (Houndsmill: Macmillan).

Grimmett, J. J. (2001), 'Why Certain Trade Agreements Are Approved as Congressional-Executive Agreements Rather than as Treaties', *CRS Report for Congress*, 97–894.

Gundelach, F. O. (1979), 'Prospects for the Common Agricultural Policy in the World Context', in Tracy and Hodac (eds.), *Prospects for Agriculture in the European Economic Community. Cahiers de Bruges* NS 38 (Bruges: De Tempel).

Hall, P. A. (1986), *Governing the Economy: The Politics of State Intervention in Britain and France* (Cambridge: Polity Press).

—— (1989), 'Conclusion: The Politics of Keynesian Ideas', in Hall (ed.), *The Political Power of Economic Ideas: Keynesianism across Countries* (Princeton: Prince University Press), pp. 361–91.

—— (1993), 'Policy Paradigms, Social Learning, and the State. The Case of Economic Policymaking in Britain', *Comparative Politics*, 25/3: 275–96.

Halpin, D. (2005), 'Agricultural Interest Groups and Global Challenges: Decline and Resilience', in Halpin (ed.), *Surviving Global Change? Agricultural Interest Groups in Comparative Perspective* (Aldershot: Ashgate), pp. 1–28.

Haniotis, T. (2007), 'The 2003 Reform of the European Union's Common Agricultural Policy and its Relevance To the U.S. Farm Policy Debate', in Arha, Josling, Sumner and Thompson (eds.), *US Agricultural Policy and The 2007 Farm Bill* (Woods Institute for the Environment, Stanford University), pp. 53–74.

Hanson, V. (2008), 'WTO Roundup', *Trade Negotiations Insights*, 7/7: 11–12.

Harris, B. and Devadoss, S. (2005), 'Why Did the Byrd Amendment Not Fly with the WTO?', *The Estey Centre Journal of International Law and Trade Policy*, 6/2: 226–50.

Harris, S. (1990), 'Agricultural Trade and Agricultural Trade Policy', in Williams (ed.), *Agriculture in the Australian Economy*, 3rd edn. (Melbourne: Sydney University Press).

Harris, S., Swinbank A. and Wilkinson G. (1983). *The Food and Farm Policies of the European Community*. (Chichester: John Wiley & Sons).

Hartwell, R. M. (1971), 'Introduction', Ricardo, *On the Principles of Political Economy, and Taxation* (London: Penguin).

Harvey, D. R. (2003), 'Agri-environmental Relationships and Multi-functionality: Further Considerations', *The World Economy*, 26/5:705–25.

Hay, C. (1995), 'Structure and Agency', in Marsh and Stoker (eds.), *Theories and Methods in Political Science* (London: Macmillan), pp. 189–206.

Heisenberg, D. (2005), 'The Institution of "Consensus" in the European Council: Formal Versus Informal Decision making in the Council', *European Journal of Political Science*, 44/1: 65–90.

Hillman, J. S. (1994). 'The US Perspective', in Ingersent, Rayner and Hine (eds.), *Agriculture in the Uruguay Round* (New York: St. Martin's Press), pp. 26–54.

Hindley, Brian (1999), 'New Institutions for Transatlantic Trade?', *International Affairs*, 75/1: 45–60.

Hoekman, B. and Howse, R. (2008), 'EC-Sugar' *World Trade Review*, 7/1: 149–78.

Hoekman, B. M. and Kostecki, M. M. (2001), *The Political Economy of the World Trading System. The WTO and Beyond*, 2nd edn. (Oxford: Oxford University Press).

House of Lords Select Committee on the European Communities (2008), Evidence of Mr Adrian van den Hoven, Director International Relations, Mr Eoin O'Malley, Senior Advisor International Relations, and Ms Schild, Junior Advisor International Relations, BusinessEurope, 24 June.

Hudec, R. E. (1993), *Enforcing International Trade Law: The Evolution of the Modern GATT Legal System* (Salem: Butterworth Legal Publishers).

——(1998), *Does the Agreement on Agriculture Work? Agricultural Disputes after the Uruguay Round*, Working Paper 98–2 (Minnesota: International Agricultural Trade Research Consortium) (http://iatrcweb.org/).

Hufbauer, G. C. (1983), 'Subsidy Issues after the Tokyo Round', in Cline (ed.), *Trade Policy in the 1980s* (Washington, DC: Institute for International Economics), pp. 327–61.

Ingco, M. D. (1996), 'Tariffication in the Uruguay Round: How Much Trade Liberalisation?', *The World Economy*, 19/4: 425–46.

Ingersent, K. A., Rayner, A. J. and Hine, R. C. (1994), 'The EC Perspective', in Ingersent, Rayner and Hine (eds.), *Agriculture in the Uruguay Round* (New York: St. Martin's Press), pp. 55–87.

Jackson, J. H. (1983), 'GATT Machinery and the Tokyo Round Agreements', in Cline (ed.), *Trade Policy in the 1980s* (Washington, DC: Institute for International Economics), pp. 159–87.

——(1997), *The World Trading System: Law and Policy of International Economic Relations*, 2nd edn. (Cambridge: The MIT Press).

Johnson, C. (1991), *The Economy under Mrs Thatcher 1979–1990* (Harmondsworth: Penguin).

Johnson, D. G. (1950), *Trade and Agriculture. A Study of Inconsistent Policies* (New York: John Wiley & Sons).

——(1973), *World Agriculture in Disarray* (London: Macmillan).

——(1975), 'World Agriculture, Commodity Policy and Price Variability', *American Journal of Agricultural Economics*, 57/5: 823–8.

Johnson, H. G. (1971), 'The Implications for the World Economy', in Evans (ed.), *Destiny or Delusion: Britain and the Common Market* (London: Victor Gollancz).

Johnston, W. and Sandrey, R. (1990), 'Land Markets and Rural Debt', in Sandy and Reynolds (eds.), *Farming without Subsidies: New Zealand's Recent Experience* (Wellington: MAF, GP Books), pp. 183–209.

Josling, T. (1993), 'Agriculture in a World of Trading Blocs', *Australian Journal of Agricultural Economics*, 37/3: 155–79.

——Roberts, D. and Orden, D. (2004), *Food Regulation and Trade* (Washington, DC: Institute for International Economics).

——and Swinbank, A. (2008), *European Union: Shadow WTO Agricultural Domestic Support Notifications*, IFPRI Discussion Paper 00809 (International Food Policy Research Institute: Washington D.C.).

——Tangermann, S. and Warley, T. K. (1996), *Agriculture in the GATT* (Basingstoke: Macmillan).

——and Valdés, A. (2004), *Agricultural Policy Indicators*, FAO Commodity and Trade Policy Research Working Paper No. 4 (Rome: FAO).

——Zhao, L., Carcelen, J. and Arha, K. (2006), *Implications of WTO Litigation for the WTO Agricultural Negotiations*, IPC Issues Brief 19 (Washington, DC: International Food & Agricultural Trade Policy Council).

Kay, A. (1998), *The Reform of the Common Agricultural Policy: The Case of the Mac-Sharry Reforms* (Wallingford: CABI Publishing).

Kerr, W. A. and Hobbs, J. E. (2005), 'Consumers, Cows and Carousels: Why the Dispute over Beef Hormones is Far More Important than Its Commercial Value', in Perdikis and Read (eds.), *The WTO and the Regulation of International Trade: Recent Trade Disputes between the European Union and the United States* (Cheltenham: Edward Elgar), pp. 191–214.

Keynes, J. M. (1936), *The General Theory of Employment Interest and Money* (London: Macmillan).

Kindleberger, C. P. (1951), 'Group Behavior and International Trade', *The Journal of Political Economy*, 59/1: 30–46.

Kjeldahl, R. (1994), 'Reforming the Reform? The CAP at a Watershed', in Kjeldahl and Tracy (eds.), *Renationalisation of the Common Agricultural Policy* (Valby/la Hutte: Institute of Agricultural Economics/Agricultural Policy Studies), pp. 5–22.

Lamy, P. (2006), 'DG Lamy: Time Out Needed To Review Options and Positions', Director-General's Statement To an Informal Meeting of Heads of Delegations in the Trade Negotiations Committee on Monday 24 July 2006, WTO News Items, http://www.wto.org/English/news_e/news06_e/tnc_dg_stat_24july06_e.htm. last accessed 18 December 2008.

—— (2008*a*), 'Lamy Calls for "Serious Reflection" on Next Steps', Chairman's Opening Remarks To a Formal Meeting of the Trade Negotiations Committee on 30 July, WTO News Items, http://www.wto.org/english/news_e/news08_e/meet08_chair_30july08_e.htm, accessed 19 August 2008.

—— (2008*b*), 'Statement by Pascal Lamy to the General Council', 18 December, WTO News Item, http://www.wto.org/english/news_e/news08_e/gc_dg_stat_18dec_e.htm, accessed 18 December 2008.

—— and Fischler, F. (2004), Letter to all ministers in WTO Members responsible for trade, pdf document downloaded from http://europa.eu.int/comm/agriculture/external/wto/index_en.htm, accessed 19 May 2004.

Legg, W. (2003), 'Agricultural Subsidies: Measurement and Use in Policy Analysis', *Journal of Agricultural Economics*, 54/2: 175–201.

Lowe, P., Buller, H. and Ward, N. (2002), 'Setting the Next Agenda? British and French Approaches To the Second Pillar of the Common Agricultural Policy', *Journal of Rural Studies*, 18: 1–17.

MacSharry, R. (1991), 'Commission Statement on the Common Agricultural Policy', Debates of the European Parliament, *Official Journal of the European Communities*, Annex 3–403: 15–17.

Mandelson, P. (2008), 'Daily update from Peter Mandelson' at http://ec.europa.eu/trade/issues/newround/doha_da/geneva08/update_en.htm (accessed 21 August 2008).

Manegold, D. (1989), 'EC Agricultural Policy in 1988–89: An Early End to Reform?', *Review of Marketing and Agricultural Economics*, 57/1: 11–46.

March, J. G. and Olsen, J. P. (1989), *Rediscovering Institutions: The Organizational Basis of Politics* (New York: The Free Press).

Marsh, D. and Rhodes, R. A. W. (1992), 'The Implementation Gap: Explaining Policy Change and Continuity', in Marsh and Rhodes (eds.), *Implementing Thatcherite Policies: Audit of an Era* (Buckingham: Open University Press), pp. 170–87.

Mauldon, R. (1990), 'Price Policy', in Williams (ed.), *Agriculture in the Australian Economy*, 3rd edn. (Melbourne: Sydney University Press).

McCall Smith, J. (2006), 'Compliance and Bargaining in the WTO: Ecuador and the Bananas Dispute', in Odell (ed.), *Negotiating Trade: Developing Countries in the WTO and NAFTA* (Cambridge: Cambridge University Press).

McCalla, A. F. (1969), 'Protectionism in Agricultural Trade, 1850–1968', *Agricultural History*, XLIII/3: 329–43.

McCrone, G. (1962), *The Economics of Subsidising Agriculture. A Study of British Policy* (London: George Allen & Unwin).

McMahon, J. A. (2007), 'Trade Policy Reform Through Litigation', *EuroChoices*, 6/2: 42–6.

McQueen, M. (1982), 'Lomé and the Protective Effect of Rules of Origin', *Journal of World Trade Law*, 16/2: 119–32.

—— (1998), 'Lomé Versus Free Trade Agreements: The Dilemma Facing the ACP Countries', *The World Economy*, 21/4: 421–43.

Meadows, D. H., Meadows, D. L., Randers, J. and Behrens III, W. W (1972), *The Limits to Growth: A Report for the Club of Rome's Project on the Predicament of Mankind* (London: Earth Island Ltd.).

Meilke, Karl (2008), 'Does the WTO Have a Role in Food Crises?', *The Estey Centre Journal of International Law and Trade Policy*, 9/2: 53–62.

Meunier, S. (2005), *Trading Voices: The European Union in International Commercial Negotiations* (Princeton: Princeton University Press).

Meyerson, C. C. (2003), *Domestic Politics and International Relations in US–Japan Trade Policy Making: The GATT Uruguay Round Agriculture Negotiations* (Basingstoke: Palgrave Macmillan).

Moravcsik, A. (2000*a*), 'De Gaulle Between Grain and *Grandeur*: The Political Economy of French EC Policy, 1958–1970 (Part I)', *Journal of Cold War Studies*, 2/2: 3–43.

—— (2000*b*), 'De Gaulle Between Grain and *Grandeur*: The Political Economy of French EC Policy, 1958–1970 (Part II)', *Journal of Cold War Studies*, 2/3: 4–68.

Morgan, D (1979), *Merchants of Grain* (New York: The Viking Press).

Moyer, H. W. (1993), 'The European Community and the GATT Uruguay Round: Preserving the Common Agricultural Policy at All Costs', in Avery (ed.), *World Agriculture in the GATT* (Boulder: Lynne Rienner Publishers), pp. 95–119.

—— and Josling, T. E. (2002), *Agricultural Policy Reform: Politics and Policy Process in the EC and the US in the 1990s* (Aldershot: Ashgate).

Murphy, S. and S. Suppan (2008), *The 2008 Farm Bill and the Doha Agenda* (Minnesota: Institute for Agriculture and Trade Policy).

Narlikar, A. (2004), *The World Trade Organization: A Very Short Introduction* (Oxford: Oxford University Press).

Noble, J. (2006), 'Commodity Focus: How does the CAP Work in Practice for Sugar?', in *Agra Europe, A Practical Seminar on Agricultural Policy in Europe: Understanding the Common Agricultural Policy*, 4–5 July (Tunbridge Wells: Agra Informa Ltd.).

North, D. C. (1990), *Institutions, Institutional Change and Economic Performance* (Cambridge: Cambridge University Press).

Norway (2001), *Coexistence in a World of Agricultural Diversity—The Right of Every Country To Safeguard Non-trade Concerns*, Discussion Paper One, International Conference on Non-Trade Concerns in Agriculture, Mauritius, 28–31 May.

OECD (1982), *Communiqué of the Meeting of the OECD Council at Ministerial Level on 10–11 May*, available at the University of Toronto G8 Information Centre (http://www.g7.utoronto.ca/oecd/oecd82.htm, accessed 29 January 2007).

Bibliography

OECD (1987), *National Policies and International Trade* (Paris: OECD).

—— (1992), *Agricultural Policies, Markets and Trade. Monitoring and Outlook 1992* (Paris: OECD).

—— (2002), *Agricultural Policies in OECD Countries: Monitoring and Evaluation* (Paris: OECD).

—— (2003), *Multifunctionality: The Policy Implications* (Paris: OECD).

OECD/FAO (2008), *Agricultural Outlook 2008–2017* (Paris: OECD/Rome: FAO).

Office of the United States Trade Representative (2005), *US Proposal for WTO Agriculture Negotiations*, 10 October 2005.

Official Journal of the European Union, various issues.

Orden, D., Paarlberg, R. and Roe, T. (1999), *Policy Reform in American Agriculture: Analysis and Prognosis* (Chicago: The University of Chicago Press).

Oskam, A. J. and Meester, G. (2006), 'How Useful Is the PSE in Determining Agricultural Support?', *Food Policy*, 31/2: 123–41.

Oxfam International (2005), *A Round for Free. How Rich Countries Are Getting a Free Ride on Agricultural Subsidies at the WTO*, Oxfam Briefing Paper 76 (Oxfam International: www.oxfam.org).

Oxley, A. (1990), *The Challenge of Free Trade* (Hemel Hempstead: Harvester Wheatsheaf).

Paarlberg, R. (1993), 'Why Agriculture Blocked the Uruguay Round: Evolving Strategies in a Two-level Game', in Avery (ed.), *World Agriculture in the GATT* (Boulder: Lynne Rienner Publishers), pp. 39–54.

—— (1997), 'Agricultural Policy Reform and the Uruguay Round: Synergistic Linkage in a Two-level Game?', *International Organization*, 51/3: 413–44.

Paemen, H. and Bensch, A. (1995), *From the GATT to the WTO. The European Community in the Uruguay Round* (Leuven: Leuven University Press).

Page, S. and Hewitt, A. (2002), 'The New European Trade Preferences: Does "Everything but Arms" (EBA) Help the Poor?', *Development Policy Review*, 20/1: 91–102.

Patterson, L. A. (1997), 'Agricultural Policy Reform in the European Community: A Three-level Game Analysis', *International Organization*, 51/1: 135–65.

Peters, G. (1988), 'The Interpretation and Use of Producer Subsidy Equivalents', *Oxford Agrarian Studies*, 17: 186–218.

Picciotto, S. (2003), 'Private Rights Vs Public Standards in the WTO', *Review of International Political Economy*, 10/3: 377–405.

Piesse, J. and Thirtle, C. (2009), 'Three bubbles and a panic: an explanatory review of recent food commodity price events', *Food Policy*, 34/2: 119–29.

Pilegaard, J. (2006), *Between Coherence and Fragmentation: The EU's Everything but Arms Initiative* (Copenhagen: Institute of Political Science, University of Copenhagen).

Putnam, R. D. (1988), 'Diplomacy and Domestic Politics: The Logic of Two-Level Games', *International Organization*, 42/3: 427–60.

Rapp, D. (1988), *How the US Got into Agriculture and Why It Can't Get Out*, Washington DC: Congressional Quarterly.

Rau, A. (1957), *Agricultural Policy and Trade Liberalization in the United States 1934–1956: A Study of Conflicting Policies*. Études d'Histoire Économique, Politique et Sociale XXI (Geneva: Librairie E. Droz).

Ray, D. E. and Schaffer, H. D. (2007), 'How US Farm Policies in the Mid-1990s Affected International Crop Prices: A Harbinger of What to Expect with Further Worldwide Implementation of WTO-compliant Policy Modifications?, in Koning and Pinstrup-Andersen (eds.), *Agricultural Trade Liberalization and the Least Developed Countries* (Dordrecht: Springer).

Rayner, T. (1990), 'The Seeds of Change', in Sandy and Reynolds (eds.), *Farming without Subsidies: New Zealand's Recent Experience* (Wellington: MAF, GP Books), pp. 13–24.

Read, R. (2005), 'The "Banana Split": the EU–US Banana Trade Dispute and the Effects of EU Market Liberalisation', in Perdikis and Read (eds.), *The WTO and the Regulation of International Trade: Recent Trade Disputes Between the European Union and the United States* (Cheltenham: Edward Elgar), pp. 109–34.

Ricardo, D. (1817), *On the Principles of Political Economy, and Taxation* (London: John Murray).

Rieger, E. (2000), 'The Common Agricultural Policy: Politics against Markets', in Wallace and Wallace (eds.), *Policy Making in the European Union*, 4th edn., (Oxford: Oxford University Press), pp. 179–210.

——(2005), 'Agricultural Policy: Constrained Reforms', in Wallace, Wallace and Pollack (eds.), *Policy Making in the European Union*, 5th edn. (Oxford: Oxford University Press), pp. 161–90.

Ross, G. (1995), *Jacques Delors and European Integration* (Cambridge: Polity Press).

Rothstein, B. (1992), 'Labor Market Institutions and Working Class Strength', in Steinmo, Thelen, and Longstreth (eds.), *Structuring Politics: Historical Institutionalism in Comparative Analysis* (Cambridge: Cambridge University Press).

Ruffer, T. and Swinbank, A. (2003), *Stock-take of the WTO Agriculture Negotiations. Implications for Developing Countries* (Oxford: Oxford Policy Management).

Ruggiero, R. (1998), Address to Danish shipowners' association, 25 March 1998: http://www.wto.org/English/news_e/sprr_e/copenh_e.htm, accessed 16 January 2007.

Sandrey, R. A. and Scobie G. M. (1994), 'Changing International Competitiveness and Trade: Recent Experience in New Zealand Agriculture', *American Journal of Agricultural Economics*, 76/5: 1041–6.

Scammell, W. M. (1983), *The International Economy since 1945*, 2nd edn. (London: Macmillan).

Schattschneider, E. E. (1975 [1960]), *The Semisovereign People: A Realist's View of Democracy in America* (Hinsdale: The Dryden Press).

Schelling, T. C. (1960), *The Strategy of Conflict* (Cambridge: Harvard University Press).

Serger, S. S. (2001), *Negotiating CAP Reform in the European Union—Agenda 2000*. Report 2001: 4 (Lund: Swedish Institute for Food and Agricultural Economics).

Shapiro, H-. and Brainard, L. (2003), 'Trade Promotion Authority Formerly Known as Fast Track: Building Common Ground on Trade Demands More Than a Name Change', *George Washington International Law Review*, 35/1: 1–53.

Skogstad, G. (1998), 'Ideas, Paradigms and Institutions: Agricultural Exceptionalism in the European Union and the United States', *Governance*, 11/4: 463–90.

—— (2001), 'The WTO and Food Safety Regulatory Policy Innovation in the European Union', *Journal of Common Market Studies*, 39/3: 485–505.

—— (2007), 'Agricultural Policy Paradigms and Canadian Agriculture', paper prepared to the international conference Agricultural Policy Changes: Canada, EU and the World Trade Organisation, the University of Victoria, Victoria B.C. Canada, 13–15 September 2007.

—— (2008), 'Canadian Agricultural Policy Programs and Paradigms: The Influence of International Trade Agreements and Domestic Factors', *Canadian Journal of Agricultural Economics*, 56/4: 493–507.

Soames, C. (1973), 'Statement by Sir Cristopher Soames, Vice-President of the Commission of the European Communities to the GATT Ministerial Meeting in Tokyo (12 September 1973)', in *Europe. Documents.* 20.09.1973, No 759, pp: 3–5, accessed at http://www.ena.lu/ on 11 December 2008.

Srinivasan, T. N. (2007), 'The Dispute Settlement Mechanism of the WTO: A Brief History and an Evaluation from Economic, Contractarian and Legal Perspectives', *The World Economy*, 30/7: 1033–68.

Steinberg, R. H. (2002), 'In the Shadow of Law or Power? Consensus-Based Bargaining and Outcomes in the GATT/WTO', *International Organization*, 56/2: 339–74.

—— and Josling, T. E. (2003), 'When the Peace Ends: The Vulnerability of EC and US Agricultural Subsidies to WTO Legal Challenge', *Journal of International Economic Law*, 6/2: 369–417.

Stiglitz, J. E. (2004), *The Roaring Nineties: A New History of the World's Most Prosperous Decade*, paperback edn. (New York: W. W. Norton and Company) (first published 2003).

Stoler, A. I. (2004), 'The WTO Dispute Settlement Process: Did the Negotiators Get What They Wanted?', *World Trade Review*, 3/1: 99–118.

Stovall, J. G. and Hathaway, D. E. (2003), 'US Interests in the Banana Trade Controversy', in Josling and Taylor (eds.), *Banana Wars: The Anatomy of a Trade Dispute* (Wallingford: CABI Publishing), pp. 151–68.

Sumner, D. A. (2005), *Boxed In. Conflicts between US Farm Policies and WTO Obligations*, Trade Policy Analysis No. 32 (Washington, DC: Center for Trade Policy Studies, Cato Institute).

—— and Tangermann, S. (2002), 'International Trade Policy and Negotiation', in Gardner and Rausser (eds.), *Handbook of Agricultural Economics. Volume 2B: Agricultural and Food Policy* (Amsterdam: Elsevier).

Swinbank, A. (1992), 'The EEC's Policies and its Food', *Food Policy*, 17/1: 53–64.

—— (1997), 'The CAP Decision-making Process', in Ritson and Harvey (eds.), *The Common Agricultural Policy*, 2nd edn. (Wallingford: CABI Publishing).

——(1999a), 'EU Agriculture, Agenda 2000 and the WTO Commitments', *The World Economy*, 22/1: 41–54.

——(1999b), 'CAP Reform and the WTO: Compatibility and Developments', *European Review of Agricultural Economics*, 26/3: 389–407.

——(2002), 'Multifunctionality: the Concept and its International Acceptability', *Journal of the Royal Agricultural Society of England*, 163: 141–8.

——(2004), 'Dirty Tariffication Revisited: The EU and Sugar', *The Estey Centre Journal of International Law and Trade Policy*, 5/1: 56–69.

——(2005a), 'The Challenge of the Agricultural Trade Negotiations in the Doha Round', in Perdikis and Read (eds.), *The WTO and the Regulation of International Trade. Recent Trade Disputes between the European Union and the United States*, (Cheltenham: Edward Elgar), pp. 87–108.

——(2005b), 'Developments in the Doha Round and WTO Dispute Settlement: Some Implications for EU Agricultural Policy', *European Review of Agricultural Economics*, 32/4: 551–61.

——(2006a), 'Like Products, Animal Welfare and the World Trade Organization', *Journal of World Trade*, 40/4: 687–711.

——(2006b), 'The EU's Export Refunds on Processed Foods: Legitimate in the WTO?', *The Estey Centre Journal of International Law and Trade Policy*, 7/2: 152–67.

——(2008a), 'EU Sugar Policy: An Extraordinary Story of Continuity, but Then Change', paper prepared for the Organized Session on *The Future of the European Sugar Market* at the XIIth Congress of the European Association of Agricultural Economists, 26–29 August, Ghent.

——(2008b), 'Potential WTO Challenges to the CAP', *Canadian Journal of Agricultural Economics*, 56/4: 445–56.

——and Daugbjerg, C. (2006), 'The 2003 CAP Reform: Accommodating WTO Pressures', *Comparative European Politics*, 4/1: 47–64.

——and Ritson, C. (1995), 'The Impact of the GATT Agreement on EU Fruit and Vegetable Policy', *Food Policy*, 20/4: 339–57.

——and Tangermann, S. (2004), 'A Bond Scheme to Facilitate CAP Reform', in Swinbank and Tranter (eds.), *A Bond Scheme for Common Agricultural Policy Reform* (Wallingford: CABI Publishing), pp. 55–78.

——and Tanner, C. (1996), *Farm Policy and Trade Conflict. The Uruguay Round and CAP Reform* (Ann Arbor: The University of Michigan Press).

—— ——(2001), 'The European Union and Eastern Europe', in Michelmann, Rude, Stabler and Storey (eds.), *Globalization and Agricultural Trade Policy* (Dulles, VA: Lynne Rienner), pp. 197–214.

——and Tranter, R. (2005), 'Decoupling EU Farm Support: Does the New Single Payment Scheme Fit within the Green Box?', *The Estey Centre Journal of International Law and Trade Policy*, 6/1: 47–61.

Swinnen, J. F. M. (2008), 'The Political Economy of the Fischler Reforms of the EU's Common Agricultural Policy. The Perfect Storm?', in Swinnen (ed.), *The Perfect*

Storm? The Political Economy of the Fischler Reforms of the Common Agricultural Policy (Brussels: Centre for European Policy Studies).

Tangermann, S. (2001), 'Has the Uruguay Round Agreement on Agriculture Worked Well?', paper prepared for the International Agricultural Trade Consortium's Theme Day Meeting *Agriculture in the WTO*, 18 May 2001, Washington DC.

—— (2003), 'European Interests in the Banana Market', in Josling and Taylor (eds.), *Banana Wars: The Anatomy of a Trade Dispute* (Wallingford: CABI Publishing).

—— (2004), 'Agricultural Policies in OECD Countries Ten Years After the Uruguay Round: How Much Progress?', in Anania, Bohman, Carter and McCalla (eds.), *Agricultural Policy Reform and the WTO: Where Are We Heading?* (Cheltenham, Edward Elgar), pp. 15–42.

Tanner, C. and Swinbank, A. (1987), 'Prospects for Reform of the Common Agricultural Policy', *Food Policy*, 12/4: 290–4.

Thelen, K. (1999), 'Historical Institutionalism in Comparative Politics', *Annual Review of Political Science*, 2: 369–404.

—— (2003), 'How Institutionalism Evolves: Insights from Comparative Historical Analysis', in Mahoney and Rueschemeyer (eds.), *Comparative Historical Analysis in the Social Sciences* (Cambridge: Cambridge University Press), pp. 208–40.

—— and Steinmo, S. (1992), 'Historical Institutionalism in Comparative Politics', in Steinmo, Thelen and Longstreth (eds.), *Structuring Politics. Historical Institutionalism in Comparative Analysis* (Cambridge: Cambridge University Press), pp. 1–32.

Thirsk, J. (1997), *Alternative Agriculture. A History: From the Black Death to the Present Day* (Oxford: Oxford University Press).

Thompson, A. (2007), 'The Power of Legalization: A Two-Level Explanation for U.S. Support of WTO Dispute Settlement', paper prepared for the International Studies Association Annual Convention, Chicago, March.

Tracy, M. (1982), *Agriculture in Western Europe: Challenge and Response 1880–1980*, 2nd edn. (London: Granada).

van Vliet, H. (2000), 'WTO Dispute Settlement and Agriculture: Lessons for Negotiators', in Bilal and Pezaros (eds.), *Negotiating the Future of Agricultural Policies: Agricultural Trade and the Millennium WTO Round* (The Hague: Kluwer Law International).

Viner, J. (1950), *The Customs Union Issue* (New York: Carnegie Endowment for International Peace).

Walsh, J. I. (2000), 'When Do Ideas Matter? Explaining the Successes and Failures of Thatcherite Ideas', *Comparative Political Studies*, 33/4: 483–516.

Warley, T. K. (1976), 'Western Trade in Agricultural Products', in Shonfield (ed.), *International Economic Relations of the Western World 1959–1971. Volume 1 Politics and Trade* (Oxford: Oxford University Press).

Warwick Commission (2007), *The Multilateral Trade Regime: Which Way Forward?* (Coventry: The University of Warwick).

Wilcox, C. (1949), *A Charter for World Trade* (New York: Macmillan).

Winham, G. R. (1986), *International Trade and the Tokyo Round Negotiation* (Princeton: Princeton University Press).

—— (2007), 'The GMO Panel in the World Trade Organization: Implications for Agricultural Policy in Developed and Developing Countries', paper prepared for the International Conference on Agricultural Policy Changes: Canada, EU, and the World Trade Organisation, Victoria, Canada, 13–15 September.

Winter, S. C. (2006), 'Implementation', in Peters and Pierre (eds.), *Handbook of Public Policy* (London: Sage), pp. 151–66.

Wooding, P. (1987), 'Liberalising the International Trade Regime', in Bollard and Buckle (eds.), *Economic Liberalisation in New Zealand* (Wellington: Allen & Unwin in association with Port Nicholson Press), pp. 86–101.

Woolcock, S. (2005), 'Trade Policy. From Uruguay to Doha and Beyond', in Wallace, Wallace and Pollack (eds.), *Policy Making in the European Union*, 5th edn. (Oxford: Oxford University Press).

WTO (1995), *Analytical Index: Guide to GATT Law and Practice*, updated 6th edn., CD-ROM (Geneva: WTO).

—— (1997), *European Communities—Regime for the Importation, Sale and Distribution of Bananas. Complaint by the United States. Report of the Panel*, WT/DS27/R/USA (Geneva: WTO).

—— (1998), *United States—Import Prohibition of Certain Shrimp and Shrimp Products. Report of the Appellate Body*, WT/DS58/AB/R (Geneva: WTO).

—— (1999a), *Committee on Agriculture: General Council Overview of WTO Activities (1999), Report by the Chairman*, G/L/322 (Geneva: WTO).

—— (1999b), *European Communities—Measures Concerning Meat and Meat Products (Hormones). Original Complaint by the United States. Recourse to Arbitration by the European Communities Under Article 22.6 of the DSU. Decision by the Arbitrators*, WT/DS26/ARB (Geneva: WTO).

—— (2000a), *Note on Non-Trade Concerns Revision*, G/AG/NG/W/36/Rev.1 (Geneva: WTO).

—— (2000b), *EC Comprehensive Negotiating Proposal*, G/AG/NG/W/90 (Geneva: WTO).

—— (2000c), *Agriculture negotiations, 23–24 March 2000. Talks Reach Swift Agreement on 'Phase 1'*, Press Release: Press/172, 27 March (Geneva: WTO).

—— (2001a), *European Communities—The ACP–EC Partnership Agreement Decision of 14 November 2001*, WT/MIN(01)/15 (Geneva: WTO).

—— (2001b), *Ministerial Conference Fourth Session Doha, 9–14 November 2001 Ministerial Declaration*, WT/MIN(01)/DEC/W/1 (Geneva: WTO).

—— (2002a), *Chile—Price Band System and Safeguard Measures Relating To Certain Agricultural Products. Report of the Appellate Body*, WT/DS207/AB/R (Geneva: WTO).

—— (2002b), *Export Subsidies. Background Paper by the Secretariat*, TN/AG/S/8 (Geneva: WTO).

—— (2002*c*), *Members' Usage of Domestic Support Categories, Export Subsidies and Export Credits. Background Paper by the Secretariat*, TN/AG/S/1 (Geneva: WTO).

—— (2003*a*), *Agriculture—Framework Proposal. Joint Proposal by Argentina, Bolivia, Brazil, Chile, China, Colombia, Costa Rica, Cuba, Ecuador, El Salvador, Guatemala, India, Mexico, Pakistan, Paraguay, Peru, Philippines, South Africa, Thailand and Venezuela*, WT/MIN(03)/W/6 (Geneva: WTO).

—— (2003*b*), *First Draft of Modalities for the further Commitments Revision*, TN/AG/W/1/Rev.1 (Geneva: WTO).

—— (2004*a*), *WTO Agriculture Negotiations. The Issues, and Where We Are Now*. Updated 1 December 2004 (Geneva: WTO).

—— (2004*b*), *Members' Usage of Domestic Support Categories, Export Subsidies and Export Credits. Background Paper by the Secretariat*, TN/AG/S/12 (Geneva: WTO).

—— (2004*c*), *Doha Work Programme. Decision Adopted by the General Council on 1 August 2004*, WT/L/579 (Geneva: WTO).

—— (2004*d*), *United States—Subsidies on Upland Cotton*, WT/DS267/R (Geneva: WTO).

—— (2005*a*), *European Communities—Export Subsidies on Sugar. Report of the Appellate Body.* WT/DS265/AB/R, WT/DS266/AB/R, WT/DS283/AB/R (Geneva: WTO).

—— (2005*b*), *Product-Specific AMS. Note by the Secretariat*, TN/AG/S/15 (Geneva: WTO).

—— (2005*c*), *Total Aggregate Measurement of Support. Note by the Secretariat*, TN/AG/S/13 (Geneva: WTO).

—— (2006), *United States—Subsidies on Upland Cotton. Recourse to Article 21.5 of the DSU by Brazil. Request for the Establishment of a Panel*, WT/DS267/30 (Geneva: WTO).

—— (2007*a*), *Appellate Body Annual Report for 2006.* WT/AB/7 (Geneva: WTO).

—— (2007*b*), *Chile—Price Band System and Safeguard Measures Relating to Certain Agricultural Products. Recourse to Article 21.5 of the DSU by Argentina. Report of the Appellate Body*, WT/DS207/AB/RW (Geneva: WTO).

—— (2007*c*), *European Communities—Anti-Dumping Measure on Farmed Salmon from Norway. Report of the Panel*, WT/DS337/R (Geneva: WTO).

—— (2007*d*), *United States—Subsidies and Other Domestic Support for Corn and Other Agricultural Products. Request for Consultations by Canada*, WT/DS357/1, G/L/812, G/SCM/D73/1, G/AG/GEN/74 (Geneva: WTO).

—— (2007*e*), *World Trade Report 2007. Six Decades of Multilateral Trade Cooperation: What Have We Learnt?* (Geneva: WTO).

—— (2007*f*), 'WTO Membership—In Brief', dated 11 January (Geneva: WTO).

—— (2008*a*), *Committee on Agriculture Special Session, Revised Draft Modalities for Agriculture*, TN/AG/W/4/Rev.3 (Geneva: WTO).

—— (2008*b*), *Report to the Trade Negotiations Committee by the Chairman of the Special Session of the Committee on Agriculture, Ambassador Crawford Falconer*, JOB(08)/95. See also the secretariat's 'unofficial notes' on the web version of this text at http://www.wto.org/english/tratop_e/agric_e/chair_report_11aug08_e.htm, last accessed 6 October 2008.

Yeutter, C. (1988), 'US Negotiating Proposal on Agriculture in the Uruguay Round', in Petersmann and Hilf (eds.), *The New GATT Round of Multilateral Trade Negotiations: Legal and Economic Problems* (Deventer: Kluwer Law and Taxation Publishers), pp. 265–70.

Young, A. R. (2007), 'Trade Politics Ain't What It Used to Be: The European Union in the Doha Round', *Journal of Common Market Studies*, 45/4: 789–811.

Young, O. R. (1997), 'Global Governance: Towards a Theory of Decentralized World Order', in Young (ed.), *Global Governance: Insights from the Environmental Experience* (Cambridge: The MIT Press), pp. 273–99.

Index